D1206946

Sustainable Lifestyles and the Quest for Plenitude

Sustainable Lifestyles and the Quest for Plenitude

Case Studies of the New Economy

Edited by Juliet B. Schor and Craig J. Thompson

Yale UNIVERSITY PRESS

NEW HAVEN & LONDON

Yale University Press books may be purchased in quantity for educational,
business, or promotional use. For information, please e-mail sales.press@yale.edu
(U.S. office) or sales@yaleup.co.uk (U.K. office).

Set in Adobe Garamond and Stone Sans types by Westchester Book Group.
Printed in the United States of America.

ISBN: 978-0-300-19232-2 (pbk)

Library of Congress control number: 2014935916

A catalogue record for this book is available from the British Library.

This paper meets the requirements of
ANSI/NISO Z39.48–1992 (Permanence of Paper).

10 9 8 7 6 5 4 3 2 1

To plenitude practitioners everywhere

Contents

Acknowledgments

The editors and authors would like to thank the Center for Humans and Nature for its generous funding of the project that made this volume possible. Juliet Schor would like to give special thanks to Brooke Hecht, who helped conceive of the project and was extremely supportive throughout. Mary Crane and the Institute for Liberal Arts at Boston College kindly funded the Practicing Plenitude conference in October 2011 at which most of the chapters were originally presented as papers. The authors are grateful to participants in the symposium and to Anja Claus and Monetta Edwards. Juliet's agent, Melanie Jackson, provided helpful advice. We are especially indebted to our editor, Jean Thomson Black, and her assistant, Sara Hoover, of Yale University Press and to our excellent copy editor, Robin DuBlanc. Finally, all the authors appreciate each other for their extensive feedback and comments on drafts.

Teresa Gowan and Rachel Slocum would like to thank the people they interviewed who graciously shared their work with them and Jack Atmore for research assistance. Karen Hébert is grateful to those involved in the Transition movement in Alaska for their generous and committed engagement in this project, both the individuals whose interviews appear in her chapter and the many others who are not identified by name. Her research would not have been possible without their generous participation and the inspiring work they have begun. She also thanks Jedediah Smith and Ashwini Srinivasamohan for their research assistance. Emilie Dubois, Juliet Schor, and Lindsey Carfagna would like to thank the members of the time bank who were interviewed, Anny Fenton and Connor Fitzmaurice for comments on the manuscript, and Abigail Letak, Alison Grewe, and Alison Wawrzynek for research assistance. They are also grateful to the MacArthur Foundation for financial support for this research, and especially to Mizuko Ito and Connie Yowell. Diana Mincyte would like to thank Zine Magubane, Sylvia Samaniego, Karen Hébert, Guntra Aistara, and Laura Sayre for their feedback on drafts of her chapter. She is grateful to her informants, who generously shared their time and stories with her, as well as to the scholars and practitioners she met at the conference who inspired her to think globally about plenitude. Bobby Wengronowitz would like to thank Gavin Van Horn, who contributed immensely to this project, assisting at all stages from conception and fieldwork to writing and editing; without him, this chapter would not exist. He also would like to thank Connie, Dennis, Jamie, and all the good folks at Experimental Station for sharing their time and space. Finally, he would like to thank his partner, Becky, who is always there for him.

Introduction: Practicing Plenitude

Juliet B. Schor and Craig J. Thompson

Two thousand twelve was a frightening year for the planet. In March, fifteen thousand temperature records were broken in the United States, and large parts of the country suffered their worst drought in fifty years (NOAA 2012). In July, 94 percent of Greenland's summer ice disappeared in four days (Slivka 2012). Two months later, the rate of Arctic ice melt hit a new high, putting the predicted date for an ice-free Arctic within a decade, rather than the hundred-year time-line originally expected by scientists (Gillis 2012). In October, Hurricane Sandy, possibly the worst storm ever to hit the Northeast, devastated the region, depositing a down payment on a future of ris-ing sea levels and increased vulnerability. By December, it was settled that 2012 would rank as the hottest year in U.S. history, by an aston-ishing full degree Fahrenheit (Gillis 2013). As British journalist George Monbiot noted, repurposing Queen Elizabeth's memorable quip, it was truly an *annus horribilis* (2012).

Monbiot is not alone in his pessimism. Scientists and policy makers are trying to come to terms with the failure of the global community to limit climate change to two degrees of warming and contemplating the catastrophic consequences of four or even six degrees. Environmental journalist and activist Bill McKibben (2012) rang in the New Year by noting that we are fighting the "laws of physics."

Exhibit 1 is the continued rise in global emissions. Not only are emissions 58 percent higher than they were in 1990, the benchmark year enshrined in the Kyoto Protocol, they are rising faster with each decade. The years 2011 and 2012 saw annual increases of more than 2.5 percent, and atmospheric concentrations of greenhouse gases now exceed 390 parts per million (ppm), considerably above the 350 ppm that many scientists say is a safe limit.[1] Modest emissions declines in wealthy countries have been insufficient to counterbalance the large increases in the Global South, especially from China and India. And some of what is easing emissions in the United States, such as the shift from coal to hydraulic fracturing for natural gas, has its own unpredictable impacts: the climate impacts of gas flaring and methane release may turn out to be worse than what they are replacing.[2]

What McKibben has called the "terrifying new math of global warming" makes clear that we need to find alternatives to fossil fuel–driven economies as fast as we can (2012). Using even the most forgiving climate change scenarios being modeled by researchers, the scientific consensus is clear: the window of opportunity for averting devastating climate impacts is closing rapidly (Peters et al. 2012). For those of us in the Global North, and especially the United States, the high emissions of the past as well as the present make it imperative that we decarbonize rapidly.

But how to do it? The economic, political, and cultural conditions necessary for a wholesale shift out of fossil fuels are formidable. The 2012 presidential election provided a hint of just how large the political obstacles may be. Romney mocked fear of rising sea levels, just a few short months before the storm surges of Sandy took lives and cost billions. Obama continued to avoid political risk by espousing his characteristically centrist "all of the above" energy stance, conveniently ignoring that the rationale for shifting to renewables was in direct contradiction to any mandates for expanded fossil fuel production. Climate change was apparently such a fearsome issue that candidates treated it as "that which shall not be named," maintaining near-total silence throughout the campaign. Globally, the failure of the Rio+20 summit to produce anything but meaningless platitudes and the utter lack of progress at the Doha round of UN talks were further indication that elites are not yet ready to get serious about climate. Media coverage of climate change issues and debates—excluding the attention-grabbing reports on the damage and human suffering wrought by superstorms—seldom broke into the mainstream news cycle. According to the nonpartisan Media Matters for America, in all of 2012, less than one hour of coverage was given to climate issues by all the major nightly new shows, and of that less than ten minutes addressed scientific findings (Fitzsimmons 2013).

This lack of urgency, or even expression of serious concern, on the part of political leaders, the corporate-dominated news media, and much of the corporate sector at large seems to be propelling action at the grass roots. Undaunted by the paralysis of the powerful, members of a group we call plenitude practitioners are taking matters into their own hands. Convinced of the need for a radical new way of living, they are transforming their lifestyles, organizing in their communities, and building a localized, alternative economy that is capable of meeting human needs with a dramatically reduced energy footprint. They are organizing themselves into Transition initiatives, community groups that work on "energy-descent plans" to manage the shift into low-carbon lifestyles. They are constructing local food economies built on farmers' markets, community-supported agriculture (CSA), urban agriculture, seasonal eating, and a farm-to-table restaurant culture, believing that these activities are the foundation of a small-scale alternative to the carbon-intensive, industrialized, fast food system that currently dominates food production and consumption. They are joining the "maker" movement, which is dedicated to expanding the art of fabrication, both with simple tools and with high-tech machinery. Plenitude practitioners are downsizing their spending and looking for new ways of accessing goods and services, such as the many online opportunities for swapping, bartering, reselling, gifting, or repurposing.

These alternative practices of plenitude are creating new ways for people to meet their needs by sidestepping malls, big box stores, and professionalized services. Engaging with locals in peer-to-peer initiatives, people are creatively reinventing their everyday consumer practices to save cash, build social ties, and reduce their ecological footprints. While plenitude practitioners are by no means politically monolithic, many share a lack of faith in the ability of large institutions, be they governments or corporations, to successfully address the ecological and economic challenges we face. Instead, they are taking on the task of building another kind of economy in the shadow of what increasingly looks like a declining system.

In the pages that follow, we will explore the worlds of these plenitude practitioners by highlighting a series of in-depth cases. Through an ethnographic approach we will watch them as they join CSAs and time banks, plan for peak oil and climate change, teach skills to impoverished inner-city youths, and defy the state in their quest to reconstruct preindustrial food chains. While our cases are mostly situated in the United States, we also recognize that this movement is global. We will look at a region of France that has been practicing a version of plenitude since the 1960s, where *alternatifs* have established high levels of community connection through barter, self-provisioning, and an oppositional ideology to the normative lifestyles of "work and spend." We will also see that this movement is diverse. While it is often thought to be exclusively the domain of the white, highly educated middle class, we find that plenitude practitioners are a more varied group. Our case studies cover a broad demographic and geographic range, testament to the mainstreaming of these practices. Trendy New Yorkers and degree-rich Cantabridgians are represented, but so too are middle-class folks from central Pennsylvania and African American youth from the South Side of Chicago. However, as we shall see, a cultural chasm also exists between rationales and cultural messages used to promote plenitudinous lifestyles and the growing ranks of Americans who are grappling with the dilemmas posed by economic insecurity, declining real incomes, and other forms of economic disenfranchisement. Any chance of mobilizing a broad-based social movement to the cause of transforming the "business-as-usual" (BAU) economy may well hinge on finding ways to bridge this gap between plenitude ideals and the everyday lives of the struggling middle class. But before we delve further into these complexities and challenges, it will be useful to situate the plenitude model within its economic and social context.

BEYOND BUSINESS AS USUAL

In 2010, Juliet published *Plenitude: The New Economics of True Wealth.*[3] The book addressed the urgency of ecological overshoot and the failures of the existing "business-as-usual" economy. Set in the context of the 2008 global financial collapse and the worldwide recession that followed, it argued that the challenges of addressing climate change and ecological overshoot during an economic downturn require going beyond conventional approaches. A new energy paradigm, though desperately needed, will not suffice. We also need a new kind of economics.

What exactly do we mean by the BAU economy? The term itself comes from the climate literature, where business as usual means staying on the current path of emissions. It is now widely recognized that for climate, BAU entails a tripling of atmospheric concentrations of greenhouse gases by century's end and catastrophic climatic changes. As applied to the economy, BAU refers to the neoliberal commitment to corporate-dominated rather than state-regulated markets; highly concentrated distributions of wealth, income, and power; and treatment of nature as a free resource to be used and abused. BAU also exhibits what we have elsewhere termed *physophilia*—the love of growth. Incessant expansion is the sine qua non of a finance and corporate-driven system. Growth (and more precisely raising the rate of growth) is invariably offered as an all-purpose solution, the cure for almost anything, from unemployment, to income inequality to social conflict. Coupled with the "externalization" of ecological resources such as atmosphere, water, and soil, BAU leads to largely unmitigated environmental damage. In the current economic system, attaining any semblance of sustainability requires regulatory and legislative interventions to modulate an inherently unsustainable growth process. But over the last three decades, the political conditions (and much of the political will) needed to enforce such constraints have been steadily undermined. The economic system itself has become an obstacle to stopping climate change.

BAU reasoning holds that protecting the environment requires sacrificing other goals such as income, jobs, or profits. Soon after winning the 2012 election, President Obama provided a stark reminder of the grip of trade-off thinking. Asked by a reporter whether and how he intends to address climate change in his second administration, the president replied: "Understandably, I think the American people right now have been so focused, and will continue to be focused on our economy and jobs and growth, that if the message is somehow we're going to ignore jobs and growth simply to address climate change, I don't think anybody is going to go for that. I won't go for that." Leaving aside the audacity of using the word *simply* (as in *simply* to save the planet from catastrophe), the statement is notable for its narrow framing of options. Obama did go on to suggest there may be a way forward within the current paradigm: "If, on the other hand, we can shape an agenda that says we can create jobs, advance growth, and make a serious dent in climate change and be an international leader, I think that's something that the American people would support" (2012).

But the imagination for following that second path has so far been confined to the energy sector: the employment-generating effects of investments in renewable energy are well documented. Clean energy technologies will be globally competitive and hence more profitable; energy efficiency lowers costs and puts more money in people's pockets. While a crash program of investment

in renewable energy sources such as wind, solar, and geothermal is imperative, promoting greener, cleaner BAU still won't get us to a sustainable
economy.

One reason is BAU's slavish adherence to growth. If clean energy does lead
to a burst of new demand, that growth will in turn enlarge the size of the
carbon footprint. Similarly, becoming more efficient can lead to rebound effects
as lower costs lead people to use more energy. More generally, experience has
shown that the rising demand for energy that goes along with growth wipes
out much of the incremental progress in reducing emissions. It also degrades
other endangered ecological resources such as water, soil, forests, and plant and
animal species.

Timing is another problem. We've got only a narrow window in which to
avert climate catastrophe. We won't make it through if we keep expanding the
size of the economy. Ultimately it all comes back to those laws of physics, as
scientists keep reminding apparently deaf economists: we just can't manage
infinite growth on a finite planet.

While scientists are focusing on the ecological impossibilities of the current paradigm, most people are noticing that it is now failing even on its own
terms. The unchecked economic and political power of the global financial
sector led to a monetary meltdown whose aftershocks are still being felt five
years later. In the United States, distributions of wealth and income continue
to worsen, unemployment remains stubbornly high, incomes are depressed,
and the conditions of daily life are deteriorating for many. Extreme concentrations of power, in the finance and energy sectors in particular, have undermined democratic control of government. In Europe, the financial market
crash rendered the single currency system unworkable, which in turn resulted
in banker-imposed austerity policies. Southern European economies have im-
ploded, calling the viability of BAU into question. Globally, rising food prices
and the failings of corporate globalization have led to little progress against
poverty, with the exception of China. Meanwhile, the Chinese are following
an unsustainable path of carbon-intensive, export-driven growth that is generating internal protests and a deteriorating natural environment.

Plenitude argued that the BAU economy was in for a rough patch, particularly in wealthy countries. That prediction was premised on two main factors.
First, the spatial configuration of the world economy has been shifting away
from the more highly industrialized areas to the Global South, especially
Asia. The United States and Europe look more and more like declining economies whose privileged position is being eroded by lower-cost competitors.

Growth in output, income, and jobs may have fallen to a permanently lower level, or what in the popular press is described as a "new normal." The prediction in the book was that growth would not rebound to precrash levels quickly and might never regain the 3–4 percent that characterized earlier decades. Second, emerging ecological scarcities have begun to permanently affect prices, as food, fuel, and other commodities become more expensive. This trend began in 2000 and is expected to intensify. In the United States, unemployment would remain high, real wages and incomes for most people would stagnate or decline, and the prices of food and energy would escalate. All of those expectations have been borne out in the years since the book was written.

While the reality of this "new normal" is evident in economic forecasts, it has not yet prompted the wholesale rethinking that is required. Nowhere is that failure more evident than in the labor market. Growth is not—and will likely not be—sufficient to absorb the more than 20 million people whom the crash left unemployed, underemployed, or marginally attached to the workforce. Youth have been especially hard hit, with unemployment among recent high school graduates running at nearly 40 percent (Van Horn et al. 2012). In the world of BAU policy making, joblessness (like nearly everything else) is solved by growth. When growth fails to appear, there's nothing in the tool kit to put people back to work. That's the world in which we now find ourselves.

THE NEW ECONOMICS

Not surprisingly, the manifest failures of BAU are giving rise to new ways of thinking. One movement, called new economics, is the intellectual home of plenitude (Alperovitz 2011; Broad and Cavanagh 2012). While new economics is itself diverse, it does embody a few bedrock commitments. It is first and foremost an ecological economics, a commitment to live within the limits of the biosphere. Its hallmark is a rejection of the trade-off between growth and environment, the no-win outlook that anchors mainstream thinking. In BAU, the environment is mainly thought of in trade-off terms, as a luxury we "consume" when we are "rich" enough. We "buy" more or less of it just as we purchase cars, shoes, or computers. In the new economy paradigm, this reasoning is upended. Nature is understood to be the basis of human survival, an input into production, rather than a consumer good. When ecosystems are endangered, so too are humans. The nation's leading progressive economist, Joseph Stiglitz, reflected this shift in thinking by beginning 2013 with the claim that climate change is the "most serious" long-term problem facing the U.S. economy.

The second pillar of new economics is its insistence on fairer, more egalitarian social relations. BAU has resulted in extreme concentrations of wealth, income, and power, and the tyranny of the 1 percent so evocatively exposed by the Occupy movement. New economics is committed to building economies characterized by widespread ownership and control of economic and ecological assets, broad distributions of skills and market power, and effective norms of fairness. These in turn foster true democracy. This paradigm also recognizes an intimate link between inequality and ecological degradation. More equal countries, regions, and cities have better environmental performance (Boyce 2007). In the United States, the concentrated power of the fossil fuel sector has been the main obstacle to addressing climate change (Dunlap and McCright 2003).

Unlike Keynesian economics, which is also committed to more equal distribution, new economics does not mainly look to the state to redress inequality through monetary and fiscal policies. It aims to remake the foundations of the economy itself, not just alter the government policies that redress its most glaring faults. New economics sees the way forward through construction of a new productive base, made up of small-scale green enterprises, community trusts, local businesses, and significantly more popular access to capital (Alperovitz 2011). It advocates for Main Street over Wall Street via publicly financed investment through institutions such as state banks, local investing, "slow money," and crowd financing. Prominent new economics projects include worker and consumer cooperatives and municipally owned enterprises, examples of democracy-enhancing economic innovations.

A good example of initiatives that combine ecological restoration, grassroots wealth creation, and democracy are what new economists James Boyce and his collaborators have termed "natural assets projects" (Boyce and Shelley 2003). Local communities gain title or access to degraded land, turn it to productive use through agriculture or urban development, and share the income that it yields. These assets are typically owned communally or through trusts, and they are managed through democratic governance and local control. Natural assets projects are triple-dividend interventions because they enhance wealth and income, restore ecosystems, and promote local empowerment. They transcend the trade-off of BAU through an "outside the box" solution, in this case giving property to people with no prior rights over productive assets.

New economics' commitment to living within ecological limits and to fair distributions of wealth and power has implications that further differentiate it from mainstream approaches. It departs radically on questions of scale. In BAU, bigger is generally better, whether it's the size of a company or the scale of the economy. Big corporations are thought to capture efficiencies that come with size. The global economy is considered superior because of its world-wide division of labor—if it's cheaper to make clothes in Bangladesh, it must be more efficient. BAU doesn't worry about the concentrations of power associated with bigness, the threats to democracy, or the ecological costs of a far-flung production system.

In contrast, new economics promotes smaller-scale enterprises and local or regionally based economies. Taking as its mantra E. F. Schumacher's "Small is beautiful," ([1973] 2000), it articulates several critical benefits that accrue from organizing economic life in ways that privilege sustainability and social connection over the BAU mandates for perpetual growth and ever-expanding economies of scale. Perhaps most important, access to wealth will be more widely and fairly distributed when enterprises are smaller. Small firms are also easier to manage democratically. Local economies are thought to be more humane, because participants have ongoing social ties and are less likely to inflict harm on each other. As we shall see in the ethnographic data from our cases, face-to-face, personalized economic exchanges have become highly valued, not just for their economic viability but on their own terms. Our informants want to know the farmer who grows their food and provides the milk they drink. We interviewed one woman who chose to have her wedding dress made by fellow time bank member to experience that personal connection. In an era of global commodity chains and lack of transparency about labor conditions or environmental impacts, increasing numbers of people prefer to support others they know and can trust.

Local or regional economies are also thought to be more resilient, because they are diversified. Bioregionalism ties economic relations to surrounding ecosystems, in the hopes that by modeling human activities on the biological rhythms and relationships of place, the result will be a more sustainable and resilient economy. Large-scale global activity is more polluting because of its high fossil fuel requirements for transport.

As Juliet argued in *Plenitude,* there's an important dimension of why small is beautiful that hadn't surfaced in the 1970s when Schumacher wrote his classic: the power of decentralized networks. Thanks to the Internet, small-scale units can be harnessed to other small-scale units to form great powerful networks capable of highly productive activity. No longer does that network need to be contained within one big enterprise (for example, a giant corporation). The power of crowds comprised of single individuals can be harnessed to create enormous value (Benkler 2006). Wikipedia, which engaged individuals in a collaborative, bottom-up process, toppled the expensive *Encyclopaedia Britannica,* proving itself to be both more productive and cheaper. The open-source software movement relies on the kindness of millions of strangers. Online opportunities open global communication and markets for small businesses, artisans, and community groups. Because the Internet drastically reduces the costs of information and communication, it makes smaller-sized units vastly more productive. This is part of why, in the last few decades, small- and medium-sized businesses have provided far more employment and dynamism in the economy than the corporate behemoths.

By combining dedication to place with a worldwide communication system, plenitude practitioners are remaking the meanings of local and global. The valorization of the local that is evident in our cases, from central Pennsylvanians' love of local produce to the neighborhood focus of the Experimental Station on the South Side of Chicago, is not a backward-looking parochialism. Rather, it's a hybrid of cosmopolitan sensibilities rearticulated through a local prism. We call it cosmopolitan localism (Carfagna et al., 2014) to signal that it mixes familiarity with global culture and a sincere dedication to what's around the corner.

THE FOUR PRINCIPLES OF PLENITUDE

So far we have been talking about the broad principles of a new economic paradigm—its stance on ecological limits, distributions of income and property, scale, and so forth. Achieving these outcomes at the macro scale involves new behaviors and lifestyles for households and individuals. Indeed, much of *Plenitude* was dedicated to discussing how people could live differently in order to achieve the goals of ecological balance, fairness, adequate livelihood, and well-being for all. It laid out four basic principles that are the foundation of a different kind of economy: work and spend less, connect and create more. Together they constitute a new economics of the household by which growing numbers of people are adopting.

The first principle of plenitude is a transition to fewer hours of work in paid employment. By transferring labor time from the BAU market into other activities, households can free themselves from dependence on one job, prepare for a more uncertain labor market, and construct a more stable foundation for meeting needs. They can also escape the "work and spend" cycle and the corporate rat race that has become a common source of alienation and discontent (Schor 1998). Plenitude practitioners are frequently people who have downshifted or who reject the corporate ladder altogether, preferring to "patchwork their careers," as one of our informants described her postcorporate experience.

From the household's point of view, the logic of less dependence on the market provides not only freedom from the alienation of corporate life but also a strategy of risk diversification. Diversification becomes especially critical during a time when BAU is yielding lower wages, more precarious employment, and higher prices for basic necessities such as food and energy. The future will be different from much of the last century, during which the market offered decent jobs, expanding opportunity, and declining costs of living for basic needs. During that period, people did what one would expect—they became more dependent on the market, as they bought more and more of what they consumed, added family earners and hours of work, and developed ever more specialized skills. Now, because labor will be less well remunerated and employment will be more volatile, it makes sense to develop other modes of earning and surviving.

Of course, the opportunity to redeploy labor time to new occupations and activities is not available to everyone. Some people need full-time work to gain access to health insurance or other benefits. Others earn so little that they cannot afford to reduce their hours. Many people are in jobs that have no downward flexibility in hours. But as we shall see from the examples in the chapters that follow, there are many paths to shorter hours. In nations where the state provides basic security, such as France, a less work-intensive lifestyle is easier to achieve. In the United States, many of our respondents have been able to downsize their spending to match their reduced earning power. They're sacrificing fast-track careers, but they're gaining time, richer social interactions, and meaning.

This brings us to the second principle of plenitude, which is high-tech self-provisioning. Making and doing for oneself, or DIY, as it is commonly referred to, is the companion principle to working fewer hours in a BAU job. If fewer hours are being devoted to the market, people need to find productive and satisfying ways of spending time, and they need low-cost methods for meeting needs. Self-provisioning provides both. Growing vegetables or even going all the way to urban homesteading, installing solar panels and earning money back from the utility, selling crafts on Etsy, and building an eco-friendly home are activities that provide access to food, energy, shelter, and cash. We find that growing numbers of people are taking up these tasks with enthusiasm, talent, and joy. Self-provisioning allows people to learn new skills, promotes independence, and yields the deep satisfaction that comes from being creative. It is also a means to incubating new businesses and starting or switching careers. The plenitude universe is populated by people who are teaching permaculture, consulting on the construction of sustainable buildings, writing how-to manuals, and helping others downsize their footprints. It's full of corporate financiers turned bakers, potters, or even closet organizers.

An important dimension of self-provisioning in the twenty-first century is that it is high tech. If self-provisioning meant a return to methods of the nineteenth century (or even earlier), it would not be an attractive (or even palatable) alternative. The philosopher Frithjof Bergmann, who coined the term high-tech self-providing, made this point many years ago. After a brutal winter in southern New Hampshire, where he was attempting to repeat Henry David Thoreau's experiment in simple living, Bergmann realized that spending hours a day cutting firewood to keep warm was neither uplifting nor liberating. His epiphany was that the knowledge-driven technologies of postmodernity now make it possible to self-provision with much less human labor. Bergmann set out to find these technologies and to assemble a set of them that allows people to meet their basic needs for food, shelter, energy, transport, and clothing with relatively little labor, and even less cash. He found innovations such as living wall gardens, which grow vegetables with water rather than soil, thereby eliminating tedious jobs such as hoeing and weeding. He discovered small-scale generators that operate on biomass. He was involved in the production of a DIY car that cost a fraction of a regular vehicle to buy and little fuel to run.

Meanwhile, many others were working on similar visions—smart, cheap, DIY ways of meeting needs. At MIT, engineers constructed "fabrication labs," which combined a set of small, relatively inexpensive machines that were capable of making much of what we need for daily life and can construct it mostly from scrap materials. Fab labs can manufacture bicycle frames, cell phones, and even prefabricated houses. The MIT group has opened labs around the world as community centers and begun a movement to teach people how to use them. Permaculture, which began in the field of agroforestry, is an approach to growing food that minimizes manual labor and relies on nature-inspired ingenuity. By exploiting the synergies that characterize all natural systems, permaculture lets animals and plants do the tasks that humans and chemicals were previously taking on. The Internet is another high-tech source of enhanced labor productivity. It makes information freely and easily available and provides opportunities for collaboration that move projects forward much more quickly. One group that was profiled in *Plenitude,* the Factor e Farm, not only relies on fab labs and permaculture principles, it also designs machinery and methods of provisioning by outsourcing innovation to an online group of volunteers who figure out the designs. In this way the group has developed a set of inventions and agricultural machines that cost little and operate sustainably. More generally, plenitude practitioners are a diverse group in terms of technology. Some are relatively low tech, preferring time-tested artisanal methods of making and doing, such as the small cheese producers or bakers in the Aude, while others are spreading the ideas of permaculture or using the Internet to organize collaborative consumption initiatives such as time banking, ride sharing, and food swapping. But even among those who are going back to the land or rediscovering old production methods, there is little technophobia or Luddism. Plenitude practitioners use technology to enhance their productivity through learning, connecting, selling, and collaborating.

One important dimension of digital technologies is the promise they hold out for sustainability. By reducing the cost of information, the Internet facilitates a shift to production methods that are rich in knowledge and sparse in the use of natural resources. That's also a key insight of permaculture, which substitutes ecological know-how for chemicals and labor. In this way, digital technology and eco-knowledge can be the bedrocks of a closed-loop, ecologically light production paradigm.

The Internet also makes possible a new social arrangement of production. Instead of the emphasis on competition that characterizes BAU markets, it facilitates collaborative peer production in which people come together to solve problems, create products, write software, and share resources. While the 1960s counterculture also embraced cooperation, subsequent technological advances turned its ideas from what seemed like utopian aspirations into an economically viable model. That cooperative spirit is an important part of how plenitude practitioners are changing the way they live and work.

The third principle is true materialism. The everyday meaning of materialism implies a strong (or excessive) desire for goods. However, those who exhibit it often find the satisfactions of their purchases to be short lived. Today's must-have item is tomorrow's cast-off, not because it has changed materially but because it is no longer fashionable, or one has grown tired of it. The most materialist among us in one sense are the least materialist in another, in that for those consumers, the symbolic qualities of goods often dominate their material attributes (Schor 2010). Among plenitude practitioners, materiality matters. They care about the texture, aroma, provenance, and feel of products. The origins and travels of goods—their biographies, to use anthropologist Igor Kopytoff's evocative term (1986)—are of concern, as are the natural and human resources that went into making them. Rejecting the fast-fashion model of the 2000s (Schor 2010), true materialists emphasize the longevity of goods, by keeping, swapping, gifting, exchanging, selling, sharing, repurposing, or reusing them.

True materialism is an ecological, social, and aesthetic commitment to respect the materiality of products and the people who made them. But it is also a pragmatic response to lifestyle choices such as working less, which may not yield much spare cash. Plenitude practitioners are supplementing their self-provisioning with the emerging peer-to-peer collaborative economy as a way to access goods and services by paying little or nothing for them. They are bartering services in the time bank, using the peer-to-peer housing site AirBnB instead of hotels, swapping food, coming together in coworking spaces instead of renting individual offices, sharing cars, and raising money on Kickstarter to launch their entrepreneurial activities. These sites also provide opportunities to supplement income, if one has a room to rent or a car to lend out.

The final principle is to invest in community, known as recapitalizing the social. In recent decades, social ties have frayed, as neighborhoods hollowed out, work pushed out socializing and family time, and civic participation waned. Plenitude recognizes not only that social connections are important on their own terms—as a foundation of health and well-being—they are vital to a healthy economy and polity. Social capital, to use the academic term, enhances resilience in the face of adverse events and fosters democracy and efficiency. The people described in the case studies that follow are mostly passionate believers in the importance of social connection, as we shall see in the face-to-face relationships they build, the meetings they organize, and the networks they participate in.

New economics sees community not just as a warm and fuzzy attribute of daily life but as a foundation for building new ways of managing resources and providing livelihoods. Organizations such as community land trusts, cooperatives, and municipally owned enterprises are alternatives to the private property model that, when operated democratically, can result in ecologically and socially beneficial outcomes. Natural asset projects, as described above, are also examples of investments in community that meet these goals. Elinor Ostrom's (1990) groundbreaking work on community management of common resources shows that private property is but one—often flawed—approach. Placing ownership and control of land and ecosystems in communities, either through nonprofits, cooperative shares, trusts, or other arrangements, is an increasingly popular way of building vibrant, sustainable, and fair local and regional economies.

Taken together, these four principles add up to an alternative lifestyle that we call the "new economics of household production." Households diversify their labor across a number of sites—they work some hours for pay in the BAU market, self-provision, share and swap, and engage in community investments that yield goods and income. The plenitude "sector" has become a place to go to avoid declining mobility in the BAU economy. Those who engage with it find exciting start-ups, peer production schemes, collaborative consumer sites, local co-ops, trusts, and nonprofits. They manage diversified income streams and sources of goods and services. They build strong social ties that serve as insurance when times are difficult. Few people are engaged in all the dimensions of the model, but increasingly its adherents are involved in multiple practices. What starts with a membership in a CSA expands to include a time bank, car sharing, and participation in online collaborative production.

The withdrawal of labor time from BAU also yields important macro or systemwide consequences. First, it redistributes the available work more equitably, thereby reducing unemployment and poverty. One reason for job scarcity in the United States is that too many of the jobs that do exist require long hours. If people opt for shorter schedules, employers can spread the work they do have over more employees. If rapid growth is not coming back, then we need creative ways to provide jobs for everyone. Reducing hours is an inescapable part of a fair adjustment to a growth-constrained future (Schor 2010, 2013; Victor 2008). The second effect is that when people work less, carbon and ecological footprints are reduced (Knight, Rosa, and Schor, 2013). The wealthy countries of the Global North whose residents work fewer hours annually have been more successful in reducing carbon emissions. This is because their economies are growing more slowly and because households with more time to spare are able to live more sustainably. Energy is a powerful substitute for time. The third effect of shorter working hours is that it preserves time for family, friends, community, and the natural world. There's no way we'll be able to regain a humane economy, a functioning democracy, or ecological sanity without reclaiming our time.

AN IDIOSYNCRATIC EMERGENCE

We have described plenitude as a "movement," but that formulation does not do justice to its experimental and pluralistic nature. It is emerging as a congeries of diverse experiments, in a variety of places, with participation from a range of demographic groups. That, in some sense, is in its very nature. Unlike BAU, this alternative does not advocate a single, best way of doing things. It believes that context matters, which means that solutions are to be found in local adaptations rather than in a globally installed monoculture. It also takes nature as a guide, and nature is nothing if not extraordinarily diverse. Pluralism is thought to yield more resilience, efficiency, and adaptability. Many of the plenitude initiatives or regions that have sprung up around the country and the world are labs of innovation, in which people try new things, adapt when they don't work, and try again.

The seven ethnographic case studies in this volume represent what might superficially appear to be an odd or even idiosyncratic collection. However, that quirkiness and diversity is representative of plenitude as a whole. Plenitude innovations are being adopted by hipsters in trendy areas of the East and West coasts as well as by inner-city residents in midwestern cities such as Detroit, Milwaukee, and Cleveland. The Transition initiatives that are being organized, largely by a middle-aged cohort, bear many similarities to the collaborative experiments of young technophiles who make up the peer-to-peer and open-source hardware movements. Enthusiasm for bicycles is common to the youth of Chicago's South Side and the Cambridge residents who revel in their "car-free" lifestyles. The desire to get off the grid that we found among Alaskan Transitioners is not so different from that of the alternatifs in France who began their journey decades ago. In the interviews we have conducted, we find that respondents link farmers' markets, CSAs, solar panels, bicycle fabrication, permaculture, and the purchase of raw milk as they create alternative, sustainable lifestyles.

The volume opens with the story of the Aude, a region of southern France whose mountainous terrain and difficult farming conditions led to an outmigration of local youth, and then an influx of 1968ers looking to create a different kind of society. These alternatifs chose the Aude because its cheap and plentiful land enabled lifestyles with relatively little cash. The first author of this chapter, Teresa Gowan, has been going to the Aude for many years, since her mother moved there, attracted to the region's lifestyle and community. The alternatifs eventually turned the region into a center of self-provisioning, local commerce, barter, and strong social connection. This French case shows one possibility for what an economy and society can look like when plenitude practices become widespread. Inhabitants of the region enjoy a tremendous amount of personal liberty and free time, revel in their creativity and artistry, and forge long-term friendships and relations of mutual aid. They also work hard, typically at some type of farming or craft work. It's not an easy life, but it does appear to be a satisfying one. Teresa and Rachel Slocum identify a number of factors that have made these alternative lifestyles possible. The first is ideological: the architects of the Aude's transformation reject capitalist values and are firmly committed to resisting what the French call the *métro-boulot-dodo* (travel-work-sleep) lifestyle, the equivalent to our "work and spend." The second is more practical. They are able to rely on state support for education and health care. While the lesson of this case is not that it is impossible to live plenitudinous lifestyles without a welfare state, it does provide a cautionary tale about attempting to leave the market without mechanisms of common security.

The second case takes us to Alaska, where we meet leaders of the local Transition movement. Karen Hébert, who has done ethnographic work in the state for years, chronicles the origins and progress of two Transition initiatives, one in Anchorage and the second in the oil town of Kenai. The Transition movement emphasizes two great challenges: climate change and peak oil. These have been especially resonant in Alaska, given warming in the Arctic and the state's dependence on the oil industry. Karen finds that the organizers of these initiatives are following plenitude principles such as leaving full-time work and self-provisioning. One couple bought a bio-shelter, an ecologically closed-loop home, which they pay for partly by leading tours through it. A number of participants are permaculture instructors who are teaching others to engage in sustainable food production. Transitioners are putting together diverse income streams from start-up careers and businesses, and building neighborhood social capital in the hopes that they can survive as extreme weather and energy shortages intensify.

The Alaskan case presents an especially challenging political context for Transition, as the conservative and libertarian culture of the state is strong.

But the overtly apolitical face of Transition, and plenitude more generally, can be an asset in places where politics is highly polarized. As the Alaskan Transitioners themselves often note—it's easy to do Transition in Portland or Seattle. Getting results in Alaska is a far more impressive achievement. Karen analyzes the accomplishments and obstacles of this movement and draws lessons that are relevant for Transition activists throughout North America.

In the next case, Juliet, Emilie Dubois, and Lindsey (Luka) Carfagna study the nation's largest volunteer time bank, which is located in Boston and Cambridge, Massachusetts. Time banks predate the sustainability movement, originally invented to address the high unemployment of the 1980s. Members join a bank and earn "time dollars" by performing services for other members. They spend their dollars when others perform services for them. All trades are based on time spent rather than skill level or the market value of the services, and everyone's time is valued equally. This egalitarian feature of the time bank is one of its most appealing features, as it stands in stark contrast to prevailing market valuations that create vast and socially illegitimate inequalities.

In our interviews with time bankers we found that they are eager to escape the marketization of services and the increasing commercialization of daily life. Many express market fatigue and are nostalgic for an earlier era when people could rely on economies of reciprocity for daily needs. For members who are rejecting full-time work, the time bank represents a way to get services without expending cash. As such, it lives up to its promise of providing an alternative to the cash economy. However, the time bank also shows the limits of egalitarian alternatives in the midst of a highly unequal market society. For some members who consider their skills very valuable, or whose high cultural capital leads them to prefer others of high socioeconomic standing, the equal valuation of every member's time presents a challenge. A subset of members seeks out other highly educated people to trade with, implicitly devaluing those whose education or social class is below their own. Creating truly egalitarian economic arrangements requires more than just fairer principles of exchange. It also requires cultural transformation and ideological commitment, an insight that also comes from the French case study.

Next, Craig Thompson and Melea Press explore the world of community-supported agriculture, or CSA, as it is commonly referred to. CSA is a form of subscription farming—members join a local farm and for a set fee they get access to a portion of the farm's output. Numbering only about 1,000 in 1999, the latest count in 2007 found 12,500 CSAs now operating. Craig and Melea have done extensive research on CSAs, from both the consumer and the farmer sides. In this piece their respondents are central Pennsylvanians, a population more mainstream and middle American than most of the subjects discussed elsewhere in the book. Interviews were conducted from first exposure to the CSA through an entire growing season to investigate members' changing relationships to food, the market, the natural world, and the people in their lives. The research revealed that a change as simple as joining a subscription farm can have profound effects. One member, who joined because he wanted to lock in a set price for his vegetables, began to care deeply about local farmers. Another, who also signed up to keep her grocery costs down, became committed to a living wage for food producers. Others began to see the connections between farming and climate change and a healthy environment, even if they originally joined because they wanted to save money or improve their health. Building on sociological accounts of contemporary life such as Ulrich Beck's risk society, Melea and Craig argue that many people feel paralyzed by the scope of the environmental, political, economic, and other problems facing the world today. Participating in a CSA allows them to feel efficacious, not just about their own lives but because they are participating in what feels like a local solution to these global issues. Climate change, exploitation of farmers and farm workers, toxic pesticides, and a range of other challenges that they had rarely thought about before were now at the forefront of their concerns.

In the next case, we meet another emerging food practice, the consumption of raw milk. Banned in most parts of the United States in the mid-twentieth century on account of bacterial contamination, the procurement of unpasteurized, or raw, milk is gaining adherents in areas of the country where alternative food practices are most extensive. Diana Mincyte, a sociologist whose earlier ethnographic research focused on raw milk economies in eastern Europe, expands her gaze to raw milk consumers in New York, a highly educated, sophisticated group that is passionate about this quasi-legal commodity. Diana finds that raw milk consumption is part of a nexus of alternative practices that include membership in procurement clubs that work directly with farmers, self-directed investigations into alternative theories of health and illness, and creative transformations of the milk into yogurt, buttermilk, kefir, and cheese. A central conclusion of this case is that participation in these alternative practices leads to a larger set of changes and resistant behaviors, much as the act of joining a CSA or a time bank transforms its members.

Diana contrasts the U.S. group with her subjects in Lithuania, where raw milk production is a vestige of premodern economies. Superficially, the mostly female farmers who deliver raw milk to city dwellers by hand could not be more different than the New Yorkers. They present as backward peasants, opposed to the standardizing and modernizing effects of European unification. But the groups share a number of features. In both cases, raw milk networks are important avenues of social connection, creativity, the shortening of commodity chains, and opposition to state policies that are directed at outlawing this supposedly dangerous product. The relative poverty of the Lithuanians, like that of the French inhabitants of the Aude, also raises an interesting juxtaposition—plenitude practitioners are sometimes voluntary downshifters whose cash incomes place them among the ranks of the poor. What is the relation between cash assets and the other forms of wealth, such as wealth of time, information, or creativity, that are so valued by this movement?

The raw milk study is also interesting because it involves legally questionable activity and, in many cases, strong antistate views. While many plenitude practitioners are critical of corporations, for this group the state is a more prominent pole of opposition. However, while they may be the most antistate of the plenitude groups we have studied, there are parallels among advocates of other practices that either defy or skirt the law. We are thinking here of the urban poultry movement, which involves violating local ordinances against having poultry in one's yard, the renting out of spare rooms through sites such as AirBnB in contravention of local regulations, renting personal automobiles when liability is not clear, and the typically unexplored tax liabilities associated with peer to peer consumption schemes. Indeed, there is a variety of legal ambiguities associated with some plenitude practices that we expect will receive more scrutiny as the scale of participation grows (Orsi and Doskow 2009).

Robert Wengronowitz's account of what is now a venerable Chicago institution—Experimental Station—draws out the links between contemporary plenitude initiatives and innovations from the 1960s. It also affirms the relevance of plenitude principles across class and race, in this case the largely African American neighborhood of Chicago's South Side. Experimental Station was started by Ken Dunn, a visionary but practical University of Chicago student in 1967 who enlisted homeless men in recycling. The name comes from a Frank Lloyd Wright speech and refers to the productive melding of art and technology under the same roof. It also signals another dimension of plenitude—the importance of experimentation and change. The Station has gone through a variety of physical incarnations as well as different directions and activities and sees itself as creating an ecology of diverse initiatives that over time add up to a living, growing alternative system. Its core is a loosely knit group of DIY adherents. In some ways, it's a microcosm of what Teresa and Rachel studied in the Aude. Bobby's case looks closely at two current projects, a racially integrated farmers' market that sits on the boundary between the South Side and the affluent, white Hyde Park neighborhood, and a bicycle shop that attracts young African American boys and girls who learn to build and repair bikes.

The findings from this case highlight a number of aspects of plenitude. First, the bicycle shop has been a successful venue, especially for young boys from the neighborhood who might otherwise be drawn into gangs and violence. Many of them are captivated by the chance to earn a bicycle of their own, which they can after putting in a certain number of hours at the shop. They go on to learn repair and construction, an example of the kind of skills and DIY capacities that many plenitude practitioners are turning to. The currency earned at the shop is bicycles, not cash, although there is some fungibility with cash as those who spend many hours can sell the bicycles they earn. The kids who populate the bike shop find mentors, community, a place to build marketable skills, and the joy of skilled labor. While the chapter is an inspiring story about addressing poverty and race through an alternative economy, it is also an example of the transformative potentials of a plenitude technology, in this case the bicycle. Bicycles have a minimal carbon footprint, are now a faster means of transport than a private car in many traffic-congested cities, combine exercise and mobility in one activity, and enable people to experience their surroundings on a human scale. They can also be constructed locally in small-scale workshops such as the one at Experimental Station. (Bicycle frames can be made from scrap metal using fabrication lab machines or by hand with materials such as bamboo. There's now a thriving world of handmade bamboo bikes, which range from the very inexpensive do-it-yourself projects available online to rather expensive professional-quality DIY versions to commercially available options.) Bobby also highlights another aspect of plenitude: the pursuit of pleasure. Whether it's through pizza nights around the wood-fired oven, cooking classes at the Station, community get-togethers, mingling at the market, or hanging out with the neighborhood kids, the people who are drawn to this space come both to make a difference in the world and to experience the deep pleasures it makes possible.

Douglas Holt's chapter on the challenges of scaling up the sustainable economy model to Main Street presents a less optimistic and more cautionary account of the possibilities of this movement. He argues that sustainability has been culturally branded by a system of discourses—what he refers to as market myths—that are resonant with a highly educated and affluent sector of society variously characterized as the cultural creative class or bourgeois-bohemians (aka bobos) but that have little relevance to the broader swath of Americans who are struggling to maintain some semblance of a middle-class lifestyle in the face of the economic collapse of 2009, imploding local economies, student loan debt, foreclosures, and declining real wages. Douglas argues that these Main Streeters, who now make up approximately 60 percent of the population, are unreceptive to standard plenitude messaging about imperatives to address climate change or combat forces of environmental degradation because they are, by sheer necessity, firmly focused on economic opportunity, particularly for their children. Accordingly, he argues, plenitude initiatives will gain traction among this socioeconomic class only when they are directly and meaningfully linked to grassroots strategies for creating local economic opportunities. At the end of the chapter, Douglas sketches an approach to Main Street that provides public employment for youth at the same time that it provides needed services and reduces ecological footprints.

In the final chapter, we also take up the question of the politics of plenitude. We begin with the question of whether plenitude, because it is primarily oriented to transformation through lifestyles and entrepreneurial activity, is a neoliberal response to the twin crises of ecology and economics. We look at dominant conceptions of the market by analyzing the influential formulation of Friedrich Hayek. While any one plenitude innovation—a CSA or a bicycle shop or an artisanal cheese maker or a raw milk consumer—may seem innocuous, or worse, reproductive of the dominant market system, we argue that these acts and projects must be seen in their entirety. Drawing on Gilles Deleuze and Felix Guattari's notion of the rhizome, we see the potential for change coming from the aggregation of many small initiatives, a kind of underground root structure that is taking hold without a centralized leadership. It's a networked revolution, if you will, that we believe has the potential to contribute to significant social transformation.

That does not mean, to return to the question with which we started this introduction, that climate change can be stopped by local action. We are at a crucial moment that demands concerted efforts by governments, and the United States and China in particular, to get the planet off fossil fuels. But we do believe that the practices and ways of being in the world that plenitude practitioners are pioneering will be an important part of how and why a different energy and economic system can work. By weaning off a carbon-intensive consumer lifestyle, embracing economic equity for all, finding means of livelihood without relying on continual growth, and using plenitude's emphasis on social connections to build political power for lasting change, we believe the movement we describe in this volume is part of the path to a sustainable, humane, and fair future.

NOTES

1. http://www.globalcarbonproject.org/carbonbudget/12/hl-full.htm.
2. In much of the contemporary news media and business press, fracking and shale oil extraction technologies are heralded as rebukes to predictions that declining oil production would profoundly and negatively impact the world economy (e.g., Brown 2012; Orszag 2012). However, peak oil more accurately refers to declining rates of production from the most accessible and cost-effective sources. In blunt terms, peak oil means the end of (relatively) cheap petroleum. In keeping with original peak oil predictions, it was expected that higher prices for raw crude would encourage more costly (and environmentally risky) modes of production, such as deep-sea oil drilling and the much-ballyhooed processes of fracking and shale extraction. While these technologies are, in the short run, minimizing the shortfalls between increasing demand for fossil fuels and the declining of rates of conventional oil production since 2005 (Deffeyes 2011), they are nonetheless costly, and many experts argue environmentally risky, adaptations to peak oil conditions. As discussed by Richard Vodra (2013), "Traditional wells have a ratio of energy returned on energy invested (EROEI) of 10-or 20-to-one, or an energy cost factor of 5 to 10%. The EROEI with fracking is in the range of 5-or 10-to-one, or a cost factor of 10 to 20%. . . . EROEI roughly correlates with financial cost, and a typical fracking oil well in Texas now costs over $10 million to drill, compared to less than $1 million for a conventional well." These exorbitant investment costs, coupled with the troubling fact that fracking wells have a rapid decline rate— creating a so-called drilling dread mill to meet production goals—suggest that the destabilizing effects of peak oil conditions on the BAU economy are being modulated but certainly not obviated by exploiting these less accessible reserves of hydrocarbons.
3. The paperback edition of *Plenitude,* published in 2011, has the title *True Wealth.*

REFERENCES

Alperovitz, Gar. 2011. "The New-Economy Movement." *Nation,* May 25. http://www.thenation.com/article/160949/new-economy-movement (accessed March 1, 2013).

Benkler, Yochai. 2006. *The Wealth of Networks: How Social Production Transforms Markets and Freedom.* New Haven, CT: Yale University Press.

Boyce, James. 2007. "Inequality and Environmental Protection." In *Inequality, Collective Action, and Environmental Sustainability,* ed. Jean-Marie Baland, Pranab Bardhan, and Samuel Bowles, 314–48. Princeton, NJ: Princeton University Press.

Boyce, James, and Barry Shelley. 2003. *Natural Assets: Democratizing Environmental Ownership*. Washington, DC: Island.

Broad, Robin, and John Cavanagh. 2012. "It's the New Economy, Stupid." *Nation*, November 28. http://www.thenation.com/article/171502/its-new-economy-stupid (accessed March 1, 2013).

Brown, Mark. 2012. "Citigroup: Shale Oil Fracking Has Killed Peak Oil." *Wired*, February 23. http://www.wired.co.uk/news/archive/2012–02/23/peak-oil (accessed March 1, 2013).

Carfagna, Lindsey B., Emilie A. Dubois, Connor Fitzmaurice, Thomas Laidley, Monique Ouimette, Juliet B. Schor, and Margaret Willis. 2014. "An Emerging Eco-habitus: The Reconfiguration of High Cultural Capital Practices among Ethical Consumers." *Journal of Consumer Culture*. 14(2): 1–21.

Deffeyes, Kenneth S. 2011. *When Oil Peaked*. New York: Hill and Wang.

Dunlap, Riley, and Aaron McCright. 2003. "Defending Kyoto: The Conservative Movement's Impact on U.S. Climate Change Policy." *Social Problems*, 47 (4): 499–522.

Fitzsimmons, Jill. 2013. "Study: Warmest Year on Record Received Cool Climate Coverage." *Media Matters for America*, January 8. http://mediamatters.org/research/.2013/01/08/study-warmest-year-on-record-received-cool-clim/192079 (accessed March 1, 2013).

Gillis, Justin. 2012. "Ending Its Summer Melt, Arctic Sea Ice Sets a New Low That Leads to Warnings." *New York Times*, September 19. http://www.nytimes.com/2012/09/20/science/earth/arctic-sea-ice-stops-melting-but-new-record-low-is-set.html?_r=1& (accessed March 1, 2013).

———. 2013. "Not Even Close: 2012 Was Hottest Ever in U.S." *New York Times*, January 8. http://www.nytimes.com/2013/01/09/science/earth/2012-was-hottest-year-ever-in-us.html (accessed March 1, 2013).

Global Carbon Budget Highlights. 2012. *Global Carbon Project*. http://www.globalcarbonproject.org/carbonbudget/12/hl-full.htm (accessed March 1, 2013).

Knight, Kyle W., Eugene A. Rosa, and Juliet B. Schor. 2013. "Reducing Growth to Achieve Environmental Sustainability: The Role of Work Hours." In *Capitalism on Trial: Explorations in the Tradition of Thomas Weisskopf*, ed. Robert Pollin and Jeannette Wicks-Limm, 187–204. Cheltenham, UK: Edward Elgar.

Kopytoff, Igor. 1986. *The Social Life of Things: Commodities in Cultural Perspective*. Cambridge: Cambridge University Press.

McKibben, Bill. 2012. "Global Warming's Terrifying New Math." *Rolling Stone*, July 19. http://www.rollingstone.com/politics/news/global-warmings-terrifying-new-math-20120719 (accessed March 1, 2013).

Monbiot, George. 2012. "Annus Horribilis." *Guardian*, December 31. http://www.monbiot.com/2012/12/31/annus-horribilis/ (accessed March 1, 2013).

NOAA. 2012. "U.S. Records Warmest March, More Than 15,000 Warm Temperature Records Broken." U.S. Department of Commerce blog entries, April 9. http://www.commerce.gov/blog/2012/04/09/noaa-us-records-warmest-march-more-15000-warm-temperature-records-broken (accessed May 21, 2013).

Obama, Barack. 2012. Remarks by the President, November 14, News Conference. *White House Office of the Press Secretary*. http://www.whitehouse.gov/the-press-office/2012/11/14/remarks-president (accessed March 1, 2013).

Orsi, Janelle, and Emily Doskow. 2009. *The Sharing Solution: How to Save Money, Simplify Your Life and Build Community*. Berkeley, CA: Nolo.

Orszag, Peter. 2012. "Fracking Boom Could Finally Cap Myth of Peak Oil." *Bloomberg*, January 31. http://www.bloomberg.com/news/2012–02–01/fracking-boom-could-finally-cap-myth-of-peak-oil-peter-orszag.html (accessed March 1, 2013).

Ostrom, Elinor. 1990. *Governing the Commons: The Evolution of Institutions for Collective Action*. Cambridge: Cambridge University Press.

Peters, Glen P., Gregg Marland, Corinnne Le Quéré, Thomas Boden, Josep G. Canadell, and Michael R. Raupach. 2012. "Rapid Growth in CO_2 Emissions After the 2008–2009 Global Financial Crisis." *Nature Climate Change* 2 (January): 2–4.

Schor, Juliet B. 1998. *The Overspent American: Upscaling, Downshifting, and the New Consumer*. New York: Basic Books.

———. 2010. *Plenitude: The New Economics of True Wealth*. New York: Penguin.

———. 2013. "Why Solving Climate Change Requires Working Less." In *Reducing Working Hours*, ed. Anna Coote. London: New Economics Foundation.

Schumacher, E. F. [1973] 2000. *Small Is Beautiful, 25th Anniversary Edition: Economics as If People Mattered; 25 Years Later . . . with Commentaries*. Vancouver: Hartley and Marks.

Slivka, Kelly. 2012. "Rare Burst of Melting Seen in Greenland's Ice Sheet. *New York Times*, July 24.

Stiglitz, Joseph. 2013. "Climate Change and Poverty Have Not Gone Away." *Guardian*, January 7. http://www.guardian.co.uk/business/2013/jan/07/climate-change-poverty-inequality (accessed November 15, 2013).

Van Horn, Carl, Cliff Zukin, Mark Szeltner, and Charley Stone. 2012. "Left Out. Forgotten? Recent High School Graduates and the Great Recession." New Brunswick, NJ: John J. Heldrich Center for Workforce Development, Rutgers University. http://www.heldrich.rutgers.edu/about-center/staff/carl-e-van-horn-phd-0 (accessed March 1, 2013).

Victor, Peter A. 2008. *Managing without Growth: Slower by Design, Not Disaster*. Northampton, MA: Edward Elgar.

Vodra, Richard. 2013. "Is Fracking a Happy Solution to Our Energy Needs?" Advisorperspectives. http://advisorperspectives.com/newsletters13/pdfs/Is_Fracking_a_Happy_Solution_to_our_Energy_Needs.pdf (accessed March, 1, 2013).

Chapter 1 Artisanal Production, Communal Provisioning, and Anticapitalist Politics in the Aude, France

Teresa Gowan and Rachel Slocum

In the absence of revolutionary change, to what extent can alternative economic practices reduce the toll of ecological devastation, rampant consumerism, and radical inequality in favor of more sustainable ecosystems and more fulfilling and equitable ways of life? What is the potential for incremental transformations of the destructive, unstable economic world system we call capitalism? Understanding how to change the world requires not only visionary thought but also *praxis,* the development of knowledge through the active process of social change. In this spirit, we were drawn to study core practitioners in one of Europe's more notable centers of small-scale local production and ecological consciousness: the French *département* of the Aude.

Here in the southwestern corner of France, remote villages depopulated or abandoned by the devastating rural exodus that took place after the Second World War were discovered by enthusiastic radicals of the generation of '68. Because the Aude was long one of the country's poorest départements, its rock-bottom land prices made it possible for these migrants of very modest means to establish themselves on smallholdings and to build a local economy around self-provisioning, small-scale market production, and exchange, which gave them unusual independence from the mainstream cash economy. From the 1970s to the present, the growing alternative economy and the comparatively lower price of land continued to attract new migrants from urban France, the Netherlands, Germany, Switzerland, Britain, and Belgium, people with an orientation toward anticonsumerism, voluntary simplicity, and ecological sustainability. While many other former strongholds of the western European alternative economy and culture have faded, the rocky hills of the Aude, and especially the area's Haute Vallée (High Valley), have retained a critical mass of *alternatif* (alternative) farmers and artisans. The collapse of the eastern bloc and state socialism brought new migrants from East Germany and Poland in the 1990s and 2000s, and even though land prices are rising, young alternatifs continue to migrate into the area.

Through an ethnography of *petits producteurs*—small-scale producers of cheese, olive oil, bread, meat, honey, and organic vegetables—we sought to understand how the Aude's economy of sustainable production, self-provisioning, and mutual help in the Haute Vallée and the Corbières—our two study sites—came to exist. What motivated these people to leave urban areas of origin and dedicate themselves to small-scale organic farming and low-tech forms of production? To what extent have they built a common culture and community, and what does it look like? How do they understand and negotiate their relationship to the formal market and the French state?

DIVERSE ECONOMIES: TOWARD A PRAXIS OF ABUNDANCE

Cases such as this one are celebrated by some and viewed with deep skepticism by others. Neoclassical economists and Marxists alike tend to reaffirm the versatility and virility of capitalism, making it appear inevitable, an unstoppable creator of landscapes. But a growing area of scholarship argues that rather than a juggernaut that flattens worlds, capitalism must be *achieved*— it does not "just happen," and it is actually a "leaky" system, its powers often dissipated (Gibson-Graham 1996; Massey 2000). Gibson-Graham and others have urged scholars to explore the multitude of "diverse economies" outside business-as-usual (henceforth BAU) capitalism, in the form of noncash exchange, self- or communal provisioning, circuits of unpaid care and household labor, and informal gifting. By studying the characteristics of diverse economies, their internal and external power relations, and their viability as objects of activism and policy, we might lend them more legitimacy within global conversations about alternatives to capitalism (Gibson-Graham 2008). Like-minded scholars have similarly begun to explore self-consciously alternative forms of economic organization, from Global North to South, especially non-market exchange in the form of bartering or "local exchange trading systems" (LETS) (Hughes 2005; Leyshon 2005).

Skeptics question the potential of alternative economies (Glassman 2003). Inevitably, they find "that for every local food co-op with a few score members, there is another Walmart superstore, stocked floor to ceiling with commodities produced by processes straight out of the pages of Marx's *Capital*" (McCarthy 2006, 99). Others point to the reliance of alternative economies on infusions of income and wealth from work in the BAU economy, on women's unpaid household maintenance and caregiving, and even indentured labor (Lawson 2005).

The reminder to pay attention to labor relations is welcome—certainly the vast history of slavery and other unfree labor should warn us against any general romanticization of economic systems outside the capitalist market. For this reason, it is probably not a bad thing for those researching diverse economies to remember the skeptical voice of theorists of the underground economy, who remind us that the commonsense opposition between the BAU and the informal economy disguises what is often in fact a close relationship. Capital outsources the lower layers of global production into the informal sector, and even more widely relies on cheap or unpaid labor in the informal economy for the subsistence of workers on very low wages (Portes, Castells, and Benton 1995).

Yet we still agree with Gibson-Graham that totalizing visions of the ever-expanding, ever-adaptable power of capital are tainted by paranoia and defeatism. Interpreting household work, informal exchange, or gifting economies solely in terms of how they benefit capital not only masks their potential lessons for sustainable local production, it devalues the immense creativity, cultural knowledge, and human connection that can potentially be transmitted and reinforced through such practices.

Capitalism's onslaught on the world's ecosystems is a major instigator of alternative economies across the Global North. With many around the world aspiring, we are told, to consume at levels practiced in the Global North (Zakaria 2011), the world is in trouble. Humanity has been warned for centuries that it will bump up against limits (Meadows et al. 1972), and this way of seeing is now supercharged by global extinction and climate change. This threat of imminent destruction requires belt tightening, even though the majority has never suffered from "affluenza." But we suspect that narratives of scarcity and frugality are not likely to enthuse majorities anywhere. Instead, mobilizing people toward different political economies requires reorienting and enriching contemporary frames of "sufficiency"—focusing less on *scarcity* and more on pleasure, community, and alternative kinds of abundance. In fact, these latter notions quite accurately reflect the intentions of the alternatifs and artisans we discuss in this chapter.

A similar focus on pleasure, community, and alternative kinds of abundance informs Juliet Schor's *Plenitude* (2010), which makes the case for the combined revolutionary potential of small-scale "bottom-up" movements away from the BAU economy. She identifies four principles. The first is "true materialism"—in the sense of passionate engagement with the materiality of the product, its natural and social history, and its future in terms of sustainability. Equally important are a "new allocation of time," "self-provisioning," and "reinvesting in community and ourselves."

Our current chapter extends Schor's schema: our study supports the idea that reversing domination by a dislocated cash nexus requires not only an *economics* but a *politics* of plenitude—more successful alternative economies are likely to be embedded in a holistic vision and culture of change that fundamentally reorients notions of work and production, wealth and security. Economic arrangements are inherently political. We slightly modify Schor's four principles, therefore, by reframing the "new allocation of time" as only one part of a more fundamental reorientation toward work and creativity, a demand for "nonalienated labor." More specifically, our case study gives us the ground to make important contributions to the concept of the plenitude economy.

First, our case demonstrates the crucial importance of initiating alternative economic practices within favorable socioeconomic conditions. The Aude was inexpensive enough to allow *les néo-ruraux* (neorurals) to settle in substantial numbers and to dig in with a tenacity that has supported successive waves of migrants. The willingness of many older Audois to accept and teach the migrants was also important.

Second, we make the point that alternative economic practices do not have to inhabit a rarified, pure space in which making a living is subordinated to ideals. Instead, we see a continuum of approaches to the market and to work itself, from "deep" alternatifs privileging radical simplicity and autonomy to others pursuing artisanal businesses oriented to high quality—they might eventually sell to a Michelin three-star restaurant or even a San Francisco boutique. Yet there is much overlap between the two orientations; it is notable that all the producers explicitly reject core elements of business-as-usual economic practice, particularly the idea of prioritizing profit over other outcomes and unsatisfying enslavement to work. What is of paramount importance is the commitment to live relatively simply, finding primary fulfillment not in profits but in what they do: the ethical, communal, and aesthetic characteristics of production are ends in and of themselves.

Third, the diverse economic practices among the Aude alternatifs are underpinned by tight networks of support and cooperation. The prevalence of gifting, cooperation, and informal exchange evident in our case constitutes a kind of communal provisioning, which is key to the high quality of life and the economic survival of petits producteurs and alternatif residents of the area, substantially lowering the cost of living. We therefore see a strong synergy between Schor's principle of (self-)provisioning and that of reinvestment in community, in that informal exchange networks simultaneously provide vital material support for households while creating and reinforcing strong social ties.

Fourth, the small producers in the Aude have benefited greatly from the strongly interventionist French welfare state. Without a variety of programs for new farmers and organic agriculture, farmland preservation, health care, social security, and child support, the modest resources and low-cash arrangements of many of our interviewees would have left them in a vulnerable and perhaps less sustainable precarity, making this alternative economy a far less inclusive project. In sum, a receptive community, inexpensive basic resources, and a strong welfare state provided the fertile ground into which plenitude practitioners' nonnormative approach to work and money could take root, grow, and spread.

SOCIAL LANDSCAPE OF THE STUDY SITE AND
RESEARCH METHODS

Our study benefited from Teresa's wealth of acquaintance and friendship in the area—her mother has lived on a smallholding in the Corbières for over twenty years, and Teresa has spent months in the Haute Vallée every summer for the last eight years. Several of the producers were already friends or acquaintances. We knew already, therefore, that our two sites had a somewhat different place within the Aude's alternative economy. The Haute Vallée is a "hippie" and "*écolo*" (environmental) center with many foreign migrants, well known within European counterculture networks. The Lagrasse area of the Corbières, more tied into the region's traditionalist wine monoculture, has also drawn '68ers and later migrants seeking to live differently, with a somewhat stronger concentration of those more likely to characterize themselves as artisans.

The watershed moment of May 1968 had a subtle but indelible effect on the character of the Aude, as countercultural migrants from urban France, Holland, Belgium, Britain, Germany, and Switzerland trickled steadily into its isolated villages and even more remote abandoned farms and barns. With their enthusiasm to experiment with a radically different way of life, this group tended to identity as "alternatifs." Some longer-standing residents, not tuned in to the same radical desires, could not fathom why anyone would choose the hard labor of the *paysan* (peasant) existence and indeed often found the lifestyles and many of the motives of the "neorurals" jarring.

The incomers stirred up the public culture of the place, challenging traditional mores as well as demonstrating new economic possibilities in the region. The first generation would never truly belong to the tight-knit village-based communities, but their higher numbers in the Haute Vallée created a stronger alternatif culture, and in the cases where they took over largely abandoned hamlets and villages, they quickly became involved in local politics.

Later waves of newcomers continued the labor-intensive work of rebuilding ruined farmhouses and creating a living, joined by some returning children of the first alternatifs. Several chose the Aude because it was more affordable than the increasingly expensive Provence to the northeast.

On the whole, the producteurs in the Haute Vallée articulated a more deeply alternative ethos than their more diversely oriented counterparts to the north in the Corbières. Across the study we found a wide range of orientations to production and the politics of *bio* (organic) agriculture. While some were involved in large-scale production and distribution, most, whether more artisan or alternatif, made their living from the earnings of their small sales at one or two markets, making the conscious decision not to expand their business or put their competitors out of business.

During the summer and fall of 2011 we conducted twenty-two life-history interviews with eighteen petits producteurs (individuals or couples), two former producteurs, and two key local activists. We defined petits producteurs for the purposes of the study as people who (1) sell at a local market, producers' shop, and/or co-op; and (2) do not sell to large-scale distributors because it does not suit their business model or their ideological position. We also engaged in participant observation of markets, co-ops, an organic fair, and a *boutique paysanne.*[1] Teresa volunteered regularly at the Espéraza co-op Amaranthe for nine months from October 2011. We recorded observations through field notes and transcribed interviews, focusing our analysis on the themes explored below.

The markets were particularly important ethnographic sites. Repositories of concentrated symbolism of "traditional" France, market imaginaries connect French identity to rural village life and to localized foods embodying specific climate, soil, and regional tradition (*terroir*), although the reality is often quite different (Fantasia 1995; Demossier 2003; Hervieu and Purseigle 2008). Weekly open-air markets persist in the postindustrial age, although they have become less central to public life and household provisioning in villages and towns alike. But in much of the Aude, with its low population density, they continue to thrive.

Lézignan's large urban market represents a typically diverse mixture of local producers and resellers of fruit and vegetables sharing space with vendors of cheap clothing, shoes, utensils, and the like. The tiny Lagrasse market represents the other end of the spectrum. Made up almost exclusively of small local producers, it caters to local people throughout the year, but its regular seven or eight stalls swell to twice that many when the clientele is boosted by second-home owners and tourists in the summer. We interviewed nine people of different ages and national backgrounds from the villages around the canton of Lagrasse in the Corbières. The Lagrasse market is too small to significantly support the area's producers, so most sell at the larger Lézignan market to the east (see fig. 1.1). We recruited the second set of nine producers at the Haute Vallée's most important market in the small town of Espéraza. Here again, many of the producteurs also sold in the markets at Limoux to the north, Mirepoix to the west in the Ariège, and in the nearby smaller market in Quillan.

INTO THE FIELDS

Lagrasse and the Corbières

The Lagrasse area of the Corbières lies some twenty miles east-southeast of Carcassonne. There, rocky hills covered with brush (*la garrigue*) surround valleys still dominated by small-scale vine cultivation. Two hours from the sea, this is a land of fierce winds (the dry Cers from the west and the Mediterranean

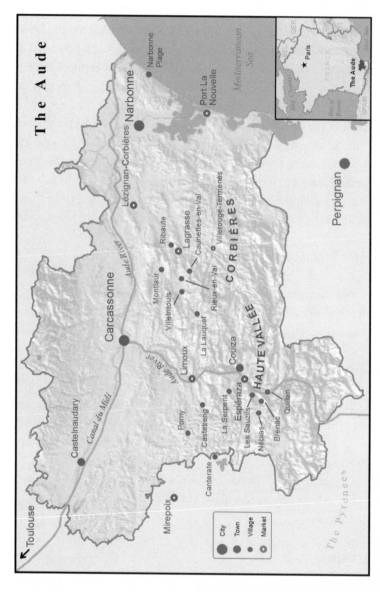

Figure 1.1: Map of the Haute Vallée and the Corbières in the Aude, France

Marin) often mentioned as one of the hardships of living in the Aude. The scent of thyme, rosemary, and fennel, indigenous to the Mediterranean, pervades the air under a sun beating hotly on soil that has withstood hundreds of years of vine cultivation. Most people live in villages and small towns of between fifty and eight hundred people. Avenues of plane trees yield to a compact mass of jumbled old row houses in tiny streets, now usually accompanied by a handful of more modern villas around the edges.

Though nothing like the remote existence of the pre-WWII Corbières, village life still feels profoundly localized. Except for the school service there is no public transit. Commerce is limited to the larger villages, and many, especially homemakers and older people with limited access to cars, rely on regular house visits from vans selling meat and fish that make long circuits from butchers' and fishmongers' shops in Carcassonne. These unique sources of food are slowly losing ground to supermarkets.

The region has been recognized for centuries for wine production; old vines have twined tightly around the cultural and economic life of the Aude, so much so that newcomers often felt cornered literally and figuratively by the vines ("coincés par les vignes"). While viniculture protected these villages from the abandonment that occurred in the Haute Vallée, its dominance hindered alternative economies. Vines took priority for prime land, taking spots near streams and rivers that might have served other purposes, such as gardening. One producer from the Corbières put it like this: "Before there were many more vines than today and so we were cornered by the vines. . . . It's wine, and then a little bit of olive oil in the last fifteen years. Really, olive cultivation is ancient in the region, but the vines took up every available spot. This wine monoculture stifled all the other uses of the land."[2] Though olive groves were once an important part of the economy, they suffered a devastating frost in 1956 that wiped out many. According to a story that circulates among the alternatifs, the conservative rural mind (or maybe the wine cooperatives) created a new truth—the region could not support commercial olive production. Half a century later, olive orchards are being restored by incomers, advised by some of the old people who have kept their olives going.

The Haute Vallée

If you drive southwest from Lagrasse for forty miles or so, the interminable bends of the Corbières Vertes will eventually lead you to the Haute Vallée of the Aude, where remote wooded hills plunge and climb into the deep valleys and massive cliffs of the eastern Pyrenees.

Figure 1.2: Landscape of the Haute Vallée at Brenac

Outside of a cluster of small towns by the Aude River, the rural exodus in the Haute Vallée was extraordinarily severe, leaving many hamlets abandoned and other villages with only a handful of aging men and women. As a result, throughout the 1970s and even early 1980s the old stone village houses (*maisons de village*) could be bought for a song, attracting a large critical mass of *soixante-huitards* ('68ers) eager to leave the industrial city to find pure air and a more "natural" way of life (Cazella 2001). Relations between the residents and newcomers were not always easy. The strong sense of village identity defined even someone from the next valley as an outsider. Both French and foreign-born newcomers had to work to gain acceptance by the local population, who remained reluctant to sell even land that had not been much used in decades. There remain tensions between this long-standing local population and newcomers, often centered on disputes over hunting, traditionally pursued across all agricultural and forest land, regardless of ownership. It is common wisdom that if one seeks only to rent or borrow land rather than to buy it, the chance of being accepted is greater.

Yet given the extraordinary devastation wrought by the radical exodus, some of the old people were willing to countenance an in-migration of strong young neighbors, no matter how strange. Farmer and baker Patrick claimed to have always maintained good relationships with the original locals (*gens du coin*), even as a member of a commune camping out in a ruined hamlet. Farmer Dédou told us how wonderful it was to be so warmly greeted as a young shepherd for hire in the late 1960s: "The old people [left in the villages] were happy to see us, because I think they were depressed to see all the children leave. Yes, they were happy in that they would say, 'My son is making a good situation for himself.' But deeper down there was a real sadness in seeing their land abandoned, their farms neglected."[3]

The Haute Vallée nowadays is still an unusual place. For a start, some of the operations are tiny—with some market traders living in rudimentary straw-bale houses or yurts on a small piece of land, bringing a small collection of varied vegetables to market. The neomedieval purism that characterized many of the earlier communes is no longer the norm, but radical simplicity still exerts a powerful presence.

One commentary, which suggests the unusual character of the Haute Vallée within the French small-producer economy, came from Suzanne, a retired producer from another part of France, who couldn't believe how inefficient and unreliable many of the small producers were in the Haute Vallée. "It is incredible, it's as if they just don't care about making money at all. They just want to be 'baba cool' and do whatever comes to them spontaneously. . . . They *work,* but they are not willing to be efficient (*efficace*). It's *not* like this in other areas. The Haute Vallée is really something else!"[4] She laughed and rolled her eyes.

Our fieldwork and interviews confirmed Suzanne's sense that the Haute Vallée culture placed less emphasis on efficiency and high returns. In many cases, this different orientation was explicitly articulated: there was a strong anticapitalist thrust to many of the interviews, and prominent graffiti marked the main roads of the area with union logos and slogans such as "*Le monde n'est pas une marchandise*" (The world is not a commodity). The alteration of the "Shell" logo to "hell" in fig. 1.3 has remained untouched for several years above the main street of Espéraza.

We begin our analysis of plenitudinous practices in the Aude with Schor's notion of "true materialism." As we demonstrate below, beginning with the Corbières' petits producteurs, true materialism involves not only the relationship between producer and product but building trusting relationships with

Figure 1.3: Espéraza, (S)hell

long-term customers founded on a sense of the importance of the simplicity of the sources and the process of production.

TRUE MATERIALISM

Holistic Commercialization

By the time we arrived at Lézignan market at 9 a.m. one Wednesday in August, there were already ten people queuing for Chantal's cheese, which she cut and wrapped while carrying on rapid, cheerful conversations with regular and new customers alike. She always quickly sells out of her fresh yogurt and *brousse* (an unaged, creamy, yet grainy cheese), and her more mature semisoft *tomme* and *tommette* are equally popular.

About forty years ago, Chantal's husband, Jean-Gabriel, decided to follow his dream in life—to become a sheep farmer. He went to school, worked for four years, and then they looked for a place to establish their own farm, "arriving in the Aude by chance." They were not wealthy enough to buy land, but they were lucky enough to encounter people who would rent them land in the brush-covered hills (the garrigue) for an eight-year renewable contract (*fermage*).[5] In order to get agricultural subsidies from France and Europe, one had to have about twenty-two hectares, which meant they had to find nearly twenty landowners willing to provide fermage to them in order to arrive at the requisite amount. Echoing Dédou's narrative, she said, "When we arrived here, there were only simple people who very much wished to give us land. They knew we needed land. [They said], 'I have a hectare, Madame, I don't know where it is but I would love to loan it to you so that you can work it!' "[6] Chantal and Jean-Gabriel did not favor industrial forms of production, nor did they want their business to get bigger. Instead, by chance again, they heard of people in the nearby Montagne Noire who were making organic sheep cheese. While other Audois considered these cheese makers "hippies" rather than serious producers, Chantal thought the cheese "was really extraordinary . . . so when we tasted that, my husband and I said, 'That's what we want to do' and so it was another adventure, enabled by the fact that I had done five or six cheese-making trainings."[7]

The petits producteurs have a passionate investment in the quality of the goods they make and the sustainability (*durabilité*) of their practice—whether woolen socks and lamb from a small sheep farm, untreated (*pas traités*) vegetables from a market garden, honey and beeswax products, or goat cheese and yogurt. They told us how the quality of their products derives from their simplicity—from the uncontaminated grass eaten by Mireille and Dédou Baudeuf's sheep to the "elemental magic" of baking described evocatively by each of the Haute Vallée bread makers. Bread makers Jan and Rolf both grow their own wheat, while beekeepers Mireille and Philippe go to the trouble of collecting single-source honey. This emphasis on the simple and authentic character of artisanal production epitomizes what Schor calls true materialism.

Chantal believes that one of the key elements of their lifestyle is to take the whole product from origin to sale: "Yesterday I watched a program on TV about the *crottin* of Chantignole. It's one of the typical forms of goat cheese. Those producers, like me, make fresh cheese, and sell it to a cheese maker to be refined. They only make fresh cheese and do not know refining themselves. And it's a pity. Because the real value of their work is created by the refining process and the sale of the finished product. And I think that if you're too big you can't do that, whereas if you are working on our scale, you can."[8] Chantal later reinforced the same point in reference to a woman who had recently started selling lamb direct from her farm in the Val de Dagne. "It's really different here to not sell to the [large] cooperative but instead to take your lambs to the abattoir and to deliver them to your customers yourself. To go right to the endpoint of the process, the sale. This is the only way for us small producers to be able to establish ourselves, and to prosper."[9]

Similar commentary linking pride in their product to the need for careful relationships with customers came from Micias and Marie, deep alternatifs who make syrup from lavender and mint that they cultivate in the hills above Lagrasse. "At first we started very small, but it's true there was a huge demand at first—people said, 'Wow, that's super'—there was such a demand that we couldn't fill all the orders. But now we've organized the production process. . . . Now, people are really looking for these ["real"] products. They encourage us: 'Ah, bravo! Continue what you're doing!' People need contact, to see the producer, to talk with the producer."[10] With Jan and others in the area they bought an old stone farmhouse where they will set up a laboratory to dry the herbs and create syrup, preferring, like Chantal, to follow the process from beginning to end.

Honey producers Mireille and Philippe told us that they treat the commercialization process very seriously, making great efforts to engage with customers as well as to find a number of points of sale. In the south, they argue, there is a sense of shame in making money, which gets in the way of the relationship that people seek with producers. "Everyone is welcome to buy our honey," quipped Philippe.[11] In contrast, Mireille described a potter whose expensive pots were much admired: the seller spent the entire day ignoring the customers, and then complained that she had made no money. To be alternatif should not mean being commercially unsuccessful—"You have to want to sell your product,"[12] insisted Mireille, expressing admiration for the business acumen of Micias and Marie and other producteurs nearby. As one means to cultivate their market, Mireille and Philippe coorganized Extraterrean, a collective that hosts short visits at area farms (farm tourism) and organizes five festivals per season featuring local wine, leather goods, and donkey milk soap as well as many foods.

For the consumer, artisanal production encourages interest in the work involved and respect for what it produces, in great contrast to the excessive consumption of anonymous packages encouraged by supermarket "special offers" and "value packs." A hunger for the "known" vegetable is evident in Isabelle's narrative: "It is increasingly older people buying our produce because it reminds them of what they grew when they had their own gardens."[13]

Direct interactions in the congenial settings of the market build social ties by developing relationships of commitment and trust, and in the process everyday bread, cheese, or onions become reenchanted, taking on far higher value for both the producer and the consumer (Hinrichs 2000; Thompson and Coskuner-Balli 2007). While more arbitrary constructions of quality and nostalgic imaginaries may be in play (Holloway and Kneafsey 2000), the sedimentation of face-to-face sales around a trusted product lifts it out of a dislocated cash nexus, building a known and situated materialism directly in opposition to the "C'est moins cher!" (It's less expensive!) of the supermarkets (see also Gilg and Battershill 1999).

Our case study suggested that a sense of commitment goes both ways. Customers develop a loyalty to their regular *marchands,* who in turn do their best to keep prices down. Mireille and Philippe, for example, had charged the same price for their honey for the past six years, and many of the others talked about striving to hold down prices during the recession.

The importance of trust and value other than price is especially true in the specific case of organic farming that we turn to next.

Organically Enchanting Connection

Organic vegetable producers Isabelle and Daniel got their first customers when Isabelle forgot the sign advertising "bio" produce at the Lézignan market. At the time, said Isabelle, people were actually afraid of eating organic food because the French agriculture department was suggesting that it might be dangerous. Now most customers buy their products precisely because they are organic.

Organic certification serves as a source of trust extending beyond personal interaction. Ecocert, a company started in France in 1991, inspects about 70 percent of the organic food industry in France and about 30 percent worldwide. Most of the producers we talked to seemed to welcome the concept of certification. Sheep farmer Dédou participated in Ecocert himself, assessing producers in other European countries as well as other French regions, and even much smaller-scale producers like bread maker Anne-Marie considered certification a no-brainer, arguing that certification was well worth the price for the added value and respect it gave the product, especially in terms of gaining new customers. Certification also created more possibilities for free labor. Many of the long-established bio farmers now take on paying *stagiaires* (trainees or interns) from public agricultural colleges as well as more informal apprenticeship arrangements. Micias sees certification of his syrups as

Figure 1.4: Mireille Baudeuf with sheep

necessary, and because of significant state subsidies, the returns from growing organically were higher than the cost of certification. Recently, however,
these subsidies have been cut, and although EU assistance will continue, some
are skeptical that the French state (compared to that of Spain, for instance) is
genuinely committed to promoting organic agriculture.

Organic labeling and certification have been critiqued in the U.S. context
because, as market mechanisms, they do not challenge the BAU economy.
On the contrary, certification acts as a barrier to entry, creates a higher price
point that can be capitalized into higher land values, increases prices for the
consumer without necessarily benefiting the producer, heightens competition

among farmers, and leads to the growth of new markets (Guthman 2004, 176). Just as large-scale organic production threatens smaller producers, in distribution, too, big organic is changing the scene. Limoux's Floréal co-operative and its Espéraza outpost Amaranthe were initiated (1981 and 2010 respectively) as a means to support smaller producers whether their organic goods were certified or not. But because of its membership in the national organic distributor Biocoop, Floréal is required to stock only certified organic, making it inaccessible as an outlet for the uncertified microproducers. Smaller cooperatives, in contrast, do not get the discounts available from Biocoop to larger purchasers. Alistair Smith, one of the founders of Floréal, contends that the certification is first and foremost a market mechanism, which means it is susceptible to lobbyists' efforts to make the standard less rigorous. He finds that Ecocert and Biocoop ultimately favor organic agribusiness. Some of the smallest-scale producers we interviewed do not participate in Ecocert, maintaining that the dominant forms of certification privilege "grand bio" (big organic) over people like them.

But ecologically sound and socially just agriculture that garners customer trust can be successful without state- or market-sanctioned certification. Some in the Haute Vallée have chosen to work with the alternative certification process provided through the bio-regionalist NGO Nature et progrès–Aude, which is very active in the area. Under an agreement with Biocoop, Floréal is able to sell produce certified by Nature et progrès. The first to establish the organic standard in France, Nature et progrès has found itself increasingly marginalized in the certification discussion because its process is more rigorous.

ESCAPING ALIENATED LABOR

Out on the main road between Carcassonne and the Pyrenees to the south stands a huge bowler hat on a pole, one of several mementos of the Haute Vallée town of Espéraza's former identity as a producer of felt hats. In the 1930s the town boasted fourteen factories employing over three thousand workers, but felt hats fell out of style in the mid-twentieth century, and the population has steadily declined since the late 1960s, leaving around twenty-one hundred residents today.

Like the other towns of the Haute Vallée, Espéraza is a tricky place to sustain a business. Population decline and poverty have been compounded by competition from the Intermarché supermarket nearby, its billboards screaming its price advantages, capped with the company slogan "Tous unis contre la vie chère!" (Everybody united against the expensive life!). The town's central streets are dominated by vacant commercial space: old-fashioned wooden storefronts empty for decades interspersed with more recent casualties. On Sunday, though, Espéraza is transformed, its lively market drawing customers from all over the Haute Vallée.

The marchands arrive early to set out their wares, and by 8 a.m. a few of the organic petit producteurs will be sitting around one of the outside tables of the central café, relaxing and talking. Over the years they have become close friends, privy to each other's family and financial concerns and helping each other out in various ways.

One of these producers is Anne-Marie Verdonque, a bread maker born into a working-class family in Lille and a woman whose life history exemplifies the strong sense of calling that many feel toward the countryside and *la vie alternative*. Thin and graceful with evident sinewy strength, "Marie" greeted Teresa at her home in a remote hamlet wearing a characteristic Haute Vallée tie-dye shirt and drawstring pants. Over a tisane, she described her life before deciding to move to the countryside: "My life was urban in every sense. . . . I lived for twenty years in Lille, so I had never grown a vegetable, I knew nothing of the countryside. . . . At the beginning I wanted to live by the sea, close to something elemental. . . . When you are a city type, you don't know how to survive up on the mountain. I was afraid of insects and mice; the world was a hostile place for me! There aren't as many insects and bugs by the sea."[14] Neither Marie nor her boyfriend found work in Dunkerque, so they moved back inland to St. Quentin, near his parents. By this point, Marie felt a powerful calling toward bread making. "Now I understand the symbolism, but at the time I just felt a pull towards bread making, I didn't know why."[15] At St. Quentin, she met a kindred spirit: "He was doing it because it was his passion. He did not really need the money, but he made bread for a few clients, so twice a week I would make the bread with him. The *pain* was the most traditional possible. You don't need much to make *levain* [a traditional sourdough], just flour and water. So you prepare your levain, which takes three days. . . . And then we sampled a bit of levain before each kneading, and it was always the same. It's very, very, very simple; it could not be simpler. . . . You just have to add water and some salt in some good flour and levain to make great bread. And so I just sort of fell into it, this story of bread and bread making."[16] Like other bread makers we interviewed, Marie loved not only the simplicity but also the universality of the baking process: "We use the four elements, earth, water, air, fire."[17] She preferred to work alone, completely immersed in the flow of the process.

Marie and her then partner wanted to move south. Initially they thought to move to Les Landes, but a chance encounter showed them that the Haute Vallée might be closer to what they were looking for. "Things here seemed so different from Les Landes, where there are big farms with lots of corn, force-feeding of geese, making *foie gras,* making lots of money. . . . Here I had found a way of life on a human scale."[18] Looking for land, they connected immediately with a couple already living in the hamlet of Les Sauzils, who enthusiastically welcomed them and helped Marie to establish herself. While the cheapness of the land was a major factor in Marie's decision to move to the Haute Vallée, even more important was the hearty welcome from the alternatifs she met, and generally the sense of community from fellow thinkers. She was not looking just for nature and a place to work but for a community that would inspire and support the life she wanted to lead.

Beyond *Métro-Boulot-Dodo*

As Suzanne Berger recounts, the European generation of 1968 rejected not only illegitimate domination and inequality but industrialized affluence itself: "What seems to have been at stake was an explosion of doubt about the quality and direction of life in advanced industrial societies, about the kind of human relationships that develop in mass consumer societies, about the irreconcilability of the kinds of organization required to run an industrial society with the values and personal relationships that are necessary for the satisfaction of deep human needs. This was a protest not against the failure of state and society to provide for economic growth and material prosperity, but against their all-too-considerable success in having done so, and against the price of this success" (1979, 32).

Like the many thousands of others who migrated from cities to remote rural areas from the 1960s onward, almost all of our interviewees described searching for a life outside the *métro-boulot-dodo* (travel-work-sleep) routine and the hyperconsumption of industrialized Europe. Dutch beekeeper Mireille had wandered south in search of something different:

I was working in the library in Holland and I wanted to do something with nature and couldn't find some way because there was a lot of things about money and luxury and consumerist society, so I took my bike and I sold everything in Holland and I started biking. . . . I didn't really know what I wanted but I didn't

want to be in that place. When I was in Carcassonne, I had to decide if I was going to go to Spain or if I was going to work a little. It was in June and there was
Philippe sitting on a terrace; he's a beautiful man and he asked me if I wanted to
see his bees . . . and I said yes, so . . . we got together! He was working with a
big beekeeper, working on projects for Royal Jelly, and he didn't like it at all because it's very strict. You work in a laboratory, it's . . . [only] a little part outside. I
stayed with him and slowly we were together and after two years of Royal Jelly
we decided to create our own honey business.[19]

Many of the petits producteurs were eager to articulate that their sense
of calling had been sustained by the feelings of well-being and pleasure
engendered by the work process itself. Working in the open air on their
hilltop farm makes farming joyful, said Dédou and Mireille. Isabelle sees
a unity between the ecological imperatives behind her work, her family's
health, and her pleasure in the work. Having studied agronomy, she believes
that not only would industrial agriculture turn Europe into a "poubelle" (gar-
bage can), but that pesticides are hazardous to the health of farming households
and, through genetic effects, to the health of their children and grandchildren. "Where is the pleasure in farming with gloves, a mask, and protective
glasses? It's crazy!"[20]

Many of the alternatifs are very conscious that they are not only rich in
their access to "unspoiled" nature but extraordinarily rich in *time* compared to
most French people of modest means. Jean-Baptiste prides himself in working
fewer hours than his parents, for example. They are very aware of the endless
speedups in workplaces, the intense Taylorization of the household, and the
wholesale commodification of time.[21] They often evoked the crazy pace of life
in the big towns, stating that even when they themselves came under considerable time pressure, they resisted performing "busyness." The dominant
aesthetic of social interaction is notably relaxed and congenial, and it is seen as
not only rude but unhealthy to rush around talking on one's cell phone, for
example.

One of those most determined to fight the tyranny of busyness is musician
Patrick Terris, one of the longest-established vendors at Espéraza market. His
small stall presents his spice bread and cakes as well as mustard and juice
made by his octogenarian parents and his ex-partner Claude, all former members of the Canterate commune. Patrick's business is small and his income
very modest, yet he deeply appreciates his way of life, for which he abandoned
Paris in his early twenties. He gets to work in the tranquility and beauty of
Canterate, to see his many friends at the market, and he has enough time to

Figure 1.5: Patrick Terris' stall, Espéraza market

play multiple instruments with different groups. Even after thirty-five years, Patrick's usual response to being asked how he is doing is that it is hard to be unhappy with the good fortune of being greeted every day by the snowy peak of Saint Barthélemy.

Other producers have brought a more driving work ethic to their artisan or alternatif existence, throwing themselves into highly labor-intensive projects. Nonetheless, even for these very hard-working people, the politics of anti-consumerism and critiques of workaday formal labor remain very strong. Dynamic Isabelle refuses requests from shops to sell her produce because "We don't *want* to be bigger. . . . We don't desire to drive kilometers to deliver vegetables. We do two markets and sell everything."[22]

What all the alternatifs seem to appreciate in their daily lives is not only the meaningfulness of their work but an extraordinary degree of autonomy over *how* and to some extent *when* they do their work. Work is fine, even enjoyed and sought, but the state of involuntary busyness demanded by *un job* (referred to with a grimace) is widely deplored. Bread maker Rolf expressed very clearly the link between true materialism and liberation from alienated labor. For him, the character of his rich dark bread directly expresses his own autonomy: "I try to make the right bread for *me*, and I offer it. I don't ask people what they want, I don't make thirty varieties. I don't let myself get torn in different directions by demand. But I do it the best I can, and I find people do want it. It's in balance, and that's really important to me. I have to work through my fear. If I were to be afraid of not being able to make my living, at that point my product would no longer be any good. That's how I see it."[23]

New Allocation of Time

If true materialism gives the artisanal or homemade product a value beyond pure cash, meaningful and pleasurable work, time riches, and substantial autonomy in the artisanal process are equally important in distancing the life of the producer from the reductionism imposed by the cash nexus. With what Schor calls the "new allocation of time," the producers' rejection of métro-boulot-dodo breaks down the market's intense divide between work as cash generation and leisure as cash depletion. There is no longer anything to be gained from stripping down home life to squeeze out every bit of cash-generating labor in order to bring in the leisure commodities that have come to stand in for quality of life.

RESISTING ALIENATION FROM NATURE

Each of the principles of plenitude can be read as a response to the four forms of alienation Marx describes in his *Economic and Philosophic Manuscripts* (Marx 2007, 67–80). Rather than the worker being alienated from the *product* of his labor, true materialism ties the maker into a lasting relationship with her creation, one that ultimately can extend to include the consumer. Similarly, the "new allocation of time" (which we extend out to demands for fulfillment, pleasure, and autonomy) pushes back hard against the second form—alienation from the *process* of working.

Marx's third consideration is that the privatization of nature under capitalism divides us from our "species-being," from our deep human need to directly interact with the natural world as the "material, the object, and the instrument" of our creativity (2007, 74). Schor's corresponding principle is to increase self-provisioning or, perhaps more accurately, household provisioning.

Again, the plenitude principle was already well developed by our interviewees. In settling in the rural Aude, the migrants saw not only the unspoiled visual beauty of the Corbières' rocky garrigue or the spectacular cliffs and forests of the Haute Vallée—they saw a possibility to *participate* in nature, to work with land and beast in a collaborative and sustainable fashion. First, this meant living very simply. Many started by jointly renting or buying land without official permission for building, on which they first put trailers, yurts, or other basic housing. Nine (Isabelle, Beatrice, Rolf, Patrick, Claude, Brigitte and Gerard, and Dominic and Myriam) had started their lives in the area as members of communes slowly reclaiming ruined or abandoned hamlets. In their commune at Canterate, for example, Claude and Patrick waited eighteen years for running water. Years ago, mason, cheese maker, and musician Sylvain Dumas lived in a house without electricity and running water. When asked why he chose to live that way, Sylvain said, "It was the time—1970, 1968; they said it was 'forbidden to forbid' (*interdit d'interdire*). Yes, the way I lived was marginal but more tranquil."[24] Today, Philippe and Mireille live happily in a two-room house with a hand pump for water and no shower, electricity, or cell phones. Dominic and Myriam, and later their son Micias, gradually built simple wooden houses around old traveler vans gone to ground.

The most direct way to resist the domination of industrialized capitalism and soulless affluence is to create a way of life less dependent on fossil fuels, not only through bio production but more generally by drawing life's necessities more directly from nature in the form of garden vegetables, fruits, healing plants, forest mushrooms, and firewood. Directly gleaning from nature remains central to the alternatif lifeworld, and gathering, gardening, canning, and other simple home-based making of all kinds remain ubiquitous, as does the creation of aesthetic and artistic objects and spaces with material gleaned from nature. Aiming for complete self-sufficiency, however, is generally seen as both impossible and unnecessarily isolating.

COMMUNAL PROVISIONING AND THE
ECONOMIC GROUNDING OF SOCIAL TIES

Schor's fourth principle—reinvestment in community—addresses the culminating violence done to human subjectivity under the dehumanizing calculations of the cash nexus, Marx's "alienation of man from man" (2007, 77). As we suggested at the beginning, we saw a strong relationship between informal provisioning and communitarianism, or at least the building of strong social ties. The passionate desire for home- or commune-based self-sufficiency (*l'autarcie*) has given way over the years, replaced by communal provision through local production and consumption (Cazella 2001). Much of this production and consumption, however, occurs outside of market exchange.

The generation of 1968 was driven by a strong sense of communal life as the most ideal form of social arrangement. Initially, the '68ers organized communal living and working practices around their shared radical understandings. While a couple of our interviewees would disagree, most felt that these formal projects had been less successful than communities built around informal communitarianism, where they worked together more incrementally and with less of a grand design (see also Gibson-Graham 2003).[25]

It makes more sense in this case to examine the wealth of communal provisioning rather than separately discussing reinvestment in community. By showing the integration of the two, we can illustrate the economic grounding of community—with the implication that an alternative economy may in fact be predicated on an alternative community and vice versa. In particular it is worth exploring in some detail the question of *le troc,* informal exchange outside the money economy, a primary form that enables communal (rather than self-) reliance.[26]

Le Troc

In the Haute Vallée many interviewees mentioned how the cost of living was unusually "cheap." It is true that rents tend to be lower than average, and certainly far lower than in the big city, but neither utilities nor gas nor supermarket products are any cheaper than anywhere else in France. Life becomes much more affordable for those who do some self-provisioning and spend no-cost leisure in nature, but another reason life is affordable is the ubiquity of informal exchange, which enables even the poorest within the alternatif social networks to gain from occasional work or household-level production without getting tangled up in voluminous French law.

Producers share tools and exchange labor and products. In an arrangement that has lasted several years, Rolf has kept Max permanently supplied with his rich black bread in exchange for all the vegetables he needs. Patrick exchanges the permanent use and upkeep of a tractor for help with his cows. The troc economy extends far beyond the market producers themselves. A woman in Lagrasse practices midwifery and receives food in exchange; another does the books for a small business and receives veterinary care for her animals. In the Val de Dagne, scores of parents over the years have exchanged plowing, building, vegetables, gardening, bread, or carpentry for music lessons from Tessa, Teresa's mother.

The strength of troc may be due to a synthesis of paysan practices with the countercultural principles of the incomers. Sitting in her sunny living room full of the signs of her busy life as a fruit farmer and community organizer, Claude explained how the commune that revitalized the abandoned hamlet of Canterate had organized exchange in quite a schematic way, only to be educated into a broader, more informal way of looking at it by the older country-people nearby:

So, at Canterate we already had a book of troc where each double page represented the person with whom you exchanged, so what I had got from Monsieur X would be on the left, and what Monsieur X had got from me on the right. From time to time we would do the books and see where we were in cash equivalent.

But you know, it's pretty typical for the countryside, to troc. I had never done it before, but right from the beginning, when we arrived in 1980, we had these old neighbors [in the next hamlet], very old-fashioned, who came to us to propose that we grow potatoes together. Because we, at that time, had lots of working hands, but they had a tractor. So the idea was that we would work together. We would buy our plants, and they theirs; we had our land, they had theirs; but we would cultivate them together at our place, and together at theirs. And it was fantastic—we had such a great time together.[27]

Claude's dynamism propelled her vision of no-cash exchange to larger projects. "The most extraordinary thing I was part of, as a member of Canterate, was the *système d'échange local,* the SEL. So you're interested in how we survive around here? Well the SEL was incredibly important for that. . . . So the SEL is a system of multilateral troc—the idea came from the UK, you know? And the first SEL in France was created . . ."—Claude paused for effect— "here! At Canterate!"[28]

The SEL attracted five hundred members across the Ariège and the Aude, and the organizers quickly started work on expanding the scheme to other areas of France, with Patrick Terris even appearing on national television. Members could give a good or service to one person and receive from another. People would advertise in the bulletin with services or goods offered, whether it was gardening, chocolate cakes, apples, regular rides to Toulouse, or a massage. The organization (which had no paid staff) also put on popular markets in which commodities were exchanged using each member's credit of *grains de sel* (grains of salt)—the scheme's alternative currency.

Claude was the president for the first four years, then secretary for another four, but she lost the energy for it, and the organization declined. However, some Haute Vallée people are still involved in the SEL movement, and more generally the enthusiasm of the early years gave a big boost to awareness of the possibilities of troc, leaving behind all sorts of relationships that still function well. For example, Claude described how she really needed help with the blackcurrant crop after the departure of one of her troc partners. She used the SEL scheme to bring people to help with the harvest, paying them in jam or cassis cordial. Over the years they became friends, and she still uses the same arrangement for the harvests. Most small-producer harvests are lubricated by troc, as are many building projects.

Not only did the SEL do much to develop the local exchange economy, it also created a wealth of new connections, particularly welcomed by newcomers. Discussing the analysis of systems of local exchange, French sociologist Smaïn Laacher (2002, 82) notes, "Too often the questions of their relevance have been of an economic nature: the economic role of the currency, the monetary value of goods and exchange services, etc." But these systems also enable the creation of highly concrete social ties by providing a space for "experimentation with new forms of social relations within a non-monetary economy" (83).

FROM TROC TO THE SOCIAL STATE

Although many of our interviewees were highly critical of the forms of production and exchange under globalized capitalism, they were much less likely to radically reject the French state. To be sure, alternatifs regularly excoriated the role of the French and other European governments in promoting the interests of supermarkets, banks, energy companies, and other forms of capital, producing overconsumption at home and war and vast global inequality abroad. Yet many of the same people were supportive of the state's social and regulatory functions.

"In France, if you don't have any money, you do fine in terms of health care—it's all free," said Rolf. "And the same in terms of finding somewhere to live. It's paid for."[29] For the French producteurs, and to some extent for immigrants like Rolf from other EU countries, it seems simple common sense that the social state is desirable and in many cases essential to their own survival—providing pensions; supporting households with children; subsidizing housing, energy, and food for the unemployed; and covering the majority of health care and higher-education tuition costs for the entire population. Indeed, we wondered if this relationship was thought of as so commonsensical it was underexamined—only rarely did people consider that these sources of support might be fundamentally jeopardized by the consequences of casino capitalism or neoliberal turns within French government.

Used to the more unequal, precarious landscape of the United States, we were struck by the relatively light financial pressures described by many parents, whose difficulties were along the lines of providing their children with trips to the cinema or name-brand clothes. The children of the petits producteurs live simply, but their activities don't cost their parents much. Like other rural kids, they are transported by public buses for school or sport, and their parents can rely on the high-quality and cheap French health system. Myriam shrugged, "No, the children really were not much expense at all until they were at the *lycée* [high school] and we had to deal with the problem of name brands. And that's when having to drive them around became more of a problem. But it was just a few years, really."[30]

With the economic crisis slowing down sales, many newer petits producteurs have become more reliant on a state benefit started in 2009, the RSA (Revenu de solidarité active), which boosts the income of self-employed people below the poverty line as well as supporting the unemployed. Within the more alternatif networks, at least, there seemed not to be too much embarrassment about claiming RSA benefits, as long as you were seen to be making something of your life. "It's really for people who *work*. There are a bunch of us petits producteurs around here who receive the Revenu de solidarité active," one producer told us, emphasizing the "active." This producer may have been keen to distinguish himself from the pre-2009 form of welfare, the RMI (Revenu minimum d'insertion), with its connotations of "passivity." "We are like the farmers—we get help because we are working and producing things. (*ça fait vivre le coin*)," he said earnestly. "The RSA is keeping our area alive at the moment. So, for example, you tell them you can make €300 a month, they give you another €360. If you're a couple with a child you would get a lot more, but of course you have to subtract your rent." [31] While many in the *coin* (immediate local area) have their financial woes, the safety net under them is substantial compared to that in most other countries.

Meanwhile, some of the most alternatifs continue to get by almost completely outside of the formal economy through a mixture of self-provisioning and troc, exchanging informal work for food, a place to stay, or other goods. Such was the case of Kasiem, an enthusiastic eco-builder and self-proclaimed autodidact whom we met when he was exchanging work with one of the Haute Vallée's most successful organic vegetable growers, Max. At the time we talked to Kasiem, he was working on Max's impressive ecological farmhouse, reinforcing its walls with tough hemp outside and local earth within. Via troc, Kasiem got to live on Max's land in a trailer with views of the foothills of the Pyrenees to the right and his handiwork to the left, eating Max's produce and reading and socializing in his leisure time.

Thin and athletic, with a cheerful and expressive face, Kasiem explained that the work of farming itself did not inspire him. "I need to be creative!" He explained what drew him toward eco-building. "I love to be able to come back to something, look at it and say, 'I did that.'"[32] Showing us the mechanisms of a dam and irrigation system on the land, an earlier project he did for Max, Kasiem explained that he has taught himself ecological practices from all over Europe, loving the challenges presented by alternative building. Offering troc building, Kasiem is able to make enough of a living each summer in the Aude to get by and even travel throughout the winter months. Highly decommodified artisans like Kasiem seem to serve as anchors for the alternatif character of the Aude, not only as vital labor support for the petits producteurs but as icons of liberation from the BAU economy.

Stagiaires (unpaid trainees or interns) are another critical source of labor for some of the more established producers. These are more often than not informal apprenticeship arrangements, but stagiaires also come from the agronomy programs of nearby colleges. Also important are WWOOFers (worldwide opportunities on organic farms), volunteers who exchange manual labor on sustainable farms for room and board, making a connection with farming life and sometimes learning the skills to begin their own small businesses.

REJECTING THE CASH NEXUS

Marx theorized that the cash nexus mediates value in a capitalist economy, obfuscating the political, social, environmental, and cultural relations active in production and reducing both goods and their makers to a market value. Any transaction pursued through the exchange of commodities automatically becomes defined by these exchanges.

As we have seen, the Aude petits producteurs, in tandem with the broader communities they serve, have developed a multitude of practical strategies to resist the flattening effects of cash. Their "true materialism" manifests in a deep identification with the product through its life course, with the assumption that the labor of making and selling should be fulfilling, autonomous, and unalienated.

The alternatif worldview is reinforced by the strong currents of French antiglobalization discourse (Waters 2010) in regional and national media, generally reinforcing the ideals of *décroissance* (degrowth), downshifting, and anticonsumerism (Latouche 2006). An eponymous biweekly (*La décroissance*) has become an important point of communication and discussion, reaching with its unpretentious tone the younger and often less well-educated members of the community for over a decade. Much more than in the United States, a discussion of alternative economies has been reaching a number of publics across France, with discussion led by the Parti pour la décroissance, the Confédération paysanne, the Institute of Social and Economic Studies for Sustainable De-growth, and numerous public intellectuals.

The Dangers of Debt and Cash

Our interviewees seemed attuned to these debates—some in an impressionistic way, others highly informed. Perhaps unsurprisingly, the topic on which people expressed themselves most forcefully was the need to distance oneself from the domination of money. Marie, like most, explicitly told us that she was not looking to have money; that money was *not* her wealth. "But in a world of money you need your feet on the ground. . . . You have to pay for insurance, for stuff, a car, so you also have to earn money. I'm not interested in filling my pockets. Screw that."[33]

There was a particular wariness of the danger of debt. Dédou argued forcefully that the most important advice he would give newcomers is to start very small. Bank loans, he explained, force farmers into mainstream farming and marketing both directly (through loan stipulations) and indirectly (by creating a need for substantial immediate returns).

Mireille and Philippe started out with an eighty-year-old extractor and a truck that had to be pushed to start, adamant that they would not become indebted. Most beekeepers use a mechanical arm to do the heavy lifting involved in keeping bees, but Philippe and Mireille refused to borrow the €14,000 to buy one. In fact, they do not use stagiaire labor because it would be unfair to ask unpaid workers to do such heavy lifting. "We had the same idea: we didn't want to borrow any money because we were both too afraid of debt. Having the big machines or big investments, that would change our life. So we decided to do everything by hand. . . . When we went to the market, we saw people who were unhappy because they had risked investing a lot of money [into their business]. We said to each other, no way. We never want to get into that system."[34]

TOWARD A POLITICS OF PLENITUDE

What does this study of the petits producteurs of the Aude suggest about anticapitalist, or at least *less* capitalist, futures? Over recent decades, low-cost entry into small-scale production has become harder to achieve. First the Lagrasse area and then the Haute Vallée became increasingly popular with tourists and second-home owners, especially with British émigrés excited to find such a relatively affordable French property market. This immigration has had uneven effects for our interviewees, stimulating the market for summer apartments (*gites*) and for some products, but producing a substantial surge in property prices that makes it harder for newer producteurs to establish themselves. On top of the increase in property prices, the great recession added an additional burden. As we listened to these producers, we were struck by the incredible difficulties some of them face.

Nevertheless, poorer French people have been moving back to rural areas over the last twenty years (Pagès 2005), attracted by the lower cost of living, and the current economic crisis seems to have accelerated that trend in both the Corbières and the Haute Vallée, with scores of young people, both French and international, starting microproduction in very marginal circumstances. Will they succeed? Is it still possible for young people to start with literally nothing but a tent and a backpack? It seems clear that those who live very cheaply without feeling "poor" can do so more easily in the Aude than in most places in the world because of liveable unemployment and child benefits, socialized pensions, and cheap health care. This close relationship between basic state entitlements and creative economic experimentation suggests that a "politics of plenitude" would do well to consider that social insurance itself is a form of collective provisioning, and that even minor government support can be of vital economic importance.

To the naysayers who see neoliberalism behind every door, we do indeed find much to be enthusiastic about in the alternative economies of the Aude, with their well-developed and articulated practices of true materialism and unalienated labor. Like both Schor and Laacher, we see a strong symbiosis between distance from the BAU economy and the restoration of richer webs of human connection. The centrality of collective provisioning via troc, coup de main (lending a hand), noncompetition, and volunteer-run co-ops encourages people to understand individual survival as part of a collective enterprise, thus strengthening community with relationships that are particularly reciprocal and productive, rather than oriented primarily around individualized consumption. The diverse economic practices among the Aude *alternatifs* are tied together by *communal* provisioning. This case refines our understanding of long-standing debates around the necessity and desirability of self-sufficiency. While raising questions about the cost of living for those who do not or cannot participate in such exchange networks, the Audois experience suggests gifting may be fundamental to long-lasting alternative economies.

Our scale of analysis—looking into the lives of individual producers—reminds us that BAU domination occurs through the everyday life of individuals as well as through the great institutions dominating the world system. The explicit decision to participate in an *alternatif* way of life seems to have given the small producers of the Haute Vallée and the Corbières a particularly strong sense of well-being and more confidence in their survival, underlining the inherently politico-cultural character of economic arrangements. Access to the land itself, with its manifest no-cash pleasures and opportunities for self-provision, the widespread culture of barter and coup de main and, to variable degrees, the support of the French state all allow petits producteurs to distance everyday life from the anxiety created by consumerism and the other distortions of human experience imposed by the cash nexus in capitalist society. Pursuing plenitude is not just an economic strategy but an anticonsumerist politics and aesthetics, as beekeeper Mireille articulated succinctly: "The base of capitalism is consumption. I think you have to fight against this capitalist system. You have to find a way to be creative without consumption because it is creativity that brings happiness [*bonheur*], not money."[35]

NOTES

Note: the order of authors is alphabetical, representing equal authorship.

1. The organic fair in Couiza is organized by the NGO Nature et progrès. The "boutiques paysannes" and "maisons du terroir" are shops that provide a venue for small-scale producers to sell their local products using a cooperative management system. The stores generally have very limited hours and are open only in the summer.

2. Given the inherent imperfections of translation, we will include a transcription of the original French for the quotations in this essay. "Mais avant il y avait beaucoup plus de vignes qu'aujourd'hui, et donc nous étions coincés par les vignes. . . . C'est le vin, après un peu l'huile d'olive, récemment, car l'huile d'olive ça a quinze ans, il faut pas croire que ça date. Enfin ça date de très longtemps l'huile d'olive mais les vignes avaient pris toute la place. La monoculture de la vigne a étouffé toutes les autres cultures."

3. "Les personnes âgées [celles qui sont restées au village] étaient heureuses de nous voir arriver, parce que je crois qu'elles étaient déprimées de voir tous les enfants partir. Oui, elles étaient heureuses car elles disaient 'Mon fils a désormais une meilleure situation,' mais au fond d'elles-mêmes il y avait une véritable tristesse de voir leur terrain abandonné, leur ferme négligée."

4. "Oui, ils travaillent, mais ils ne sont pas prêts à être efficace. Ce n'est pas comme cela dans d'autres domaines. La Haute Vallée est vraiment quelque chose d'autre!"

5. *Fermage* was established to protect the person who would farm the land, because once the land is established under this contract, it can be rescinded only with an eighteen-month notice. Furthermore, if the contract is nullified, it must be done in order to farm the land or to pass it on to children; it cannot be withdrawn for sale.

6. "Quand nous sommes arrivés ici, il n'y a que les gens simples qui voulaient bien nous donner des terres. Ils savaient qu'on avait besoin de terres. 'J'ai un hectare, madame, je ne sais pas où c'est, mais je veux bien te le prêter, pour que tu puisses travailler!'"

7. "Donc on est allé chez eux, on a goûté leur fromage, et ça a été pour nous la révélation. C'était extraordinaire, vraiment. . . . Donc quand on a goûté ça, on s'est dit avec mon mari: 'C'est ça qu'on veut faire.' Et donc c'est une autre aventure qui s'est mise en place, car moi j'ai eu la chance d'avoir fait des formations fromagères, plusieurs, peut-être cinq ou six."

8. "Hier je regardais à la télévision une émission sur le crottin de Chantignole. C'est une des formes typiques du fromage de chèvre. Et les producteurs comme moi font du fromage frais, et le vendent à un fromager qui l'affine. Eux ne font que le fromage frais. Ils ne l'affinent absolument pas. Et c'est dommage. Car la valorisation de leur travail est faite par l'affinage et la commercialisation d'un produit fini. Et je pense que si on est trop gros on ne peut pas faire ça, et si on est à notre échelle, on peut gérer ça."

9. "C'est extraordinaire ici de ne pas vendre à la coopérative, d'aller à l'abattoir avec ses agneaux et de livrer les gens. Alors eux ce sont de l'agneau, les autres ce sont du veau, voyez le produit fini. Aller jusqu'au bout de la commercialisation. C'est la seule façon pour nous en petite production de pouvoir se développer, de pouvoir se maintenir."

10. "On a commencé vraiment tout petit et c'est vrai que d'un coup on a eu de la demande, les gens ils ont dit, 'Ah, c'est génial' et donc, plein de demande, et nous, on n'a pas réussi à suivre au niveau de la production. Donc maintenant on a organisé la production. . . . Maintenant les gens recherchent vraiment ça [les produits des petits producteurs], les gens nous encouragent, 'Ah, bravo! Continuez à faire ce que vous faites.' . . . Les gens ont besoin de contact, de voir le producteur, de discuter avec le producteur."

11. "Tout le monde est bienvenue pour acheter notre miel."

12. "Tu dois vouloir vendre ton produit."

13. "On a beaucoup . . . de clients nous qui sont des gens . . . du troisième âge, beaucoup de personnes âgées, . . . parce que c'était comme leur jardin avant, nos produits."

14. "Urbaine en tout cas, urbaine mais on s'était quand même rapprochés de la nature et de la mer. Mais moi j'ai passé vingt ans à Lille donc je ne savais pas faire pousser un légume, je savais rien de la campagne. . . . Au départ je voulais vivre à la mer, près d'un élément. Mais après quand t'es citadine, tu sais pas ce qu'il faut faire à la mon-

tagne. J'avais peur des insectes, des souris, c'était un monde hostile pour moi. A la mer il n'y a pas trop de bêtes encore."

15. "Maintenant je peux comprendre le symbolisme, mais à l'époque où j'avais envie de faire du pain, je ne savais pas pourquoi je voulais faire du pain."

16. "Lui il faisait ça car c'était une passion, il n'avait pas spécialement besoin d'argent, mais il faisait du pain pour quelques clients qu'il avait, et donc deux fois par semaines j'allais faire du pain avec lui. Et donc le pain le plus traditionnel qui soit, il n'y a pas besoin de grand chose pour faire son levain, il faut juste de la farine et de l'eau. Donc on prépare son levain, ça dure trois jours, et ensuite on prélève avant chaque pétrie un bout de levain et c'est toujours la même chose. C'est très, très, très simple. On ne peut plus simple. Le produit en lui-même contient tout ce qu'il faut pour faire un bon pain. Il suffit d'ajouter de l'eau, du sel dans une bonne farine et du levain pour faire un bon pain. Et donc je suis un peu tombée dedans, cette histoire de pain ça m'a vraiment plu."

17. "On utilise les quatre éléments, il y a la terre, l'eau, l'air, le feu."

18. "Oui voilà, tout à fait. Et puis on sentait que dans ce pays, contrairement aux Landes où c'est des grandes exploitations avec beaucoup de maïs, on gave les oies, on fait du foie-gras, on fait de l'argent quoi. . . . On exploite. . . . Ici on trouvait plus un mode de vie à échelle humaine."

19. Mireille spoke English for this part of her interview and then switched to French. This particular quote was in English.

20. "Quel est le plaisir de faire de l'agriculture avec des gants, des boites, des lunettes, c'est fou quoi!"

21. "Taylorization" refers to the breakdown of any work into discrete small tasks, following engineering principles. In the household this means strictly rationing the amount of time spent on each activity, whether cleaning, bedtime stories, or meals. The approach was the brainchild of Frederick Winslow Taylor, who first applied these practices to industrial production (Hochschild 1997).

22. "Nous on n'a pas très envie de faire des kilomètres pour donner des légumes, on fait deux marchés et on vend tout. Il faut être beaucoup plus grand . . . et on ne veut pas."

23. "Moi, je fais peu de pain, je vends tout mon pain mais j'exige que les gens le prennent comme il est. Je ne fais pas trente variétés. Je ne demande pas aux gens ce qu'ils veulent, tu vois, je ne me laisse pas tirailler par la demande—c'est moi qui propose mais comme je le fais au mieux je trouve aussi des personnes qui le veulent. J'essaye de trouver un équilibre, et pour ça c'est très important que je travaille ma peur. Si j'avais peur de ne pas pouvoir vivre de ce que je fais, alors je ne pourrais pas faire des produits de qualité, c'est comme ça que je le vois."

24. "C'était l'époque . . . la fin des années 1970, 1968, on disait qu'il était interdit d'interdire. . . . Oui, la façon dont je vivais était marginale mais plus tranquille."

25. The sense in which we understand the centrality of gifting and cooperation within the alternatif economy as "communitarian" therefore differs in character from the American moralism of Amitai Etzioni (1994) or Robert Bellah (1992) as well as from more tightly organized forms of socialist collectivism.

26. *Troc* is slang for "exchange." It derives from the verb *troquer,* to exchange, and indicates an exchange of goods or services without the use of money. The closest equivalent in English of a troc system is "barter." As we emphasize, the culture of troc in the
Aude tends to be highly informal.

27. "Avant le SEL on avait un cahier de troc, c'est-à-dire qu'on avait un cahier sur
chaque double page, on avait une personne avec qui on troquait. On notait chaque
fois donc, non, double page, c'est ça. Sur la page de gauche c'est ce que moi je
prends a Monsieur X, et sur la page de droite ce que Monsieur X me prend. . . .
Pour chaque personne avec qui on avait des échanges on note tout sur ce cahier . . .
c'était en argent, équivalent en argent. On était très content avec ça. Ça marchait
bien. D'ailleurs c'est assez typique de la campagne, je pense à cette idée de troc,
moi, je connaissais pas, moi je n'avais jamais pratiqué le troc avant, mais on a eu ça
dès le début, quand on est arrivé ici en 1980, ce sont nos voisins qui étaient de vieux
paysans, très, très âgés, qui sont venus nous voir pour nous proposer de faire de la
pomme de terre ensemble, parce ce que nous on avait plein de main d'oeuvre, on
était très nombreux a l'époque, eux ils n'étaient pas nombreux mais eux ils avaient
un tracteur, eh donc, l'idée c'était de faire ensemble les pommes de terre. Ils nous
ont achetés nos plants, eux ils ont acheté leurs plants, nous on a nos terres, eux ils ont
leur terre, mais on cultive ensemble chez nous et ensemble chez eux. C'était superbe,
c'était génial."

28. "L'expérience extraordinaire que j'ai faite à l'époque où j'étais à Canterate c'était encore avec le système d'échange local, le SEL. Donc le SEL est un système de troc
multilatéral—l'idée vient du Royaume-Uni, vous savez? Et le premier SEL en France
a été créé . . . ici ! A Canterate!"

29. "En France, si tu n'as pas d'argent, déjà au niveau médical ce n'est pas mal, parce que
là en France tu as tout gratuit. Quand on n'a rien, c'est, plutôt au niveau de la santé,
eh, c'est plutôt bien, tu te trouves aussi un logement. Le minimum est toujours donné
par l'État."

30. "Non, les enfants n'étaient pas vraiment beaucoup de dépenses du tout jusqu'à ce
qu'ils soient au lycée et nous avons dû faire face au problème des grandes marques.
Et c'est à ce moment d'avoir à conduire eux autour est devenu plus un problème."

31. "Ça fait vivre le coin. C'est vraiment pour les gens qui travaillent. Lorsque tu pro-
poses un travail de €300, ils te donnent des €360 supplémentaires pour vivre. Il y a
plusieurs personnes dans le coin qui reçoivent ce revenu solidaire actif. C'est comme
les agriculteurs—on a de l'aide parce qu'on a des activités. On est assez nombreux, en
effet. Ça fait vivre le coin."

32. "J'ai besoin d'être créatif! J'aime bien revenir vers quelque chose, le regarder et me
dire, 'Je l'ai fait!' "

33. Et non. On fonctionne dans un monde d'argent donc il faut aussi avoir les pieds sur
terre, il faut gagner de l'argent, car on nous demande de payer les assurances, les
trucs, les machins, il faut aussi gagner de l'argent. Je cherche pas à m'en foutre plein
les poches. Je m'en fous.

34. The first part is in English. Then: "On a toujours eu la chance qu'on était bien ensemble et que quand on était au marché on a vu tous les gens qui avait investi beau-

coup d'argent et qui étaient très malheureux à cause de ça. On se dit jamais on va rentrer dans ce système. Ça c'était clair."

35. "C'est la base du capitalisme, c'est la consommation. C'est la consommation. Mais ça c'est toujours un choix de vie après. Les gens s'ils veulent ils peuvent faire quelque chose encore. Ils sont encore assez libre de faire ça. Il faut surtout que tu luttes. Moi je trouve qu'il faut lutter contre ce système capitaliste. Je pense trouver la créativité dans la vie sans consommer. C'est la créativité qui amène le bonheur, ce n'est pas l'argent."

REFERENCES

Bellah, Robert N. 1992. *The Good Society.* New York: Vintage.

Berger, Suzanne. 1979. "Politics and Antipolitics in Western Europe in the Seventies." *Daedalus* 108 (1): 27–50.

Cazella, A. A. 2001. "Les installations agricoles nouvelles: Le cas des agriculteurs néoruraux dans L'Aude." *Espace, populations, sociétés* 19 (1–2): 101–8.

Demossier, Marion. 2003. "Rural France in Europe: New Challenges." *Modern and Contemporary France* 11 (3): 265–78.

Etzioni, Amitai. 1994. *The Spirit of Community: The Reinvention of American Society.* New York: Touchstone.

Fantasia, Rick. 1995. "Fast Food in France." *Theory and Society* 24 (2): 201–43.

Gibson-Graham, J. K. 1996. *The End of Capitalism (as We Knew It): A Feminist Critique of Political Economy.* Cambridge, MA: Basil Blackwell.

———. 2003. "Enabling Ethical Economies: Cooperativism and Class." *Critical Sociology* 29 (2): 123–61.

———. 2008. "Diverse Economies: Collaboration and Community in Economic Geography." *Human Geography* 32 (5): 613–32.

Gilg, A. W., and M. Battershill. 1999. "The Role of Household Factors in Direct Selling of Farm Produce in France. *Tijdschrift voor Economische en Sociale Geografie (Journal of Economic and Social Geography)* 90 (3): 312–19.

Glassman, J. 2003. "Rethinking Overdetermination, Structural Power and Social Change: A Critique of Gibson-Graham, Resnick and Wolff." *Antipode* 35 (4): 678–98.

Guthman, Julie. 2004. *Agrarian Dreams: The Paradox of Organic Farming in California.* Berkeley: University of California Press.

Hervieu, Bertrand, and Francois Purseigle. 2008. "Troubled Pastures, Troubled Pictures: French Agriculture and Contemporary Rural Sociology." *Rural Sociology* 73 (4): 660–83.

Hinrichs, C. Claire. 2000. "Embeddedness and Local Food Systems: Notes on Two Types of Direct Agricultural Markets." *Journal of Rural Studies* 16 (3): 295–303.

Hochschild, Arlie. 1997. *The Time Bind: When Work Becomes Home and Home Becomes Work.* New York: Macmillan.

Holloway, Lewis, and Moya Kneafsey. 2000. "Reading the Space of the Farmers' Market: A Preliminary Investigation from the UK." *Sociologia Ruralis* 40 (3): 285–99.

Hughes, Alex. 2005. "Geographies of Exchange and Circulation: Alternative Trading Spaces." *Progress in Human Geography* 29 (4): 496–504.

Laacher, Smaïn. 2002. "Les systèmes d'échange local (SEL): Entre utopie politique et réalisme économique." *Mouvements* 19 (1): 81–87.

Latouche, Serge. 2006. *Le pari de la décroissance.* Paris: Fayard.

Lawson, Victoria. 2005. "Hopeful Geographies: Imagining Ethical Alternatives." *Singapore Journal of Tropical Geography* 26 (1): 36–38.

Leyshon, Andrew. 2005. "Introduction: Diverse Economies." *Antipode* 37 (5): 856–82.

Marx, Karl 2007. *Economic and Philosophic Manuscripts of 1844.* Mineola, NY: Dover.

Massey, Doreen. 2000. "Entanglements of Power: Reflections." In *Entanglements of Power: Geographies of Domination/Resistance,* ed. Joanne P. Sharp, Paul Routledge, Chris Philo, and Ronan Paddison, 279–86. London: Routledge.

McCarthy, James. 2006. "Neoliberalism and the Politics of Alternatives: Community Forestry in British Columbia and the United States." *Annals of the Association of American Geographers* 96 (1): 84–104.

Meadows, Donella H., Dennis L. Randers, Jørgen Randers, and William W. Behrens III. 1972. *The Limits to Growth: A Report for the Club of Rome's Project on the Predicament of Mankind.* New York: Universe Books.

Pagès, Alexandre. 2005. *La pauvreté en milieu rural.* Toulouse: Presses Universitaires du Mirail.

Portes, Alejandro, Manuel Castells, and Lauren Benton. 1995. *The Informal Economy: Studies in Advanced and Less Developed Countries.* Baltimore: Johns Hopkins University Press.

Schor, Juliet. 2010. *Plenitude: The New Economics of True Wealth.* New York: Penguin.

Thompson, Craig J., and Gokcen Coskuner-Balli. 2007. "Enchanting Ethical Consumerism: The Case of Community Supported Agriculture." *Journal of Consumer Culture* 7 (November): 275–303.

Waters, Sarah. 2010. "Globalization, the Confederations Paysanne and Symbolic Power." *French Politics, Culture and Society* 28 (2): 96–117.

Zakaria, Fareed. 2011. *The Post-American World: Release 2.0.* New York: Norton.

Chapter 2 The Social Forms of Local Self-Reliance: Complexities of Community in the Alaskan Transition Movement

Karen Hébert

In 2011, Anchorage resident Michelle Wilber quit her "dream job" doing energy-efficiency outreach for an organization promoting renewable energy. She got part-time work so she could devote the remainder of her day to activities to make her household and community more sustainable and resilient. These activities include tending her sizeable permaculture garden, preparing locally sourced meals for her family, and undertaking construction projects to improve the energy efficiency of her four-plex apartment building in hopes of turning it into a cohousing arrangement that is "as green as possible." Wilber also continued her involvement in organizations such as Spenard Transition, a neighborhood group whose efforts include an initiative to make area roads more friendly for biking and walking. Wilber's commitment to these activities, as she describes it, stems both from "personal leanings" and the more "global perspective" she developed over years of education and critical thinking, which instilled in her a sense of "responsibility to right what I see as wrongs." For this reason, she explains, she pushed herself, ordinarily somewhat shy, to join groups so that she could engage with these issues in a "larger social way."

Wilber's pursuit of diverse forms of alternative local provisioning and household self-sufficiency through collective, community-building endeavors mirrors the approaches of the broader organizations in which she has become involved. Spenard Transition is an offshoot of the larger Anchorage Transition, a group that is associated with the Transition movement that began in the United Kingdom in 2005. Transition is an international network that "supports community-led responses to climate change and shrinking supplies of cheap energy, building resilience and happiness" (Transition Network 2011b). The explicit linking of community engagement with ideals of self-reliance, expressed by official Transition materials and practitioners alike, prompts questions about the kinds of selves and communities that are both presumed by and generated through such strivings. In the context of concerted efforts to relocalize systems of production and consumption for community resilience, which people and places are imagined and experienced as part of the local community? How are various groups enlisted in change that aims to be at once individual and societal? And what are the implications for individuals, communities, and the social movements they are working to build?

These questions are especially pertinent in Alaska, where emergent trends that celebrate the adoption of more flexible patterns of work in order to live more lightly on—and off—the land have somewhat deeper roots and meanings. The pursuit of self-provisioning has for some time attracted a wide spectrum of adherents across very different social groups. Alaska Native people have long practiced subsistence hunting, fishing, and gathering along with participation in certain kinds of market work; and many of the state's more recent transplants, whether they identify as left-leaning hippies or antigovernment off-the-landers, moved to Alaska precisely to pursue deliberate alternatives to "nine-to-five" employment and to practice patterns of living more closely connected to the rhythms of the natural world. While aims of self-sufficiency, particularly in the face of climate change and peak oil, may seem downright paradoxical in a state that is overwhelmingly dependent on payouts from major oil companies and the federal government, a common commitment to self-reliance is often very self-consciously held up as the essence of what it means to be Alaskan. (See Haycox 2002 for a fuller examination of this tension.)

How do the mostly urban Alaskans involved in the Transition movement negotiate these tensions in their everyday efforts to build community self-reliance? How do members of particular initiatives, who are working together with the intent of galvanizing an even larger social group, reconcile the potentially divergent sociopolitical visions and projects that underlie Alaskan aspirations for local self-sufficiency? Further, what does the experience of those involved in Alaska Transition efforts reveal about the character of the "grassroots innovations" (Seyfang and Smith 2007) associated with experimental formations such as the Transition movement more generally?

I approach these questions through an ethnographic exploration of the practices and perspectives of participants involved in Transition initiatives in Alaska, drawing together and comparing the experiences of participants in Anchorage Transition and its offshoots with those active in Kenai Resilience, a Transition-affiliated group on the somewhat less urban Kenai Peninsula, a few hours' drive from Anchorage. Research into these networks was conducted through semistructured interviews of individuals and groups, informal conversations, and participant observation across some of the social settings in which Transitioners circulate, from bike-friendly progressive potlucks to weekend organizing meetings to volunteer hours at the local botanical garden. This chapter also draws upon over a decade of ethnographic research conducted on provisioning practices in more rural Alaskan communities, which I bring to bear in my analysis of the Alaska Transition groups whose activities I investigated in 2011 and 2012.

Like many parts of the United States, Alaska has witnessed a surge in practices intended to promote sustainability and resilience—or, at the very least, these have gained greater visibility and are being met with newfound excitement. Much as Juliet Schor argues in *Plenitude* (2010), such creative transformations of the work-and-spend, business-as-usual economic order tend to be experienced not as forms of deprivation by those who are putting them into practice but as practical ways of making life more rewarding, socially connected, and meaningful. Many of the Alaskans whose stories are reflected in this chapter have been inspired by the same ideas and materials that have sparked broader trends of the sort Schor and others have observed—the relocalized eating experiments of best-selling author Barbara Kingsolver (Kingsolver, Kingsolver, and Hopp 2007), for example, or lessons from *The Transition Handbook: From Oil Dependency to Local Resilience* (Hopkins 2008), which led to the creation of the Kenai Resilience group when it was discussed at a community forum. Those practicing plenitude in Alaska are plugged into new social media outlets and inhabit a blogosphere as lush and colorful as their rapidly expanding backyard gardens. As these details suggest, and as Transition practitioners themselves seem well aware, the communities that are taking shape through these local efforts involve complex patterns of both linking to and delinking from global flows, and present scholars with a suggestive case for the study of communities and social movements in formation.

In the sections that follow, I first provide a snapshot of the Transition movement and an overview of the emerging body of scholarship that aims to understand it. I then situate the Transition movement in Alaska, a very different setting than the towns of southwest England where Transition first gained prominence. This two-part section describes efforts to launch and sustain local groups in the Anchorage area and in the smaller and somewhat more rural city of Kenai, respectively. Here, I underscore dynamics, tensions, and challenges that are associated with the Transition movement broadly but are particularly at issue in Alaska. The following section offers a further comparative discussion of the two initiatives, widening the frame of analysis to consider the social formations on different edges of Transition in Alaska as it is currently practiced, including efforts to spur sustainability through for-profit ventures and more radical off-the-grid experiments. I also take up the backdrop of Alaska Native subsistence lifeways, which are occasionally mentioned as an inspiration but almost never incorporated into Transition work in a robust or sustained way. The chapter points out that certain tensions of Transition as currently practiced reflect features of the "upper-middle-class standard lifestyle" that at least some participants joined the movement in order to avoid.

In conclusion, I argue that the challenges revealed through an analysis of Transition in Alaska are indicative of the difficulties in reconfiguring not merely mainstream relations of production but also dominant systems of meaning. I ask whether some of the same social forms that may explain the growth, appeal, and success of the Transition network might also serve to diminish its potential for personal fulfillment and more radical social transformation. At the same time, however, I follow Alaskan participants themselves by pointing out that the changes sparked by Transition efforts have consequences far beyond those that may be immediately apparent.

SITUATING THE TRANSITION MOVEMENT

Transition and Its Travels

In the origin story repeated throughout Transition materials and secondary literature, the movement began through a permaculture course taught by instructor Rob Hopkins, credited as the movement's founder, in the Irish town of Kinsale in 2005 (see especially Hopkins 2008, chapter 9). In Hopkins's class, instruction in the principles of permaculture, an approach to the more sustainable design of human systems such as settlements and agriculture, was joined with concerns about climate change and a keen attention to the issue of peak oil, the idea that fossil fuel production is now at or near its point of terminal decline and so the end of cheap oil is nigh. Seeking models for "how the town of Kinsale might successfully make the transition to a lower-energy future" in these circumstances, Hopkins's students developed the Kinsale Energy Descent Action Plan (Hopkins 2008, 123). They relied on their own research and the work of thinkers such as Richard Heinberg in his book *Powerdown* (2004), which advocates economic contraction and relocalization, and "communities responding by building local infrastructure and self-reliance," or "lifeboats" for a postcarbon landscape (Hopkins 2008, 123). When Hopkins moved shortly thereafter to the town of Totnes in southwest England—an area known as a hotbed for environmental activism and alternative living, described to me by one British activist as "sort of the California of England"—his earlier work in Kinsale formed the basis for the broader Transition model for "community-scale responses to peak oil and climate change" (Hopkins 2008, 133).[1]

Totnes was the first "Transition town," a catchy moniker still widely used to describe the movement, even though the "Transition network," as the organizational hub has come to be known, has sought to shift the emphasis toward "Transition initiatives," with its somewhat broader geographical compass; "Transition culture" is also increasingly used to characterize the movement (Mason and Whitehead 2011, 512). Although the name refers to a "transition" to more sustainable forms of living, it appears to have been adopted coincidentally and largely independently from the academic literature that emerged during this same period on "sustainability transitions" (Haxeltine and Seyfang 2009, 7).

As Hopkins outlines in his hefty handbook (2008, chapter 10), four key assumptions underlie Transition initiatives:

1. That life with dramatically lower energy consumption is inevitable, and that it's better to plan for it than to be taken by surprise.
2. That our settlements and communities presently lack the resilience to enable them to weather the severe energy shocks that will accompany peak oil.
3. That we have to act collectively, and we have to act now.

4. That by unleashing the collective genius of those around us to creatively and proactively design our energy descent, we can build ways of living that are more connected, more enriching and that recognize the biological limits of our planet. (134)

As suggested by these assumptions, the resulting Transition model fuses, on the one hand, an underlying motivation of imminent, "inevitable . . . shocks" that form the basis for an almost apocalyptic future vision with, on the other hand, "a positive, solutions-focused way of gathering those around you together" to imagine and build "a post-oil world that is actually preferable to the present" (133). Transition materials recognize the challenge of negotiating this tension, alerting aspiring organizers that their awareness-raising activities will "need to bring people up to speed on Peak Oil and Climate Change, but in a spirit of 'we can do something about this' rather than doom and gloom" (Transition Network, 2011a). It thus focuses energies on "positive visioning" (Hopkins and Lipman 2009, 7) and highly practical and concrete activities that help pave the way for communities' "collective adventure" (Transition Network 2011a).

The Transition model, not unlike the process for becoming an official Transition initiative, is a flexible but fairly structured affair. The model encompasses a twelve-step process that includes initial phases of creating a steering group of key organizers (and planning for its eventual demise), followed by raising awareness of core issues; networking with existing groups and organizations; establishing theme or interest groups to tackle particular community concerns; developing open forums for visioning and also generating highly visible progress on practical projects; and encouraging various forms of reskilling and bridge-building with local government (Transition Network 2011a). Although official materials describe the steps as "ingredients" that can be creatively adapted rather than rigid, linear stages (Transition Network 2011a), the echo of twelve-step programs is not accidental. The transition to greater resilience is conceptualized as both personal and societal, and, as Hopkins explains in the *Handbook* (2008, chapter 6), the theory of behavior change that informs the Transition model draws from psychological insights that have been used in the formulation of addiction treatment. The ultimate goal is for each initiative to move from these activities to the development and implementation of more concrete energy-descent planning, involving "new infrastructure and practices to replace the incumbent regime when it fails to function" (Seyfang and Haxeltine 2012, 385). While the movement encourages broad interest in its concepts and model, it also has established somewhat formal criteria for the designation of official Transition status, which requires trainings and commitments by key organizers, and provides funding and other means of support in turn. Innumerable groups associated with Transition—including all the efforts taking place at present in Alaska—are registered only as "mullers" rather than "official" Transition initiatives.

From the beginnings of Transition town Totnes in October 2005, the model has spread quite rapidly across the United Kingdom and the world, making it widely heralded as one of the fastest-growing social movements in recent years. At present, there are 445 "official initiatives" listed on Transition Web sources (Transition Network 2013). These are heavily concentrated in Europe and the English-speaking world, specifically Canada, the United States, Australia, and New Zealand, with a handful of mullers and an even more limited number of official initiatives across much of Asia, Africa, and South America. In the United States, there are currently 114 official initiatives on record and 214 mullers, including Anchorage Transition and Kenai Resilience (Transition Network 2013). Because registering as a muller requires simply an engagement with Transition materials and the completion of an initiative profile—not insignificant tasks but ones more easily and flexibly accomplished than gaining official status—this category captures a far broader range of efforts than those found among the ranks of official initiatives. Moreover, a closer look at the experience of mullers, those at the fringes of the movement, in this case in Alaska, promises to shed light on both the diversity of approaches that have taken inspiration from Transition as well as the degree to which these can be readily accommodated under the existing model.

Making Sense of Transition

Given the newness of the Transition movement, there is not yet a large scholarly literature on the topic. But because of its prominence and rapid expansion, especially in the English-speaking world, academic analyses are being published apace.[2] A number of common themes emerge across the sweep of disparate studies, much of this foreshadowing dynamics, tensions, and challenges manifest among the groups in Alaska taking their cue from the broader movement. Multiple analysts of Transition point to tensions between the monolithic and absolute grand narrative that inspires Transition action and the push for creative, bottom-up responses to it. Amanda Smith suggests this has parallels in an uneasy mesh between the managerial models and formalized criteria that organize "official initiative" status, on the one hand, and the grassroots dynamism that these are intended to harness and cultivate, on the other (2011, 101). Nick Stevenson expresses uneasiness with the "disconcert-ing language of certitude" the movement embraces (2011, 76), and Alex Haxeltine and Gill Seyfang voice discomfort with the use of "apocalyptic future scenarios as a motivator" (2009, 18). Given the ominous overtones of the broader narrative motivating the movement, Transition efforts often re-flect a "tacit and sometimes overt" emphasis on "personal and family survival" (Barry and Quilley 2009, 4–5). As John Barry and Stephen Quilley observe, this emphasis does not always "sit easily with green activist principles of liberalism, global engagement and universalism, civic altruism and demo-cratisation" (5).[3] As coming sections detail, nearly all of these matters became the stuff of everyday negotiation and debate in the work of both Alaskan groups.

In the scholarly literature, these points connect to more general concerns about the movement's perceived lack of critical attention to power, capital-ism, and class politics. A key feature of Transition initiatives is the develop-ment and adoption of practical measures for everyday change, so goals are framed in positive—rather than oppositional—terms. Further, the move-ment eschews political affiliations and positions in favor of broad-based, nondivisive community action. At times, the "lack of oppositional energy" in everyday settings means that initiatives risk being reduced to a "bland local consensus of inaction" (Mason and Whitehead 2011, 511). Whether the move-ment is interpreted as "apolitical" (Haxeltine and Seyfang 2009, 7; Smith 2011, 102) or "depoliticised" (Trapese Collective 2008, 6), some of its sharpest critics have singled out its seeming refusal to recognize the violence by which capitalist relations are formed and maintained, and the degree to which the interests invested in the perpetuation of existing structures of power will fight to maintain them (Rotering 2011; Trapese Collective 2008). Others, however, maintain that the movement's "radical, utopian vision of a society which has transitioned to a post-carbon economy based on inclusion, local distinctive-ness, equality and freedom" (North 2010, 591) is what makes it undeniably and critically political.[4] Even among Alaskan groups embracing the Transi-tion movement's vision of organizing across the political spectrum, each group's role in issues perceived as political became a salient topic of con-versation among members, suggesting that the debates that have emerged in Transition scholarship are simultaneously playing out among movement par-ticipants.

The final set of critical engagements involves the role of "the local" in Transition concepts and the kinds of communities that are built through it.

On a very practical level, the movement has encountered problems in establishing the geographical and social scale at which community-level initiatives are to operate, as evidenced in the terminological shift away from Transition towns. Yet efforts to scale the original model up or down to encompass human settlements of all sorts have met with more mixed success, and initiatives in major cities have tended to splinter off into particular neighborhood efforts (Smith 2011, 102–3), a trend especially manifest in the Anchorage area. A notoriously troubled term whose referent is hopelessly indistinct, "community" has been lambasted by scholars who argue against the "militant particularism" (Harvey 1996) or the obfuscating romantic associations that so often accompany its deployment (Joseph 2002). As Gordon Walker points out, the notion of community that animates new carbon governance schemes has an array of meanings—distinct actor, scale above household but below government, territorial place, social network, collaborative process, and civic-minded collective identity—which are "differentially and selectively enrolled" by given initiatives (2011, 777–79).

A privileging of the "local" community in Transition efforts further complicates the picture, given the equivalent slipperiness of that concept and the degree to which it has been dismantled as a reified opposite to an equally troubled notion of the global. In the face of these critiques, Peter North seeks to rehabilitate the movement's more "intentional" localization and carve out a space for the local that is not simply synonymous with the sort of autarky conjured by Heinberg's "lifeboats" (2010, 592), a move that parallels E. Melanie DuPuis and David Goodman's (2005) attempt to promote a more "reflexive localism" in their critical engagement with local-food initiatives. Alongside the conceptual conundrums introduced by the centrality of the local community in the Transition model, analysts have also shown how its notion of resilience is heavily equated with the relocalization of systems of production and consumption "in a rather unquestioning way" (Haxeltine and Seyfang 2009, 14–16).[5]

The relationship of the people inside the movement to those outside it is a recurring topic of concern for analysts and adherents alike, including those in Alaska. Even though demographic data on membership are scarce, there is a general consensus that the movement on the whole, particularly in the United Kingdom where it has garnered most analysis, has tended to attract members of the "educated middle class" who hold rather unrepresentative "post-materialist" values (O'Rourke in Bailey, Hopkins, and Wilson 2010, 601; Stevenson, 2011, 12). As Smith notes, a longtime issue within the movement has been "membership diversity, or rather the lack of it": preliminary findings from an internal diversity study indicated that 95 percent of respondents identified as white European, and 86 percent held postgraduate degrees (2011, 102). This dovetails with the greatest challenge expressed by UK Transition initiatives, as documented by the first formal survey of coordinators in 2009: growing the movement. Over three-quarters of survey respondents indicated these difficulties, and nearly one-third recognized a need to reach out to a wider, more diverse community, including those "outside the 'green-belt'" and "beyond the 'usual suspects'" (Seyfang 2009, 11).[6] Although the ethnographic sections to follow depict the heterogeneity that exists among participants in Alaska, group membership on the whole, and perhaps in the leadership in particular, nevertheless confirms the picture of the Transition movement as a mostly white, highly educated, middle- and upper-middle-class group, most identifying as politically progressive: "demographic outliers," as one member of Kenai Resilience put it. Yet precisely because these social facts are so stark, such issues, along with the others described above, have not been ignored or submerged to other concerns but have been confronted head-on in the work of both Transition groups.

LOCATING TRANSITION IN ALASKA

Anchorage

It was only as I drove up the steep incline to the bio-shelter that Cindee Karns calls home, located off Prudhoe Bay Drive on the forested outskirts of Eagle River to the north of Anchorage, that I realized that the Prudhoe Bay Transition, whose name I had seen amid Anchorage Transition materials, refers to a neighborhood spin-off group like Spenard Transition rather than any effort to wean Alaska from dependence on its best-known oil field. It was still quite early in the morning, but Karns, an energetic former eighth-grade teacher, greeted me warmly and brightly. We had arranged for the early-hour conversation because she was set to depart later that day for a town several hours away to lead a sixteen-day permaculture course along with Rico Zook, a permaculture designer, consultant, and instructor who was taking a break from a brisk schedule of international projects to help run the Alaskan effort in his first visit to the state. Karns beckoned me into her kitchen, where Zook stood before an open laptop, paperwork assembled in preparation for the trip, a pot of cooling oatmeal on the stove. After a quick peek at the greenhouse plantings and fish pond—I would get a full tour later of the workings of what is, apparently, the only bio-shelter in Alaska—Karns, Zook, and I settled into a wide-ranging conversation about Transition, permaculture, and beyond.[7]

Karns was among a handful of Anchorage-area residents who first began talking about starting a local Transition initiative in 2009, and she has been perhaps the most visible leader of Anchorage Transition since. While her prominent leadership role may make her experience somewhat unusual, the personal questioning that brought her to participate in Transition in the first place echoes the story of a great many people involved in the movement in Alaska: "What can *I* do? How can I change *my* life?" For Karns, this particular intersection of the personal and the political began when her children had finished college, her husband got a job in Anchorage, and she was able to retire from teaching. Raised in Fairbanks and at the time living in the politically conservative and car-dependent Fairbanks suburb of North Pole, Karns welcomed a move to the Anchorage area, telling her husband, "We can choose a *sustainable* place this time." Priced out of the walkable neighborhoods of downtown Anchorage, Karns and her husband were eventually able to purchase the Eagle River bio-shelter, a "dream home" that had fallen into foreclosure, as most prospective buyers proved more intimidated than excited by the idea of maintaining two in-home composting toilets and a DIY water-recycling system fashioned from hardware-store supplies.

Like Michelle Wilber and many other core participants in Alaska Transition efforts, Karns had for some time been involved in permaculture, and in this respect the origin of Transition in Alaska parallels that of the movement itself. There is a fairly active permaculture community in Alaska, with a listserv membership of over five hundred (O'Malley 2011) and a lively Web site that coordinates discussion and the activities of local groups (http://akpermaculture .ning.com/). The network calls itself the Alaska Permaculture Guild, which is actually a play on words, since "guild" is one of the core design principles in permaculture, drawn from ecology, which refers to a group of species that work well together. The guild hosts monthly potlucks in Anchorage, which attract around thirty people at any given time, a subset of a larger group that cycles in and out of permaculture-related activities.

As Karns, Wilber, and others clarified, the Transition and permaculture groups pursue distinct but often intersecting agendas, as do those involved in the Alaska Bioneers. The Bioneers group is part of the larger U.S.-based nonprofit that seeks "practical environmental solutions and innovative social strategies to restore Earth's imperiled ecosystems and heal our human community"

(Bioneers 2011). The Alaska Bioneers' activities are largely geared around organizing a major annual statewide conference for the sharing of sustainable living practices that hosts several hundred attendees; it is held at the same time as the larger national conference, in recent years linked to it via live video streaming. The annual Bioneers event was the occasion for the first conversations about doing Transition in Alaska, and it represents the main opportunity for members of geographically separated groups, like Kenai Resilience and Anchorage Transition, to get together and swap stories, strategies, and challenges.

In our morning conversation, Karns narrated a history of Anchorage Transition that I would hear repeated in others' iterations—its progression from discussions at the 2009 Bioneers meeting to an early reading group held at the public library, followed by awareness-building community movie nights and a series of four classes, all meant to spur what Transition materials describe as a "Great Unleashing," an event intended to transform the groundswell of interest ideally generated by the prior activities into an action-oriented plan for the group's next period of work (Hopkins 2008). Karns's narrative reflected the exhilarations and frustrations of grassroots mobilization, both the excitement of finding "like-minded people" after living in "the conservative capital of the USA" and the challenges of attempting to build interest in a city of nearly three hundred thousand people. As Karns related, she and her fellow organizers would host twenty-five people at a movie screening, many leaving with enthusiastic plans to participate in Transition efforts, only to have none of them show up at the next meeting. She became fond of repeating a remark made to her by a Fairbanks organizer, who quipped that working in Anchorage must be "like punching the Pillsbury Dough Boy"—that is, trying to move a mass that would seem to absorb even a forceful impact, always returning to its original doughy state.

It was these difficulties in provoking citywide galvanization that prompted the aspiring Anchorage Transitioners to contact founder Rob Hopkins for guidance. At the next Bioneers meeting, the group arranged for a conversation with Hopkins himself via videoconference—apparently his only mode of long-distance travel. No doubt because of lessons learned from the struggles of other groups, Hopkins counseled them to "stop trying to organize the city," as Karns put it. Instead, he advised convening smaller groups on particular interests or topics, which was the inspiration for the series of courses as well as the neighborhood-focused campaigns. According to Karns and others, the classes were generally regarded as a great success, much more so than the movie nights, in large part because they energized a continuing conversation among committed participants. However, they also exposed differences in conceptions of community and organizing tactics among those who had taken a leadership role in the initiative.

While the courses attracted a critical mass, the participants did not draw from the disparate crowd that attended the movie nights, for example, but rather from the familiar faces of those who circulated at permaculture pot-lucks and Bioneers meetings. As she reported it, Karns saw the more insular nature of the community that was forming as part of Transition activities as a shortcoming, prompting her to reach out to casual acquaintances and neigh-bors to make them aware of Transition events, and encouraging others to do the same. Yet in the conversations about consciousness-raising among core group members that followed, it became clear, at least to Karns, that not everyone saw their mission as she did hers: a self-proclaimed "evangelist" to the wider community. Reflecting that it was perhaps her time in smaller towns that made her less uncomfortable or intimidated in reaching out to others with potentially divergent views, Karns explained that she did not worry about being perceived as "radically green," which she suspected was the source of at least some members' uneasiness. While Anchorage Transitioners as a group appear to firmly embrace the movement's larger message empha-sizing both an urgent planetary crisis and a positive future vision—a combi-nation that seems to account for much of the movement's appeal among the Alaskans with whom I spoke, along with its ready-to-adopt method for com-munity change—there is far less consensus among those involved on a range of matters of both philosophical and practical import.

The core members of Anchorage Transition differed not merely on whether they should evangelize but about how awareness is best built, among whom, and the extent to which consciousness-raising should take precedence over other goals, such as skill building and household self-sufficiency training. This relates to further differences in opinion as to how much to emphasize the message of crisis and impending catastrophe in community-building efforts, reflecting tensions in the motivations of the movement itself. Despite the overlap among those involved in Transition, permaculture, and the Bi-oneers, the Transition movement is known for attracting a more community-oriented set. As Wilber clarifies, "Transition Town is really, really about making sustainable, resilient, integrated communities. It's for joiners, for people [who], if the shit hits the fan, want to be out there giving food away to neigh-bors and teaching them how to garden." She contrasts these "joiners" to the "survivalists," those who similarly believe in peak oil but respond by saying, "We're all going to need our stockade, fifty-pound bags of grain, and a bunch of guns," people who are erecting "big wire fences around their gardens and stockpiling below ground." Yet Wilber's effort to elaborate on this point makes clear that the lines that distinguish the joiners from the survivalists can be somewhat blurry. She describes her boyfriend, for instance, as having libertarian leanings along with more green tendencies: despite his keen interest in permaculture, local foods, sustainable living, and cohousing arrangements, he does not describe himself as environmentalist. And Wilber herself admits to being a bit of a "doomer" and "not always sure what category to put myself in either."

It is perhaps the range of perspectives held among and by group members that has provoked an abiding division over how much the Anchorage Transition group should be involved in matters of local politics or align itself with particular political positions or orientations. A number of participants confided to me that they felt they came to the group's central issues from different starting points than other members, whether more politically conservative stances or merely less easily categorized adherences. At one permaculture potluck, which took the form of a progressive (in the sense of traveling) multi-course dinner and garden tour covering four different Anchorage households, an attendee pulled me aside to mention that she would have responded somewhat differently to one of my casual questions over a quinoa salad had there not been others within earshot whose sensibilities she may have offended. While social occasions afforded opportunity for more subtle negotiations of political alignments and interpersonal relations, public action in the name of the group made such matters more fraught. Karns told me that others disapproved of her decision to speak out as a member of Anchorage Transition in a newspaper editorial against what was widely regarded as an unscrupulous effort by Anchorage business owners to overwrite key provisions of a city planning document that had been developed through broad-based community participation. Karns's views on the topic itself seemed less the concern than the appropriate role of the Transition group in matters perceived as overtly political.

These disagreements had echoes in the divergent perspectives held by group members on the relationship Anchorage Transition should have to the broader Transition movement and its model for change, and specifically whether the local group should make it a priority to pursue official status. While added training and access to funds and other forms of support was a draw, the cost and logistical challenges of becoming official seemed daunting, and some questioned whether the local group's aims might be met more readily through other avenues and investments. Participants also revealed varying degrees of comfort with key concepts in the Transition lexicon. For example, one group member, a retired geologist who described how her scientific background made her skeptical of the certitude contained in certain sweeping claims, argued for group flyers to highlight "the end of cheap oil" as opposed to "peak oil."

In addition to exposing varied viewpoints among the leadership, the Anchorage Transition initiative's community-building forays also highlighted challenges of building group leadership itself, given the limited time many employed members had to devote to Transition activities on top of their often substantial prior commitments to other volunteer efforts and family responsibilities. While the idea of downshifting from wage work that Michelle Wilber put into practice held appeal, most of the key organizers in Anchorage either felt financially unable to do this or already had this flexibility— because they were retired, for example. Moreover, a number had turned their interests and skills into for-profit businesses, such as consultancies on permaculture or sustainable living. Karns, for example, offers bio-shelter tours to schoolchildren and other groups through a business called Alaskan Eco-Escape; and others who might be recruited to take on a leadership role were even more consumed with their private ventures, at least according to one newer core group member. While there have been a few waves of key players in Anchorage Transition over the past few years, the group finds itself yet again asking how it might use the limited time and energy of committed participants to catalyze "renewed interests and efforts" within the city.

While struggles to sustain and build leadership are no doubt familiar to many grassroots organizing efforts, these issues have contributed to ongoing internal conversations about the mission and future of the group. A recent effort to hold a formal Transition training, a required step in gaining official status, fell through due to concerns about the cost and the varying levels of interest among members in pursuing the formalized route. Even those pushing for the training acknowledge that the goal would be primarily to reenergize the group for more activities ahead versus sparking a "Great Unleashing," which one member described as just an "event for the sake of following a format." Meanwhile, several core members have begun to advocate for directing more energy toward individual members' "own self-sufficiency in terms of food and energy," such as preparing for anticipated future shocks.

Although advocates for these perspectives acknowledge that, like Rob Hopkins, the ultimate end is to engage "the community as a whole," they also note that individual and household efforts might offer a more effective starting point and could serve as a model for broader change. As explained by Sharon Ferguson, who first brought the Transition movement to the attention of those at the 2009 Anchorage Bioneers meeting, some of those in the core group have largely given up on trying to engage the wider community at the present moment. "If we lived in Portland, or Eugene, it would be another story," she remarked, but "we can only do what we can do among like-minded people." Thus, while the members of Anchorage Transition continue to discuss the future of the group, attempts to build connections on smaller scales are gaining force. Ferguson is working closely with a few other members on increasing household resilience, for instance. She has launched a reskilling group intended to boost larger Transition efforts by building and sharing hands-on, practical skills for self-sufficiency, which she sees as more valued in Anchorage than in many "Lower 48" cities. At the same time, Karns is continuing to develop the Prudhoe Bay Transition group, now an active neighborhood presence, through potlucks, tool sharing, Facebooking, and even a talent show. As another core member communicated to me via e-mail: "Folks going in their own (not surprising for AK!) directions have caused me to characterize the official movement as 'sputtering,' yet I have seen much commonality of interest in localization and stronger roots here." As the following section explores, the challenges and debates experienced by Anchorage Transition involving issues of scale, time, and community have also factored into the work of the Kenai Resilience, whose negotiations of both related and dissimilar dilemmas provide as much a point of contrast as comparison.

Kenai

The road from Anchorage to Kenai, a city of about eight thousand people 150 miles south on the Kenai Peninsula, wends its way through what many in Alaska consider some of the most spectacular country in the state, a panorama of rugged coastline, surging rivers, and picturesque mountain valleys. Kenai itself lies on the flats near the mouth of the Kenai River, a commercial and sports fishing hub and a depot for nearby Cook Inlet oilfields. Given its location along the Alaskan road system and its relative proximity to Anchorage (a three-hour drive), the Kenai Peninsula is not exactly remote by Alaskan standards. The city of Kenai and neighboring Soldotna are actually considered urban clusters in U.S. censuses (State of Alaska 2011).

While Kenai has certain features in common with Anchorage, a number of significant factors—including its smaller size, more rural feel, and immediate connection to working sites of Alaskan oil production—make Kenai a rather different place to organize around Transition themes. For one, negotiating ideological divides is an even more delicate matter, given the heightened range of perspectives and experiences that draw Kenai residents to Transition topics. The region is home to many avid subscribers to survivalist and libertarian credos, which run strong in Alaska to begin with, and even more countercultural expressions of movements that would seem to be on the opposite end of the political spectrum, to the extent that these distinctions even apply to social formations that defy easy classification in linear terms. In practice, this means that right-wing gun-rights advocates and residents of a macrobiotic intentional community have been known to mill about together at Kenai Resilience events. While this creates certain challenges for leaders, it also offers a broader and more dynamic base for gaining traction for the initiative. Those involved in Kenai Resilience reported that Anchorage Transitioners are almost always impressed by the group's organization and the vibrancy of the alternative and off-the-grid experiments that are happening there.

On an overcast Saturday in August 2012, I connected with members of the Kenai Resilience steering committee at a meeting held in the home of Heidi Chay. Chay, who runs a professional mediation service and a commercial fishing operation with her husband, a former local assemblyman, was an expert host, summoning six other group members to the weekend event, furnishing free-flowing coffee and hearty lentil soup, and helping facilitate the in-depth conversation about Transition that moved from her living room to her kitchen table over the course of several hours. Although a number of those on the steering committee were acquaintances with a variety of social ties before joining the group—Kenai is a small enough place that this is often the case, they noted—they had each come to participate from different starting points. Kate Veh, who sparked the first public discussions of Transition in Kenai, is a lifelong Alaskan with no prior involvement in sustainability issues who was shocked into action by a newfound awareness of peak oil concerns. Michelle Martin, a recent transplant from the Lower 48, was drawn to participation after her experience of living lightly on the land in a walkable Pittsburgh neighborhood came to an end at the same time that she began to gain appreciation for local fish and game harvesting and the practical skills this entailed. Chay was well acquainted with peak oil and related ideas and had learned of Transition while doing research on intentional communities during a year living in Spain. At least two other members came to the group in part through their engineering backgrounds and involvement in regional energy issues, which had instilled in each a concern for efficiency and economy as well as an interest in environmental problems and solutions.

During the group meeting, Veh related the genesis story of Kenai Resilience, which I had heard from others before. "I learned about peak oil and basically panicked," Veh explained, describing how she started to look around her and envision what things might be like in fifteen years, which provoked a feeling "like the world was sort of crashing down." When she stumbled upon Rob Hopkins's handbook and YouTube videos on the Internet, she realized "there's a solution to this," noting that Hopkins's manual "gives the format for how to proceed." As Martin recalled, Veh held up a copy of *The Transition Handbook* at a community forum in the winter of 2008–9, explaining that she was worried about what its contents meant for the future world that her two young children would inhabit and was seeking help in starting an initiative. Although Martin had been concerned about issues of climate change and her carbon footprint before she moved north, this was her first real exploration of peak oil, which seemed especially disconcerting to her since, as she put it, Alaska lies at "the end of a long supply chain." New to town at the time—she had moved with her husband, a public defender with family in Anchorage—she was eager to dive into community involvement. And so Kenai Resilience was born.

With a kickoff retreat at nearby Ionia, the macrobiotic intentional community (discussed in greater detail below), and initial events on ocean acidification and climate change, Kenai Resilience began its work. According to the steering committee, one of the major accomplishments during the group's first year and a half was gathering together a virtual community for the exchange of information and more, facilitated by building an e-mail listserv of about three hundred people and a Web site template for U.S. Transition initiatives. Assembling an online presence had the effect of making visible a group with common interests and concerns that turned out to be far larger than most people realized existed locally. After conversations with other Alaskan Transition-minded groups at the 2009 Bioneers meeting, Martin became even more convinced of the importance of listservs and social media as she learned more about the tactics of other initiatives, so she began a regular Kenai Resilience e-newsletter.

In addition to building the group's newsletter and Web presence, the primary activity of Kenai Resilience to date has been a series of monthly potluck dinners, usually organized around a presentation by a guest speaker on a particular topic of interest. Sessions over the past two years have addressed issues of food security, energy, local currencies, time banking, and homesteading, to name but a few. Attendance has been solid, with successful events having around two dozen people, most from a core group of regulars but always with a handful of new or occasional attendees as well.

The group's early experience with climate change–themed events set the course for its activities during the years to follow. Among the group's first public efforts were successful meetings organized around the risk of ocean acidification, which is linked to climate change. Inspired by these initial discussions, a member of the Kenai City Council brought forward a compact on climate change being developed by Alaskan coastal communities at the time, with contentious debates about national cap-and-trade policy unfolding in the background. The compact issue quickly became a flashpoint for volatile local politics surrounding the Cook Inlet oil industry, and the subsequent events the fledgling Kenai Resilience helped to organize on these issues became mired in angry exchanges between those promoting the compact and other members of the public who came to speak out in opposition, possibly goaded to action by oil companies themselves. As steering committee members reflected, the disappointment of these initial events undoubtedly led the group to shy away from more explicitly political or locally divisive concerns, even if this was never established through any formal decision. In addition, it suggested to at least some group members fairly early on that the Transition model might not prove the most appropriate for structuring the longer-term work of Kenai Resilience.

In contrast to the Anchorage group, the Kenai Resilience has more decisively abandoned plans to pursue official status. As Martin summarized, looking back, despite initial excitement about the prospect of Transition training, "it was clear from the early stages that the Transition model wasn't going to work here locally." Although the group took inspiration and instruction from the movement's message and techniques, she explained, "we live in a community where a huge part of the economy is oil, and trying to convince people that might not be the case is a hard road around here." Maybe "in a liberal town in England you can make this happen," she mused. But in Kenai, the chamber of commerce issues statements that convey the city's ongoing support for the oil industry, and the recent resumption of Cook Inlet drilling has been greeted with enthusiasm by most people locally, who welcome the return of jobs to the region. Indeed, as member Kristin Mitchell, a physician trained on the East and West coasts, reminded the group, "The whole philosophy of the state is resource extraction, and we hear that from the very highest levels . . . the idea that there would be a different way to manage or marshal our resources or care for our environment, it's very contentious."

Much of the group's conversation centered on the challenges of doing Transition, or something along its lines, in what one member dubbed "the oil capital of Alaska."[8] The cities of Seattle, Portland, and San Francisco were referenced a number of times as points of contrast: left-leaning metropolises where the views and voting behaviors of most among the steering committee would be far more typical than in Kenai. It soon became apparent that most of the group identified as some variant of "left of center," "progressive," or "liberal," and recognized one another as such from common involvement in various local organizations. Veh, however, was fairly quick to interject that she was "not all *that* liberal," but "probably a little more over to the other side," laughing along with the rest of the group with what seemed equal parts discomfort and amusement. If Veh had to negotiate her less predictable political leanings within the group, others had to manage the fact of their involvement with Kenai Resilience in professional settings where left-leaning politics could not always be readily acknowledged. One steering committee member, who teaches engineering at a local community college, described a "culture war in microcosm" in his workplace, where he routinely feels the need to stay silent when colleagues joke about politics or discuss the prospect of holding a wise-use rally "to counter all the sustainability stuff."

While these moments dramatize the perils of everyday action in a polarized political landscape, all the group members expressed strong agreement that Kenai Resilience efforts were also emboldened by its small-town location and the appeal of its mission among a broad cross-section of people. Heads nodded vigorously when David Thomas, an environmental engineer originally from California who sits on the board of the local electric cooperative, explained that there was "more ability for disparate groups to overlap . . . in a small town," likely due to both the proximity of people with politically and philosophically divergent views as well as an ethic of civility that leads most people to avoid divisive topics in everyday interactions. Reflecting on his routine civil exchanges with, for example, "drill-baby-drillers" in Kenai, he noted, "I definitely in my day-to-day life have conversations with, recreate with, find alliances with a wider spectrum of people than I ever did in a metropolitan area."

Conversation grew even more animated as the Kenai Resilience members described the overlapping interests that linked this broad spectrum in the region, a "bimodal" pattern that attracted adherents to sustainability from both the Left and the Right, along with a sizeable group of "anarchist-leaning" libertarians who "wouldn't align themselves with either end of political spectrum, really." Some had been surprised when a speaker at one of the potlucks, a local farmer known for his extreme libertarian and antigovernment views, devoted much of his presentation to condemning regulations that forbade the sale of raw milk, since they tended to associate enthusiasm for raw milk with more progressive political leanings. (See Mincyte's chapter 5 in this volume on the opposition of libertarians to raw milk regulations.) The steering committee's forays handing out flyers around town for Kenai Resilience events had exposed the group to the range of viewpoints held by the region's residents, including those so committed to self-sufficiency that "cooperation doesn't enter in." However, as Martin argued to general agreement, "There sure are a lot of people here, no matter how they label themselves, who are concerned about the same things that the Transition movement is concerned about," and "most of them are community-minded people." As another member commented, "We can talk to people in the community who aren't of our political bent but who will agree that it's time to quit worrying about whether the government is going to do anything about this and just go do it."

In the same way that garden tours and household food production proved popular for broad-based community building in Anchorage, Resilience members reported that the issue of food security was "really taking off" in Kenai, becoming important "on both ends" of the political spectrum. Seizing upon this trend, the group assembled a local-foods directory that has gotten a fair amount of circulation. Chay noted that many more people had begun to grow their own food in recent years, laughing with others as she pointed out the irony that this trend for self-sufficiency has been spurred in Alaska by a "big injection of USDA money," which came in the form of a program offering training and subsidies for the construction of covered greenhouse structures known as high tunnels. Despite the enduring contradictions of pursuing self-reliance in a state so heavily dependent on oil revenues and federal government programs, Martin saw quite quickly when she moved to the state that relying on local resources is "a big part of being Alaskan," a fact especially visible in local activities to produce and preserve one's own food. In her view, these are precisely the skills that are important for the Transition group to tap into and help encourage further among people in the wider region; "Whether they want to identify with the Kenai Resilience or not," Martin noted, "they have skills and use them."

Beyond the challenges of communicating Transition's peak oil message to an oil-industry town, the group widely acknowledged that despite some successful outreach efforts, "no one had the time or the energy" to take on further responsibilities to build the group to the next level, which is "such an integral part of Transition." In this respect, the experience of Kenai Resilience closely paralleled that of the Anchorage Transition group. "You need to gather a lot of energy to put on one of these 'Unleashing' events," Chay explained, "and we haven't mustered that level of energy." So the group has remained in a "very extended public education phase," the first phase outlined in Transition materials.

Rather than ramping up to official status, the strategy of the group involves building on existing strengths: taking whatever steps it can to draw attention to "what is already going on" locally and to connect interested community members with one another, in part through the ongoing potluck series and electronic communication efforts; addressing already-identified priorities, such as increasing capacities for local-food provisioning, for example, by gaining access to a slaughterhouse for meat processing and a state-approved kitchen for canning; and shoring up regional residents' already quite successful efforts to make a "sustainable situation on your own little homestead." Martin, who recently had a baby, told the group that she hoped to recruit new group members to help with these plans, those who might not already be, as another put it, "spread so thin," identifying young people and retirees as targets. Others joked that perhaps the solution was to endow an executive director.

Although the leadership of Kenai Resilience widely acknowledged that the group remained more in an awareness-raising phase as opposed to an action-oriented one, there was a good deal of general agreement that the group had done important work in its brief existence, particularly in ways that might not get "chalked up in anyone else's mind [as] a Kenai Resilience result or achievement." Members attributed accomplishments in other spheres to their involvement in the group. This included Thomas's efforts to transform energy decisions through his work on the local board, where he has played a role in successful campaigns—against supporting coal power, for example—that would not have been possible just a few years previously. A number of members pointed to highly personal transformations, such as their own relationship to consumerism. This echoes Anchorage participants' views that some of the most powerful changes resulting from Transition involved the expansion of personal capacities, whether their own or others'. While some Kenai Resilience participants expressed frustration about not being able to do "more" in their own lives and for the group, most affirmed a sense of the usefulness of having done something. As Veh remarked, "It takes several repetitions of an idea before something takes form in a community . . . so that's where I see our group"—interjecting "a bit of an idea" about sustainability "into an oil-based economy, which is really hard."

MAKING SENSE OF TRANSITION IN ALASKA

Despite their different histories, both groups mulling Transition in Alaska have experienced a common arc, in which initial ambitions for galvanizing community-wide action through a formal "Great Unleashing" have been tempered and replaced by more modest goals. Awareness-building outreach in socially and politically diverse settings is still conceptualized as part of the work of each group, but both Anchorage Transition and Kenai Resilience have also embraced a strong push toward enlisting collective resources to shore up the efforts of individual households to cultivate a "sustainable situation on your own little homestead," as Martin put it, whether through food provisioning or other skill-building endeavors. While a focus on promoting practical tools for self-reliance has clearly been central to Transition from the start—both to the broader movement and quite prominently in the Alaskan iterations—its positioning as the ultimate goal for current group activities by many participants seems noteworthy, especially given the absence of a clear path for propelling the other phases of community action outlined in Transition materials. Transition's ready-to-use methods for instigating broad-based, community-led change may have originally inspired the Alaskan groups to frame their efforts in the movement's terms, but the challenges of realizing its ingredients in Alaska have perhaps revealed Transition's limitations as a general model.

It remains possible, however, as suggested by Kenai Resilience members, that organizing around matters of household self-sufficiency may, somewhat paradoxically, offer the most promising avenue for creating connections across social, political, and philosophical divides—that is, for building a community that does not yet exist, despite overlaps in geographical space and some converging interest in sustainability. What possibilities and limitations for transformation, then, does this particular mode of community making afford? This is a critical question not merely for Alaskan efforts, since innumerable projects for social transformation at present seek to forge common ground by addressing material concerns of apparent universal import. Food, for example, has become the subject of campaigns far and wide for many of the same reasons it has been taken up as a focus by Kenai Resilience, even though some of the group's leaders are more interested in issues like urban sprawl and walkability. Half a world away in the United Kingdom, food and gardening represent "far and away the most popular practical ways for Transition initiatives to start engaging people in hands-on action" (Seyfang 2009, 13). While food may be a universal human need, its incorporation into vastly different webs of meaning and networks of social relations makes it an especially rich site for examining variance among communities generated through a common focus on sustenance.

Consider, for example, the activities of a number of for-profit businesses that have grown up alongside the permaculture and Transition movements in and around Anchorage, tapping into and helping to foster urban residents' aspirations to shift to more environmentally sound and socially fulfilling ways of living centered on skill building for local provision. I was reminded of the potential force of these growing networks as I sipped homegrown, homemade rhubarb juice while waiting for the start of a garden tour at the cheery and inviting home of Saskia Esslinger and Matt Oster, who run a business called Red Edge Design. Esslinger teaches courses in permaculture, Oster works as a licensed contractor and energy rater, and together they offer consulting services to others looking to follow their lead in transforming houses into sustainable "urban homesteads for modern living." While Esslinger would host a similar garden tour free of charge the following week for the members of the permaculture guild, in which she has long been a key player, this $20-per-person public tour was geared toward Anchorage residents who were somewhat newer to gardening, chicken raising, composting, greenhouse building, and other related pursuits. Esslinger ably guided a group of over ten people through her compact property on an unassuming suburban street in midtown Anchorage, where a fence made from recycled windows encloses a combination greenhouse–chicken coop and a garden that last year yielded over a thousand pounds of vegetables and berries.

Esslinger's garden had already been the subject of a fair bit of local media coverage, as Anchorage's most dramatic example of the newfound popularity and visibility of efforts to relocalize food in Alaska. Esslinger and Oster were central figures in the Alaska Food Challenge, a concerted effort by about thirty people to commit to eating as locally as possible for a year. They hosted the challenge kickoff party and were "among the most die-hard" of its participants, newspaper articles reported (O'Malley 2011). No doubt many on the tour had followed Esslinger's blog posts over the course of the previous year. The group (mostly women) peppered her with questions about planting techniques and vegetable bed preparations in addition to comparing notes with one another on topics such as how to house recently acquired chickens. Her guidance clearly energized those present, who seemed to leave enlivened and inspired to put the innovative ideas they had learned into practice in their own homes. If in fact they did so, it would represent an actualization of Esslinger's intent for her home and entrepreneurial activities: "This is about people, place, and profit. The triple bottom line."

While Esslinger remains involved in a variety of local organizations dedicated to sustainability, such as the permaculture guild, she confessed that her paid and unpaid time in the garden, not to mention caring for her infant son, are "a lot of work." Indeed, although for-profit ventures like Esslinger's may well do a good deal of the consciousness-raising and skill building that groups like Anchorage Transition seek to effect, they also represent yet another way in which potential recruits for membership and leadership roles are beset by competing demands for time and energy. Like Transition coordinators in the United Kingdom, nearly 30 percent of whom identified lack of time as a major challenge to their efforts (Seyfang 2009, 10), participants in Alaskan groups expressed discouragement that they and others did not have more time to spend on Transition efforts as well as their own sustainability-minded activities. While Wilber's new job at three-quarters time and half pay has made her "money poor," she finds the real problem is that despite the many joys of pursuits like child care, gardening, biking, and home improvement, "it's still too much" in terms of time spent working. As she proclaims: "I love every piece of what I do. I am never bored. But it would be nice to have more time to do everything." Martin, too, who works at a local nonprofit full-time in the summer and part-time in the winter, reports that she does not have the time to get out the Kenai Resilience newsletter as regularly as she would like, nor does she feel she is doing as much as she could to change her own lifestyle, though she has done some gardening, joined a small CSA, and cooks almost entirely with local meats. In feeling that she might be doing "more," Martin echoes Wilber, who also expresses guilt or bashfulness about the orientation of her overwork: "I'm not out there helping the world, building orphanages. . . . I'm just feeding myself. In some ways that sounds selfish." What seems noteworthy here is that Schor's (2010) and others' analyses tend to highlight the pleasures of downshifting from nine-to-five jobs and redirecting time toward more personally fulfilling and meaningful ends. Yet the perspectives gleaned from Transition leaders, while not denying these gains, point to somewhat more fraught relationships with work, responsibilities, and achievement, especially among women with young children.

While the residents of Ionia, an intentional community located not far from Kenai in a rural area, are no strangers to the time demands of self-reliance, they have opted to conceptualize and configure their activities toward sustenance rather differently. I came to Ionia on the invitation of Kenai Resilience member Eliza Eller. While Eller was helping to prepare the community-wide macrobiotic midday Sunday meal, I got a tour of the community and its activities from one of the founders, Barry Creighton. Ionia was formed by a small group who met in Boston in the 1980s while pursuing a macrobiotic approach to mental and physical health issues. Realizing that it was next to impossible to fit two-hour organic and macrobiotic meal preparations into the lifeways of an expensive urban metropolis, the group members decided to pursue a more radical, communitarian living experiment for themselves and their families, eventually finding their way to the Kenai Peninsula. Given the region's libertarian off-the-grid efforts, they were optimistic, it turns out more or less rightly, that their own enclave might be able to exist undisturbed there as well. Creighton showed me Ionia's extensive gardens and the new barn and granary under construction, which would enable the community to store more of its own foodstuffs. Self-sufficiency was the goal, Creighton explained, though he quickly acknowledged that it was an ideal that never would or could be fulfilled. Ionia has long been the recipient of government and private grants for mental health and other causes, which residents readily acknowledge as critical to the community's successes to date. While Ionia is not closed off from the wider world—as suggested by its partnership with Kenai Resilience and an openness to visits like mine—residents have adopted a life based on a thoroughgoing rejection of categories like "work" and "weekends," as Creighton reminded me, chuckling when I inadvertently used these terms in one of my questions. The greatest thing about the founding of Ionia, he explained, "was having our time."

Yet another counterpoint to the modes of self-reliance and community building associated with Transition initiatives can be found in the subsistence lifeways that are a cornerstone of Alaska Native identity and widely practiced across the state, especially in rural areas. In Alaska, "subsistence" refers not to eking out a meager living off the land, but rather to a set of highly politicized claims to resource rights by Alaska Natives based in a constellation of natural and social relationships and cultural traditions (Berger 1985; National Research Council 1999). As it is referred to in everyday contexts, "doing subsistence" involves activities like fishing or "putting up" fish—typically, cutting, drying, and smoking them—picking berries, hunting and processing moose or caribou, maintaining traplines, and the like. In addition, it entails distributing the products of this activity along lines of kith and kin, forging and renewing community ties built from relations of reciprocity. The main goal of subsistence, then, is not mere household survival but the sustenance of the social community through the exchange of culturally valorized foods. Given that subsistence as practiced today generally demands some access to cash income for inputs like guns and fuel for boats and snow machines, the creative combinations of work within and beyond market channels associated with new social formations (Schor 2010) have long been observed in rural Alaska (Langdon 1986; Wolfe 1984).

As these overviews of different modes of local provisioning suggest, some of the same practices, from vegetable gardening to fish canning, can underpin substantially different social relations, forged in dissimilar kinds of communities and associated with divergent strategies for reconciling the time-consuming aspects of living off the land. Although Transition participants occasionally gesture to Alaska Native subsistence lifeways as a source of inspiration for their own efforts, there appears to be little if any serious engagement with these cultural forms in the everyday activities of the two groups. This does not seem a coincidence. While Transition members describe the importance of social networks and provisioning skills for building local resilience, these do not depend on the same degree of shared commitments and generalized reciprocities that bind other communities. This may be one of the Transition movement's strengths, enabling members to reach out across divides of class, culture, and political persuasion. But it also would seem to keep adherents themselves ensnared in certain core contradictions of what one group member termed the "upper-middle-class standard lifestyle," a way of living that this participant, for one, was deliberately seeking to reject through her involvement in Transition.

CONCLUSIONS

In detailing the work of two Alaskan groups associated with the Transition movement, this chapter traces the accomplishments and challenges that have accompanied efforts to build community resilience by strengthening forms of local self-reliance. While scholarship on the Transition movement is expanding, social research is scanty on how its designs and methods are taken up in settings that have little resemblance to the small, politically progressive towns that incubated its rapid rise. Given the celebration of self-reliance across the political spectrum in the so-called Last Frontier of the United States, not to mention Alaskans' complex relationship to the oil industry that fills state coffers, Alaska makes a provocative site for examining how goals of community building and self-reliance are negotiated amid broader campaigns for sustainability. As the preceding pages chronicle, the Transition-themed groups in both Anchorage and Kenai wrestle with thorny questions of community on a regular basis: who should be the target of outreach initiatives, for example, and how to stimulate a collective push for change at individual, community, and societal levels. The experience of each group indicates that the questions that animate theoretical discussion in the scholarly literature about the means and ends of the Transition movement are also the stuff of pressing everyday concern and debate among its participants.

Although the paths taken by the Anchorage and Kenai groups diverge in a number of respects, both have shifted from initial goals of community-wide organizing to more modest aims intended to build resilience incrementally through more circumscribed projects—household skill building in an area of popular interest, for example. In each case, Transition's ready-to-use method for instigating broad-based change motivated the formation of the group but was soon revealed to have only moderate purchase for collective mobilizing in Alaskan settings, perhaps pointing to the limitations of the Transition approach as a general model. Individually and together, Alaskan group members reflected upon the many frustrations, impasses, and detours they had experienced in their Transition work, which on a personal level often took the form of not having enough time or energy to realize lofty goals. Yet there was also a palpable sense of satisfaction among core members in their group's achievements to date and a visible optimism about future efforts, whatever those might entail.

What can we conclude from these findings, which seem to point in a number of different directions? On one level, participants' experience of doing Transition in Alaska suggests that some of the same social forms that may explain the growth, appeal, and success of the Transition network may also serve to diminish its potential for personal fulfillment and more radical social transformation. Many of the movement's central charges—reaching across ideological divides, avoiding more overtly political matters, folding group efforts into the existing work of broad-based coalitions, and focusing on self-reliance skill building—do not necessarily require or precipitate transformations in dominant systems of meaning, such as the rethinking of concepts of work, time, and community that underlie the business-as-usual order. Nevertheless, on another level, it remains the case that the changes sparked by Transition efforts have consequences far beyond those that may be immediately apparent, as group members were quick to point out. These include action outside of formal Transition channels as well as more personal transformations, which were identified as an important outcome of Transition work by participants in both Anchorage and Kenai. Such examples of flourishing or incipient "actually existing sustainabilities" (Krueger and Agyeman 2005) signal that more modest shifts in practices, from personal consumption habits to regional energy policy, may already be making way for broader social change. From this perspective, organizing around matters of local self-sufficiency may prove a more ready means, at least in the Alaskan context, not simply to galvanize community resilience but to bring into being a resilient community of a sort that does not yet exist.

NOTES

1. Since the economic crises that began in 2007, growing financial instability has become more prominent in Transition's mobilizing narrative (Smith 2011, 101).
2. This literature includes conference papers and theses (e.g., Cohen 2010; Goldwasser 2009; Mcdonald 2009), reports from academic centers (Haxeltine and Seyfang 2009; Seyfang 2009; Seyfang et al. 2010), statements by activist groups (Rotering 2011; Trapese Collective 2008), and articles in scholarly journals (Bailey, Hopkins, and Wilson 2010; Chatterton and Pickerill 2010; Mason and Whitehead 2011; North 2010; Pickerill and Maxey 2009; Seyfang and Smith 2007; Smith 2011; Stevenson 2011; Seyfang and Haxeltine 2012). Several studies come in the form of "auto-ethnographies" in which authors are movement participants, most as some form of "sympathetic critique" (North 2010).
3. Several assessments note the potential undemocratic aspects of the movement's structure and influences, pointing to Heinberg's position that "we must be prepared to give up 'at least some human rights'" in the transition to a postcarbon future (Heinberg in Stevenson 2011, 71).
4. The movement's position vis-à-vis the state and more local political structures has also been scrutinized along similar lines. Interestingly, while some assessments note that its directive to "build a bridge" with local government opens avenues for co-optation (Smith 2011, 102) and vitiates radical potential (Trapese Collective 2008, 30), others argue the movement needs a *more* thoroughgoing "analysis of the role that the state might play in securing its ends" (Stevenson 2011, 77).

5. Haxeltine and Seyfang note that although the *Handbook* does draw on academic work on resilience, all the resilience indicators it outlines are framed in terms of the degree to which they foster local provision, which makes for an unsophisticated concept of resilience that deflects attention from the important real-world trade-offs and conflicts that communities will undoubtedly encounter in their pursuit of resilience (2009, 16).

6. Even more broadly, commentators have observed that the intensely local focus of initiatives, while conferring certain positives, can also limit the potential to develop ethics of care for distant others (Mason and Whitehead 2011, 511) and obscure the political economic processes that have done much to create far-flung local worlds (Trapese Collective 2008).

7. According to the designer of this particular bio-shelter, R. L. Crosby, "A bioshelter is an integrated house/greenhouse/aquaculture system designed to emulate natural living systems in which the subsystems interact with each other to collectively create a self-regulating whole. The goal is to simulate the thermodynamic efficiencies of a complex ecological food chain" (Crosby 2012). The Karns's home has no well or septic system; it collects rainwater that goes through a filtration system to be repeatedly reused.

8. Other Alaskan communities could clearly vie for this title, such as Valdez, the terminus of the Trans-Alaska Pipeline, or Prudhoe Bay, the oil industry extraction hub.

REFERENCES

Bailey, Ian, Rob Hopkins, and Geoff Wilson. 2010. "Some Things Old, Some Things New: The Spatial Representations and Politics of Change of the Peak Oil Relocalisation Movement." *Geoforum* 41 (4): 595–605.

Barry, John, and Stephen Quilley. 2009. "The Transition to Sustainability: Transition Towns and Sustainable Communities." In *The Transition to Sustainable Living and Practice Advances in Ecopolitics,* ed. Liam Leonard and John Barry, 1–28. Bingley, UK: Emerald Group.

Berger, Thomas R. 1985. *Village Journey: The Report of the Alaska Native Review Commission.* New York: Hill and Wang.

Bioneers. 2011. "Bioneers: Revolution from the Heart of Nature." http://www.bioneers .org/ (accessed October 14, 2011).

Chatterton, Paul, and Jenny Pickerill. 2010. "In, against and beyond Capitalism: The Messy Spaces, Practices and Identities of Everyday Activism in the UK." *Transactions of the Institute of British Geographers* 35 (4): 475–90.

Cohen, Danielle K. M. 2010. "Reaching out for Resilience: Exploring Approaches to Inclusion and Diversity in the Transition Movement." Department of Geography and Sociology / Humanities and Social Sciences, University of Strathclyde, Glasgow.

Crosby, R. L. 2012. "What Is a Bioshelter?" http://biorealis.com/bioshelter/BioshelterNarr .html (accessed February 2, 2012).

DuPuis, E. Melanie, and David Goodman. 2005. "Should We Go 'Home' to Eat? Toward a Reflexive Politics of Localism." *Journal of Rural Studies* 21 (3): 359–71.

Goldwasser, Mia. 2009. "The Transition Movement in Australia: An Analysis of the Progress, Challenges, and Future of Transition Initiatives." Independent Study Project (ISP) Collection, paper 643. http://digitalcollections.sit.edu/isp collection/643 (accessed March 1, 2013).

Haxeltine, Alex, and Gill Seyfang. 2009. "Transitions for the People: Theory and Practice of 'Transition' and 'Resilience' in the UK's Transition Movement." Tyndall Working Paper 134, Tyndall Centre for Climate Change Research, University of East Anglia, Norwich, UK.

Haycox, Stephen W. 2002. *Frigid Embrace: Politics, Economics, and Environment in Alaska.* Corvallis: Oregon State University Press.

Heinberg, Richard. 2004. *Powerdown: Options and Actions for a Post-carbon World.* Gabriola Island, British Columbia: New Society.

Hopkins, Rob. 2008. *The Transition Handbook: From Oil Dependency to Local Resilience.* Totnes, UK: Green Books.

Hopkins, Rob, and Peter Lipman. 2009. *Who We Are and What We Do.* Totnes, UK: Transition Nework.

Joseph, Miranda. 2002. *Against the Romance of Community.* Minneapolis: University of Minnesota Press.

Kingsolver, Barbara, Camille Kingsolver, and Steven L. Hopp. 2007. *Animal, Vegetable, Miracle: A Year of Food Life.* New York: HarperCollins.

Krueger, Rob, and Julian Agyeman. 2005. "Sustainability Schizophrenia or 'Actually Existing Sustainabilities': The Politics and Promise of a Sustainability Agenda in the US." *Geoforum* 36 (4): 410–17.

Langdon, Steve J., ed. 1986. *Contemporary Alaskan Native Economies.* Lanham, MD: University Press of America.

Mason, Kevin, and Mark Whitehead. 2011. "Transition Urbanism and the Contested Politics of Ethical Place Making." *Antipode* 44 (2): 493–516.

Mcdonald, Niamh. 2009. "The Role of Transition Initiatives in Local Authorities' Responsiveness to Peak Oil: A Case Study of Somerset County Council." PhD diss., Bartlett School of Planning, Faculty of the Built Environment, University College London.

National Research Council. 1999. *The Community Development Quota Program in Alaska.* Washington, DC: National Academy Press.

North, Peter. 2010. "Eco-Localisation as a Progressive Response to Peak Oil and Climate Change: A Sympathetic Critique." *Geoforum* 41 (4): 585–94.

O'Malley, Julia. 2011. "Farmers on the Block: One Couple Aims to Eat Local All Year." *Anchorage Daily News,* July 24, 2011.

Pickerill, Jenny, and Larch Maxey. 2009. "Geographies of Sustainability: Low Impact Developments and Spaces of Innovation." *Geography Compass* 3 (4): 1515–39.

Rotering, Frank M. 2011. "Post Carbon Institute: Blind to Capitalism and Power." http://www3.telus.net/needsandlimits/pdf_files/articles/PCI_blind_to_capitalism_and_power_feb_2011.pdf (accessed February 23, 2013).

Schor, Juliet B. 2010. *Plenitude: The New Economics of True Wealth*. New York: Penguin.

Seyfang, Gill. 2009. "Green Shoots of Sustainability: The 2009 UK Transition Movement Survey." Working paper, Centre for Social and Economic Research on the Global Environment, University of East Anglia, Norwich, UK.

Seyfang, Gill, and Alex Haxeltine. 2012. "Growing Grassroots Innovations: Exploring the Role of Community-Based Social Movements in Sustainable Energy Transitions." *Environment and Planning C: Government and Policy* 30: 381–400.

Seyfang, Gill, Alex Haxeltine, Tom Hargreaves, and Noel Longhurst. 2010. "Energy and Communities in Transition: Towards a New Research Agenda on Agency and Civil Society in Sustainability Transitions." Working paper, Centre for Social and Economic Research on the Global Environment, University of East Anglia, Norwich, UK.

Seyfang, Gill, and Adrian Smith. 2007. "Grassroots Innovations for Sustainable Development: Towards a New Research and Policy Agenda." *Environmental Politics* 16 (4): 584–603.

Smith, Amanda. 2011. "The Transition Town Network: A Review of Current Evolutions and Renaissance." *Social Movement Studies* 10 (1): 99–105.

State of Alaska, Department of Labor and Workforce Development. 2011. "Urban and Rural—Classification for Alaska." http://labor.alaska.gov/research/census/urbrur.htm (accessed March 1, 2013).

Stevenson, Nick. 2011. "Localisation as Subpolitics: The Transition Movement and Cultural Citizenship." *International Journal of Cultural Studies* 15 (1): 65–79.

Transition Network. 2011a. "12 Ingredients." http://www.transitionnetwork.org/support /12-ingredients (accessed March 1, 2013).

———. 2011b. "Welcome—Transition Network." http://www.transitionnetwork.org / (accessed October 14, 2011).

———. 2013. "Transition Initiatives Directory." http://www.transitionnetwork.org/ini tiatives (accessed February 23, 2013).

Trapese Collective. 2008. "The Rocky Road to Transition: The Transition Towns Movement and What It Means for Social Change." http://trapese.clearerchannel.org/resources /rocky-road-a5-web.pdf (accessed February 23, 2013).

Walker, Gordon. 2011. "The Role for 'Community' in Carbon Governance." *WIREs Climate Change* 2:777–82.

Wolfe, R. J. 1984. "Commercial Fishing in the Hunting-Gathering Economy of a Yukon River Yup'ik Society." *Études/Inuit/Studies* 8 (supplement): 159–83.

Chapter 3 New Cultures
of Connection in a Boston
Time Bank

Emilie A. Dubois, Juliet B. Schor, and Lindsey B. Carfagna

If the watchword of global capitalism is greed, as declared by *Wall Street*'s Gordon Gecko, the mantra of the plenitude economy is share—as in sharing one's car, one's home, one's food, and one's time. These practices, once unthinkable in a middle-class America obsessed with privacy, acquisition, and protection of property, create what *Forbes* magazine called "an economic revolution" (Geron 2013) as millions of people are learning new ways to access goods and services as well as deploy the assets and skills they already possess. The sharing economy is growing at an estimated 25 percent annually and is predicted to exceed $3.5 billion in 2013. It's an opportunity for changing how people spend, earn, and live that should enable the expansion of plenitude lifestyles.

The sharing economy is conventionally defined as including a wide range of initiatives, from those that represent marginal twists on business-as-usual offerings to radical alternatives.[1] Zipcar, an early example of car sharing, has evolved into a conventional car rental that offers services by the hour rather than the day. Owned by Avis now, it is not a true example of sharing. By contrast, another early initiative, couchsurfing, is a network of couch lenders and the travelers who stay with them (without payment) that has remained closer to its origins. Couchsurfing is one example of what anthropologists call a gift economy—there's no price or formal market involved. People offer their homes to strangers—that is, they share them—mostly for the purposes of meeting them and doing them a good turn. It's a stark alternative to a conventional market exchange.

The sharing economy includes traditional cases in which assets or goods are literally shared among peers, such as land sharing (which matches land-owners with prospective gardeners) or neighborhood sharing, in which people lend the proverbial "cup of sugar" in whatever form is needed, such as lawn mowers or photographic equipment. It also refers to shared ownership of goods, a less common but expanding practice, which usually involves peer-to-peer relationships. The Internet has been key in the rise of peer-to-peer economies because it simplifies the logistics of sharing goods and ownership and provides mechanisms such as ratings systems that help build trust and reputation among strangers. Craigslist and eBay are early examples of online peer-to-peer initiatives that specialize in the resale of used goods. Couchsurfing uses a peer-to-peer structure, as do AirBnB (a for-profit lodging service), Relay Rides (people rent out their own cars), and Sidecar (people offer rides in their cars, donations suggested). The sharing economy also emphasizes reuse of goods rather than buying new, and it is remaking modes of service delivery. The options range from low-cost concierge-style services such as Zaarly and TaskRabbit, which facilitate errands or other services done by nonprofessionals (peers), to time banks, which are service-exchange communities that operate without money according to principles of equal time exchange. Members trade equal hours of work deployed for different tasks in time banks.

We use the term *connected consumption* to describe many of the initiatives in the sharing economy from the consumer's side. Connectedness refers to both the digital and the social aspects of these practices. For consumers, these practices make it possible to access a wide range of quality goods and services much more cheaply than in the BAU economy. They also facilitate local, face-to-face connected relationships. From the provider's side, these innovations open up a variety of ways to earn cash income or access to goods or services through barter. People are renting out their cars, homes, and other assets to make ends meet. They are selling and trading their time for cash and services. They are swapping food and used goods. They are saving money by not having to buy things. Taken together, this new set of initiatives and practices is enabling people to work less by choice, to take a chance on a new career, small business, or a start-up, or to live a life of lighter ecological impact.

The sharing economy and the connected consumption portion of that larger entity attract participants via three main motivations. The first, just noted, is economic. Peer-to-peer economic activity shifts value away from middlemen toward consumers and producers, making alternative lifestyles possible. As Schor predicted in *Plenitude* (2010), underemployment and falling or stagnant incomes have affected growing numbers of people.[2] For them, sharing is a way to live well on less money or to earn money with assets they already own. A second motive is ecological. These initiatives aim to reduce carbon footprints: through sharing transport, reducing waste, increasing the utilization of existing assets (which reduces the demand for building new), and reusing goods. Third, many participants are interested in meeting people, creating social connections, and deepening their ties to social networks (Belk 2010). Nostalgia for an earlier era when people knew their neighbors and could rely on them permeates the sharing economy. Some sharing initiatives, such as the time bank, the subject of this chapter, explicitly attempt to re-create those informal social ties. We have found that while the sharing economy is by no means confined to young people, they have been its innovators and early participants. They're more digitally connected and more open to strangers and lifestyle experimentation. Many have not yet constructed normative middle-class lifestyles, and they are among those most affected by precarious economic times. In our time bank case, we focused explicitly on members who are under thirty-five years old to understand how they experience and participate in the sharing economy. Finally, despite the discourse of innovation that surrounds the sharing economy, mutual aid and asset sharing are long-standing activities, especially in low-income communities (Stack 1974). In this sense the sharing economy is a remix of already existing practices rather than a recent invention. What is different is that the digital environment allows strangers to establish these kinds of relations. Its popularity among highly educated, higher-income groups is also new.

In this chapter we present findings from a case study of one sharing institution—a large, volunteer-run time bank—that embodies a mix of these old and new dimensions. As we explain in more detail below, time banks are membership organizations in which people trade services with each other. Started in the 1980s, they predate the Internet and the start-up culture of the sharing economy, but they reflect many of its characteristics. No money exchanges hands, but there is a currency of hours: earned by providing services and spent by receiving them. Unlike many of the start-ups in the sharing economy, time banking has an explicitly egalitarian structure that assigns equal value to each person's time and skills, situating it at what Viviana Zelizer, in her discussion of local monies, has called the "ideological extreme" (2010, 325). While this structure may be "extreme," we have found that it is an important part of what draws people to the bank, a related finding to that of Gowan and Slocum (chapter 1 of this volume), who identify adherence to the anticapitalist ideology of 1968 as one of the factors that has led to the success and longevity of the alternative economy in the Aude. Because the time bank has an explicitly critical ideology, and because it is so devoted to a transformative and antimarket discourse, it is an interesting U.S. case for examining the opportunities and obstacles faced by plenitude-style institutions that attempt to undermine the foundations of neoliberal capitalism. If time banks result in robust trading economies, their members can opt out of or minimize market-based provisioning of services. They can also reduce their income requirements, build social capital, and help members acquire new skills. Therefore, key questions we address in this chapter are whether the trading economy of our bank is robust and whether it conforms to the ideological principles on which it is based. We expect that robustness will be hard to achieve because there is a large chasm between the egalitarian trading ratio of the time bank and standard market valuations for many of the services being offered.

The time bankers we studied express a high degree of ideological support for the stated goals of the time bank. They like that every member's time is valued equally and that the market does not determine the "worth" of someone in the community. Members are passionate about creating local alternatives to impersonal global markets in which knowing the people who provide goods and services is the norm. They are resistant to the trends of outsourcing or professionalization of services. Yet participants come to the time bank with highly variable levels of cultural, social, and economic capital and different levels of engagement with the market economy. They have different expectations about the quality of the services they are to receive and varied levels of comfort with the idea of nonprofessionals providing services. As we shall see in the ethnographic data, these standards are sometimes eroded in actual trading situations. We discovered that the socially transformative aspects of time banking were inhibited when members used conventional market criteria to dictate with whom and how often they traded. Furthermore, the volume of trades in the time bank is not always robust. The divergence between

of time banks, and laid out plans for establishing local branches (Cahn and Rowe 1996; Cahn 2000). Later reports detailed the inner workings of time bank exchanges and hypothesized about the social benefits time banking could offer should the practice become mainstream (Aldridge et al. 2001; North 2003; Seyfang and Smith 2002). Some articles, especially those within gerontology, found that time banking yields positive physical and mental health impacts for adults, as measured by improvements in self-efficacy and community engagement (Bailis and Chipperfield 2002; Collom 2008; Collom, Lasker, and Kyriacou 2012; Seyfang 2003). More recent academic studies on time banking have moved from descriptive to analytic accounts. Carfagna et al. (2014) explore the emerging taste regimes of high-cultural-capital time bankers. Zelizer (2005) discusses time banking within her analysis of circuits of commerce to highlight both the potential benefits to members and possible pitfalls of participation. Seyfang (2006) and Fenton (2013) discuss the role of time banking in building social capital. This chapter provides insight into the ideological motivations that lead people to join time banks, detailing the interplay between ideological motives and utilitarian approaches to trading and the complex class dynamics that characterize participation.

WHY BARTER WHEN YOU COULD BUY?
THE MOTIVES OF TIME BANKERS

We have noted that members are drawn to the indirect barter of time banking because they find its egalitarian values and ideological commitments appealing. In that sense we can say that all the people we interviewed are "ideological" time bankers—they believe in the equal value principle, they embrace its promise of enhanced community, and they are hopeful that it can provide economic value for unemployed or cash-constrained members. Virtually all of our informants discussed time banking's appeal in these or related value, moral, or ideological terms. Even time bankers who adopt a transactional approach, by which we mean that they aim to extract as much value as possible when they trade and who expect efficiency and professionalism, report that their membership was motivated by the egalitarian ethos of the time bank.

At the same time, the meanings of time banking are polysemic, that is, members understand what the practice symbolizes in a variety of ways. Most like that it is an alternative to "business-as-usual" economic arrangements in which a conventional market calculus governs social relations, although their views range from full-blown critiques of capitalism at one end of the spectrum to a few who treat the time bank more as a way of "giving back" to mitigate the worst outcomes of the market. Some are unhappy with the long commodity chains of global capitalism, preferring a smaller-scale, face-to-face economy in which they know where, from whom, and the conditions under which products originate. Many tie the BAU economy to ecological degradation, discussing how suburban living, excessive consumerism, or other factors are destroying the environment. For these members, the local boundaries of the time bank are an antidote to a resource-intensive lifestyle. The equal trading ratio is also a strong ideological draw. It matches the everyday humanistic values that many time bankers articulate and represents a stark alternative to the hegemonic valuation of people according to what their labor can command on the market. Some believe time banking can be a solution to personal financial distress. Others, considering themselves relatively privileged, gravitated to the time bank out of a sense of empathy and ethical responsibility toward others as well as the belief that it is part of an institutional alternative to a destructive economic system.

One of the most commonly expressed sentiments was the disintegration of social connection and a lack of place-based social networks. Time bankers often talked about getting back to the way America "used to be." As Sonia, a freelance copy editor, explained: "I actually really miss that sort of southern way of treating your neighbors and things. . . . I'm used to knowing my neighbors and helping them. And you should help your neighbor. It's kind of a religious idea." Others echoed Sonia's sentiment, calling time banking a "holistic approach of taking care of life and communities" or drawing a connection between that holistic approach and the "self sufficiency . . . trend going on where people want to be off the grid [and] more into local community." Respondents began their explanations of time banking by pausing to articulate a community orientation that almost without notice had slipped out of their lives. For a few, this sentiment led them to relate to the time bank largely as a volunteer activity or community commitment, becoming the kinds of members who often don't redeem the hours they've earned, favoring giving back over cashing in.

Our respondents fall into two broad groups in their ideological orientations to the time bank. Many exhibit what we term "market fatigue." A smaller subset expressed more coherent anticapitalist politics either rhetorically or in terms of their actual lifestyle practices. They see the time bank as part of an emerging alternative economy that they can participate in and thereby reduce their exposure to the BAU market. There are also a number of members who are drawn to the time bank for economic reasons: it allows them to have a higher real standard of living than they could manage through cash purchases alone.

THE MARKET AND ITS DISCONTENTS

The creep of marketized services was something that two-thirds of our time bankers resisted, in part because they are critical of paying for services that there are other ways of accessing. Many expressed a weariness with the market and were put off by the requirement to earn never-ending flows of cash to "live life" in an outsourced world (Melissa). They complained about the rising trend of paying for "professionals" to provide the same services that might have been exchanged between family members or neighbors in previous generations. These time bankers represent a backlash to a phenomenon sociologist Arlie Hochschild described in her 2012 book *The Outsourced Self* as the commercialization of everyday practices of social life such as courtship, marriage, parenthood, and elder care. Hochschild's research finds that a carousel of attractively packaged services assembled by paid providers is replacing the home-crafted, unpredictable, and flawed service relationships of the past. Her respondents expressed a mix of attitudes toward the marketization of services—most were relatively comfortable with well-established forms of market provision such as child care but regarded the frontiers of outsourcing (for example, paying people to visit loved ones in nursing homes, paying to have someone scatter the ashes of a dead relative, renting wombs for surrogate pregnancies) with ambivalence. However, Hochschild's informants are participating in these new markets, unlike time bankers, who actively reject them. Our respondents prefer "insourcing" through exchanges that are casual and personal. Their desire for professionalized services is weak and their preference for local provisioning is strong. A do-it-yourself (DIY) ethic guides their desire to contribute to a robust local economy in which nonprofessionals come together to make and do for each other in relationships of reciprocity and connection. Consider Mandy, a twenty-eight-year-old Asian American time banker who grew up in a small southwestern town. The daughter of a chemist, Mandy majored in neuroscience in college, first worked as a genetics researcher, then shifted career tracks to pursue a degree in social work. Now a coordinator at a nonprofit that pairs foster children with mentors, Mandy touched upon several of the dimensions of market fatigue we observed.

Mandy considers the functionality of goods over their form, prefers meaning and personal connection to the status value and professional quality of service exchanges, and is guided by an ethic of egalitarian relations. Her experience in the time bank helped her appreciate the value of "two-way" exchange, which "seems to be a much more balanced and healthy relationship where both parties feel important and valued." In Mandy's view, this "bidirectional" nature of time bank exchange creates "a lot of mutual respect for everyone and it's not as hierarchical as the economy system . . . of regular financial markets."

Her preferences became clear as she discussed the planning of an intimate yet typically outsourced event—her wedding. She explained that for her and her fiancé, "ultimately what's important . . . is that it's meaningful." Of course the rhetoric of meaning swirls around most outsourced weddings as well, but Mandy's case is unusual in its allegiance to the DIY ethos. She and her future husband have "really foregone a lot of the formalities." She explained, "We're not having wedding parties . . . we don't have a color scheme . . . we're not doing centerpieces . . . the dress code is 'be comfortable' . . . [and] it will be a backyard wedding at a personal family friend's." Unable to find a wedding dress that was both personal and that she could be assured was ethically produced, she turned to local talent to "time bank her wedding dress." Mandy and her fiancé both "like the time bank concept anyway of the dress" because of the relationship she has developed with the dressmaker, her assurance of its fair production, and because it "felt like" her. Unlike a dress plucked off of a rack at Kleinfeld's (an upscale Manhattan wedding dress shop), Mandy's dress will be valuable because it will be a product of local hands and of the contributions to the community she has made earning the hours to have it sewn. Mandy preferred a "simple linen dress," reasoning that it would not "make our wedding feel more meaningful if I have another layer to this dress, or some fancy embroidery." Unsurprisingly, Mandy appears genuinely puzzled by the appeal of "brand-name" labels and feels thankful that the time bank decelerates exchange and, in doing so, allows her to spend time developing relationships of gratitude and respect as she pursues a life that "feels good."

When we spoke with Victoria, another participant who is pursuing alternative ways to obtain services, she articulated her desire to be a productive member of a local service economy. A recent college graduate whose speech was as lucid as it was impassioned, Victoria contrasted her views to those of her parents, explaining that her modus operandi was unique in a family that preferred outsourcing. She highlighted her dual motives: to obtain services and goods from local sources and to contribute to the production of local value. She described a recent disappointing exchange she had getting her car repaired by a commercial mechanic: "I didn't even have to talk to him after he fixed my car. So there was so little interaction there, and there was something very important that happened. I put a lot of money into him fixing my car, and there was nothing really there afterwards. That's a lot of trust, like I had no real relationship. It's crazy but it's actually really normal." Victoria was bothered by the lack of personal connection to her mechanic and the logic underlying the disjointed exchange. As a result, she reported that she hoped to go the DIY route for future repair projects.

Victoria also described a related shift in how she has begun to take a stand against market-based criteria that focus on the rarity, complexity, or professionalism of a good or service. As with Mandy, her preferences relied on criteria that captured creative intent and connections between producers and consumers. She spoke about learning to whittle as a way "to really create something and put time into something." Though she admitted that "the things I have carved to this point are not beautiful at all," she claimed that their social location imbued them with an alternative value: "They are meaningful, and I think that if you give something to someone . . . it's like, oh, you put all this effort into it, and maybe there are other ways to judge something." In these and other cases, we found that time banking provided a way for members to self-provision, to access nonprofessional skills, or to participate in a local economy that "felt right" (Mandy). Mandy and Victoria measure value in large part by the relationship between producer and consumer. In their world, the value of a service increases as physical and emotional distance decreases.

More generally, we found that the practice of time banking exists somewhere between the warm, casual connection of an intimate friendship and the reserved, formal connection of market exchange. If time bankers are able to remain flexible in their expectations of professional quality, they can get services they need while building person-to-person connections. Alex, a researcher and data specialist, described the exchanges this way: "Partially [it's] about particular people, but partially it's about the context in which it [the exchange] happens. You don't have an expectation that there's a level of service that should be fulfilled, that I would when I walked into a store. So it's a sort of emotional gain I get from interacting with a person that I really like." Alex explained that while time banking doesn't provide "the best deal," peer exchanges often leave both parties "high-fiving and smiling." Rebecca articulated the dual benefits of the time bank—it "helps people live" and fills in the gaps for members hoping to build relationships with others in their community while trying to wrangle the logistics of their lives. It's there for "those little other things that it's, like, expensive to pay for . . . like taking a cab to the airport; it's nicer to have someone drive you, and it's less expensive." Rebecca's appreciation of the realities that tug at busy workaday lives and her dislike of the barriers to socialization are sentiments common to many of the members.

Leslie also expressed dissatisfaction with market options, which in her case was focused on tailoring: "I am quite short, so I have to get every pair of pants I buy hemmed, and I don't have a sewing machine. I don't know how to do it and pay $10 every time I get a pair of pants hemmed. . . . If I found a friend to do it, I wouldn't feel that comfortable asking them to hem all my pants." Like Rebecca, Leslie places time trading somewhere between the market and personal relations. She mused about the reciprocal nature of her imagined pants-hemming trade: "Then there's something like I can bake bread and somebody else might not be able to do that." She also highlighted the way the practice helps individuals recognize their skills as valuable and distinct from those of others. She concluded that, to her, it feels "so much more efficient and friendly to be doing trades like that as opposed to paying a stranger to do it for you." A national past of informal trading among kin, neighbors, and friends looms large in our respondents' imaginations. These young urbanites long to reconnect to those traditions while obtaining services from a network larger than their friends and family.

We found that the requirement to decide which services they should list on the time bank helped our participants think through their existing skills and recognize areas of personal competence. As they worked on their offers, they began to imagine ways they could help other than the services they provided as professionals. Over time, their experiences providing and accepting less-than-professional-quality services helped our participants envision a wider range of exchanges outside the cash market and allowed them to break from the naturalized logic of market exchange.

Bartering, sharing, or swapping skills are market arrangements foreign to most Americans' conceptualizations of economic relations in a world where cash trading is taken for granted. Sonia explained that "people normally think of money, the economy . . . you get a service and you pay for it." Sighing, she concluded that most "people don't even think another world is possible." But our respondents do, while identifying their issues with market ideology. For example, they expressed a strong preference for face-to-face contact with the producers of goods and services they obtained in the market. Aaron, a business developer at a technological company, notes: [It's] about knowing where your goods are produced, that they're not produced in some black box and you pay money for it and you get it, and you have no idea what happens in between. I've gone a couple times and visited my CSA farmer's farm. . . . I think knowing the person who is producing a big amount of your food brings up that level of trust between you and them. It's not going through the extra step like the supermarket." The concept underlying that "extra step" is key to an ethos of connection that is increasingly characterizing segments of consumers, especially those with high cultural capital and ecological consciousness. As Thompson and Coskuner-Balli (2007) found in their study of CSAs and we found in Carfagna et al. (2014), the embrace of local and face-to-face economic relations is part of a larger shift toward a more material, earthy, and connected sensibility that characterizes not only time bankers but participants in the sustainable local economies that have emerged in recent years.

Alternatives to anonymous and professionalized exchanges were very attractive to the people we interviewed. As Jace explains: "I love the idea of investing in a farm before the season, so they have the security of that, and you don't get that in a farmers' market, definitely." For Jennifer, a full-time nanny, "Economic transactions . . . that involve giving and taking, that don't involve money, and that don't involve paying really close attention to time" are preferable. Some of the other alternatives to the cash market she has pursued have grown out of her time bank membership: "Since starting Time Trade Circle . . . I have been doing some barter with friends directly that I wasn't doing before." The experiences of face-to-face trading and weighting people more heavily than price have helped her understand that she "really values local economy." Connected consumption's emphasis on tangible, local, and offline connection facilitated through extrageographic, online logistical platforms helps explain its rising popularity. To get these elements, time traders are willing to tolerate variable quality in the services they receive, the joint responsibility of the exchange, and place-based scarcity (or abundance) of specific services or goods.

Time bankers also favor artisanal and craft practices (Carfagna et al., 2014). The modern desire for distance from manual labor and memories of their grandparents' arduous lives as yeoman farmers play no role in our time bankers' imaginations. Rather, they embrace old-fashioned skills and practices. One middle school librarian jokingly lamented the popularity of manual labor within the time bank by describing her weakening monopoly over expertise in canning: "The thing that I've gotten the most successful trades with is canning . . . at the time that I started offering it, no one was doing that, because I've been doing that a long time, [but] it's gotten kind of hip, so there are more people out there and I have more competition now." Others want to be connected to the goods they consume on a corporeal level. Victoria articulated her discomfort at being physically disconnected from the process of obtaining food, especially with respect to the environmental impact of large-scale agribusiness. She said she had learned about some "meat that is supervised in a particular way and also slaughtered in a certain way." Taking significant personal responsibility for the act of consuming meat, she explained that she "really want[ed] to learn how to slaughter chickens in this particular way." Rebecca, a student, articulated three traits that make up this eco-habitus during her interview: the value of face-to-face trades, the importance of localism, and the idea that consuming is about more than money. She justifies paying a higher price by citing the value of interpersonal connection: "You go to a farmers' market and you get some cheese and you meet the farmer who made it, versus just going to Trader Joe's and picking up whatever is cheapest. I definitely know I'll pay more at a farmers' market . . . even if it's going to taste similar—because of, like, the experience and the sense of where your money's going versus, like, it's way cheaper to go to a grocery store and buy something there."

Others have idealized historic forms of community and networks of reciprocity. As Sam explains, "I'm really into hunter-gatherer societies, to be honest . . . for me, that's, like, real community, where you just—you're always in touch with people, and the community meets your needs, and you help the community through work, through feeding people, through—you know, if anything comes up." To this group, global supply chains denote ecological irresponsibility and a dangerous obfuscation of the conditions under which goods are produced. Therefore, the time bankers view the professionalization of the service sector and its reliance on cash as outgrowths of the fast consumption fueled by global supply chains. In and out of the time bank, they strongly prefer face-to-face interactions through which they can set the pace and tone of their exchanges.

The rising tide of insourcing and an emerging taste regime that displays an affinity for local, artisanal, and slow-produced goods both offer hope for time banking's viability as a market alternative.

ANTICAPITALIST SENTIMENT

Thirty years ago global capitalism, especially the nasty corporate-dominated variety, seemed unassailable. Margaret Thatcher famously declared that "there is no alternative," Francis Fukuyama heralded "the end of history," and free-market ideology reigned triumphant (Frank 2000). Things look very different today, after the crash of 2008. The Internet boom, soaring housing equity, tight labor markets, and the hyperconsumption of the early 2000s are distant memories. Critiques of capitalism articulated by social movements such as Occupy have been widely legitimated.

This ideological shift, which is undergirded by concern about economic inequality, social disconnection, materialist values, and expanding carbon footprints, has propelled migration toward connected consumption (Schor 2010). Half of our respondents articulated an explicit anticapitalist sentiment. In some ways this is not surprising, given that time banking positions itself explicitly as an alternative to the BAU economy and is one of the most ideologically motivated forms of connected consumption. In some cases we found that time bankers' critiques are driven by the fragility of their own economic situations or that of those around them. Often the waters of their economic futures are murky, clouded by student loan debt and destabilized by career trajectories that resemble a skipping stone rather than the single arc of the organization worker's career life. But others have highly valued skills and stable full-time jobs and are engaged in alternatives out of ideological commitment. Micah fits squarely into the latter category.

A twenty-four-year-old software developer, Micah spoke to us from the cooperative home where he lives with "eleven other roommates." Though he articulated little explicit anticapitalist rhetoric, Micah's lifestyle implicitly rejects capitalism. His room in a "three-story apartment [with] twelve bedrooms of people, chickens in the backyard and . . . a local CSA [membership]" comes with responsibility delinked from monetary exchange. Micah makes "very few purchases" and "meets [many needs] through cooperative-ish things." This means that he and his housemates spend time completing chores and cooking, participating "in a lot of other food co-ops that produce food and buy[ing] a lot of food in bulk, and we also insist on buying local, organic stuff." They run an "informal time bank" within their house, and it was through his housemates that Micah first learned of the Time Trade Circle.

Micah is exemplary in his dedication to exchange that is face-to-face, informal, and outside the well-worn tracks of the cash economy. He considers himself to be "already in a pretty demonetized state." Each week he spends eight hours providing his Web development skills free of charge and another morning he works as a volunteer language teacher at a local community center. He reported that he doesn't "feel a strong desire to earn every single penny I can get for doing my work, so that's why I already do spend a lot of time doing volunteer, totally pro bono consulting." Micah also challenged the typical arrangements for paid labor, wondering, "So if I'm a teacher, and I want to provide students with something that I like to teach, should I be charging them, or should they be charging me? Or if I really enjoy teaching it, like, what basis do I have to charge money on?" He has few things "that are currently monetized" and had to pause to think when asked about the last time he spent money. Already immersed in an extramarket existence, Micah was easily drawn to the indirect barter structure of time banking. While Micah acknowledged that it was his "relative privilege" that allowed him to push against the norms of paid employment, he still expressed hope for an economy centered on people instead of profit: "I think that the mainstream conception is that time is money, and so you invest your time in certain places in order to get enough money to spend your free time other places. So it is a very money-driven thing. But I guess it'd be really cool if the alternative was a person-based thing."

Micah believes that although time banking is focused on skills rather than people, it is a step in the right direction. He rejects "capital calculating to make ends meet" in favor of making "sure I could still survive and eat food" through "a series of relationships that I was building with people . . . whether it be mentoring or skills or sharing." Time banking fits into his plan because it is focused on sharing skills to create strong, long-lasting relationships.

Other members also try to avoid the cash nexus. Jennifer, the daughter of a Marxian economist, articulated sophisticated critiques of capitalism and belief in the view that human value stems from productive labor. Jennifer "was living for a year bartering work for housing and food, and, like, really not interacting with money at all except for health insurance." Similarly, Elaina maligned capitalism and the consumer society it breeds. "I think it just destroyed a lot of culture. I don't feel like it really makes us happy and fulfills us in any way." Rachel explained that she prefers to support "people [who] are putting an effort [in]to making something, and I'm paying them for that effort, versus, like, paying for some evil corporation far away who's never even cared about this product." Care and intention are two core concepts that surfaced again and again throughout our conversations. Our respondents' experiences of exchanges helped them think through new ways of assigning economic value.

Many time bankers reasoned that capitalism was not capable of solving the problems that humanity—and the planet—would be facing in coming years. Kristy, a community organizer and young mother, predicted: "I think we're going to have to be producing more of our own needs here locally, so we're going to have to be working collaboratively, because no one person can really do that. We need collaborative food growing, and we need to set up other ways to provide for our needs outside of the current economy." Throughout her interview, Kristy linked constraints on natural resources to the faltering of an economic model based on continual growth. She cautioned that "we're running out of resources and . . . it's creating massive inequalities that are destabilizing our society and our democracy." Participating in and supporting local, collective production helped solidify her place in the economy and set her family on a path that was achievable, understandable, and ascendant.

Rose represents a different kind of anticapitalist time banker, motivated not by a 1960s-style opposition to the system but a twenty-first-century sensibility that developed as her own career path took an unexpected turn. As she was raised in a wealthy, conservative family, Rose's break from allegiance to capitalism could hardly have been predicted, and it is largely pragmatic rather than ideological. She attended an elite college and initially went to work in corporate finance. But she left formal employment, explaining that she prefers to "patchwork my career" with several part-time jobs, including a home-organization business. Perhaps because of her unconventional work situation, she relies on time banking to meet many more of her needs than most members, incorporating at least one trade a week into her life. Rose's parents, especially her father, at first had difficulty understanding her decision to leave what they perceived as the security of one full-time traditional job for several transitory, highly variable income streams. Rose described the generational differences in this way: "I know that when my parents give me career advice they're coming from an entirely different view. . . . I know it used to be that whenever you would get fired or leave a job you could always switch to another company. Of if you had to switch to another career or industry, but you took it for granted that somebody else was going to take care of you, that kind of company care towards its employees. That's so not true anymore." Many of the young adults we interviewed expressed similar skepticism about whether big corporations would "take care" of them in return for loyal service. Despite an almost universal desire to push back against corporatization, the need to generate cash flow and access health care constrained participants' abilities to transition out of full-time work. Rose noted the importance of her partner's traditional full-time job, which comes with partner health insurance and a competitive salary. "I know a lot of people could never do what I do because it's been very risky and very scary. And I probably couldn't have done this if it weren't for my partner."

Within the time bank, Rose most often seeks out pet boarding. She reflected on her experience with ambivalence. She hasn't found a time banker who she felt cared for her dog well and though she worried about the potential risk she was exposing her dog to each time she tried out someone new, she continued her search because to her the promise of "huge savings" outweighed her concerns. Interviewees with steady employment and secure finances were less likely to repeatedly expose themselves to this type of risk. She mused about her generation's attitude to their employers and its recalculation of risk: "A lot of adults think that they're really the babies and the institutions have to take care of them, the big finance, the big banks, the government. . . . I feel that tug of war going nowhere—people need to take more ownership of their own lives." For Rose, the system of organizational allegiance necessitated by capitalism is broken. Though few other time bankers spoke in such sweeping terms, many echoed her cynicism about large institutions. The face-to-face consumption preferences of time bankers also hint at the appeal of peer-to-peer arrangements and the desire to sidestep the middleman. Localism and noncash exchanges succeed at dismantling some of the barriers to connection that young urbanites experience.

Though few in our sample are currently unemployed, the time bankers who began trading during a period of unemployment were more adventurous in the face of disappointing or "risky" trades. Those who were affected by the market's downturn via unemployment, heavy debt burdens, or the rising costs of fuel and food were engaged in a process of reimagining economic possibilities. Jace, an office manager who has an active online life as an artist, described the ways he is transforming his lifestyle: "I have a farm share with [a local farm]. I'm a member of a co-op [grocery]. I'm a member of the library. I think there's a renewed interest in farming because of—people feel that food is no longer just going to be there because the environment is in such bad shape."

For our respondents, keeping up with "the Joneses" has become a crass endeavor made undesirable by media portrayals of wealthy Americans and a belief that the "American Dream" has drifted into the category of unattainable. There is a general resignation to the sense that, globally, "it seems like corporations are running the world more and more and they have more and more power." Yet resignation does not mean acceptance. Distrust of large organizations and lack of belief in their responsibility to the people they employ loomed large for the time bankers whose market fatigue had turned into a fully articulated anticapitalist sentiment. They are critical of globalized production and of corporate impacts on the environment. However, time bankers are generally optimistic, as they describe how their lives of connected consuming are supplanting the crumbling edifice of global capitalism.

THE ADVANTAGES OF HIGH CULTURAL CAPITAL AND THE CONTRADICTIONS OF TIME BANKING

The state of our participants' finances varied, but regardless of their personal situations they were united by the belief that opportunities for economic stability should be ample and equal for all. However, our findings suggest that there are subtle and not so subtle ways that class reproduces itself in the actual workings of the time bank. Some members with high cultural capital prefer trading with others in that social stratum. Social class homophily (or love of same) is common throughout society, but the ideology of the time bank explicitly rejects this attitude. In light of their ideological commitment to the values of time banking, it was surprising to find evidence of time traders devaluing the skills of members who are not well educated, lack professional credentials in the areas they are offering trades, exhibit poor grammar, or have only rudimentary technological expertise. These sentiments were articulated at least once by almost half (47 percent) of people we interviewed.

Kelly, a self-employed bodyworker specializing in energy healing, valued time banking for the possibilities it provides to "help in different ways that don't involve money . . . expand[ing] what people have access to, and also expand[ing] the kinds of things that people feel like they can contribute to the community outside of traditional jobs." Repeating the promise of time banking put forth by its founders almost verbatim, Kelly's ideology is among the strongest of all participants we interviewed. However, her actual transactions contradicted her egalitarian stance. Kelly offered hands-on energy healing services when she began time banking but quickly realized that "the exchange ratio felt off." In the market, Kelly charges $100 per hour for her services but came to feel that it wasn't "equal to a time bank hour of value, somehow, for me to exchange for that." Kelly felt uncomfortable offering the full range of her services, given her level of expertise, refined through four years of training in energy healing and her desire to be respected as a serious practitioner. She became frustrated when time bankers seemed to be "testing out" energy healing through her services, although this was one of the potential benefits she had raised earlier in the interview when she mused about time banking's potential to be economically transformative. Kelly came to think more highly of "the value of my time in regards to the hands-on work, because I didn't want to be giving it away for free, or just for an hour of somebody else's time." While Kelly's stated values adhere to the egalitarian principle of equally valuable time, her transactions within the time bank tell a contradictory story.

Through experimentation, Kelly discovered one limitation of time banking's egalitarian structure. For her, trading increased the imagined difference between the value of her time and that of others in terms of what both are able to yield on the market. As a compromise, in exchange for time bank hours she offers free introductory attendance in some of her classes and workshops for which paying clients are charged $15 to $20 per hour. Although Kelly may lose revenue by offering spaces in her class, she reasons that the value the time bank members add through their presence increases the quality of her classes enough to make up for this potential loss.

Melissa, a suicide prevention counselor, also adheres to egalitarian rhetoric but simultaneously exhibits market-driven valuations. Although she acknowledged the time bank's potential to help people transition into new careers and even offer services they are not formally trained to give, she reported that she avoids this type of service by vetting the credentials of the members she trades with. When she wanted to "test out" a meeting with a career counselor, she didn't want to receive services from a practitioner who was also testing out his skills. Melissa remarked, "I found someone who was career counseling for twenty years, and he had this certificate or this degree, so he looked pretty legit." She continued, "I'm probably more likely to do something if it's what they do for a living, even though it doesn't have to be like that. . . . But for something like counseling or massage, acupuncture, you want them to have a degree or something like that." Melissa does not trade with uncredentialed service providers for "high-risk" trades, but she does believe in the benefit of others doing so.

Even if they avoided contracting certain services from providers without credentials, almost all of the interviewees maintained that time bank participation gave them a more multidimensional sense of value. Though some of the white-collar workers in the time bank shy away from receiving uncredentialed services, they are happy to offer such themselves. Karen, a software developer, explained that time bank membership allowed her to diversify her skill set through the tasks she performed. She often offered manual labor but not programming help. "I program all day. I don't want to program more. Changing thermostats makes people happy. It's kind of doing something physical, which I really value." Karen's focus on "making people happy" by performing manual tasks implies that software development could not make people equally happy. The services offered in the time bank, then, are subject not just to market negotiations such as Kelly's, but also to the choices of traders who withhold their credentialed skills based on their beliefs about the needs of other time bankers.

Most of the participants who enjoyed the variety of tasks membership allowed them to practice also highlighted physical activity. Others also reflected on offering services other than those for which they earn money. Corie, a full-time lawyer and social worker, said time banking was a reminder of the diversity of her skills. After posting her first offers, she was pleased that the structure of the time bank gave her the opportunity to think of skills in which she has considerable but not professional-level expertise. She explained, "It reminds you about all the areas of your life that you've actually learned things in, like gardening or home repair stuff. Things you never think of as skills because they're not on your résumé." In this way, time banking can expand an individual's sense of personal value beyond the labor he or she is able to offer in the marketplace.

Most of our participants have professional expertise backed by the appropriate credentials. Their upbringings were enriched by cultural capital, which slotted them into certain educational opportunities which, in turn, resulted in their current positions in the labor market. One might assume that this wouldn't matter in the time bank, especially when they are offering nonprofessional services. However, highly credentialed time bankers enjoyed a number of advantages that operated in subtle and extrainstitutional ways. We found that trading is partially segregated by cultural capital, and that there is higher demand for those with formal credentials and more extensive schooling.

Because there is not always robust demand for offers, these advantages translated into more opportunities to trade.

One result was that some high-cultural-capital participants became confident not only that they could offer professionalized services (if they wanted to), but that they could successfully offer services that they didn't go to school for or have much practice at. The trading potential of these members was based on their advertisements. Advertisement, we learned, was the primary medium that allowed members to communicate their legitimacy and credentials. This, we believe, leads to the relative advantage of those high in cultural capital within the time bank.

The Time Trade Circle has explicitly rejected a formal rating system of the type that is now standard on many peer-to-peer sites. In the absence of such a system, members have come up with creative ways to select and exclude potential trading partners. The vetting process our respondents described sometimes advantaged high-cultural-capital time bankers. We found that people looked for key signifiers of professionalism—personal Web sites, good grammar, external references, and even testimonials from other members about the superior service being provided. The administrators of the time bank do not object to members advertising client references on their profiles and encourage people to get in touch before a trade to ask for references or credentials. The people who can best signal their professionalism are those who have had access to professionalized lifestyles. For example, one participant explained that she negatively evaluates offers from "people who, like, didn't have basic grammatical skills," stating that she is "turned . . . off [by] people [who] don't write in complete sentences." She reflected that maybe she was "being a snob," but she believed "you could write [an offer well]" and avoid "a lot of typos or writ[ing] poorly." Our high-cultural-capital members, who have college degrees and work professional jobs (and come from families with the same background), are adept at this type of signaling. So while theoretically $1 = 1$, one high-cultural-capital hour has the potential to be a lot more attractive than one ordinary hour.

We found that the ideological breakdown of equally valued time was expressed in covert ways, such as the valuing of well-advertised, professional, and credentialed services. To the surprise of many of our participants, it was also challenged in more overt ways. In our interviews, about three-quarters of those who had previously made lengthy ideological statements about the power of such an egalitarian system then unwittingly negated those statements by saying that their time was worth more than one hour of someone else's time. Jill caught herself in this contradiction when she explained why she doesn't offer to trade the skills from her day job as a speech therapist: "Actually, no, I'm realizing the reason I don't offer that is because I think it's worth more, that I could get more money. That didn't occur to me." Many professionals who have put years of training and heavy capital investments into their careers felt that they had more to give than what was already offered in the bank. Among all of our interviewees, Jill best situated her understandings of inequality within a structural framework: "I guess I think it would be complicated to figure out how to weight more valued things. I think that would probably result in a lot of, I guess, discord. That lawyer maybe had better opportunities when they were young and a better education or maybe more money so they can be a lawyer. And it's not people's fault if they didn't have those opportunities and now aren't a lawyer."

While almost all of our participants were quick to praise time banking as a way to recognize people who were being undervalued in the market, they couldn't hide their residual belief in market preferences, which operated in taken-for-granted ways when they invalidated members who lacked professional legitimacy and credentials. Most of our participants talked about time banking as a way for unemployed people to feel they have value and something to contribute. However, the ideal of reciprocity did not always work out in practice, as more privileged members sometimes seemed to believe they had more to offer than others. While egalitarian ideology led many to time banking, participants could not always sustain that ideology when they actually got down to the business of trading.

In all cases, we found that the nature of a participant's contribution was structured by his or her relationship to the cash economy. Some members who were tired of outsourcing their lives to professionals had a more flexible rubric for the quality of services they would accept. For nonessential services, especially while learning new skills, peer-to-peer help was sometimes even preferred. However, there were limits on the quality of services time bankers tolerated. For example, the level of risk and variability of quality members were willing to incur depended on whether they had had an experience with unemployment or financial insecurity. Some experimented with time banking when they were wholly or partly without work. During those periods they were able to invest extra time into figuring out the service quality of the time bank alternative to the cash service marketplace, and these respondents now tend to take more risks when they trade. They are willing to expose themselves to the variable quality of some services offered. Rose, with her unsteady income, is willing to try out new, potentially risky dog sitters because of the savings the time bank affords.

On the other hand, interviewees with steady employment and secure finances were less likely to expose themselves to this type of risk. Jill has significant personal savings and was in the process of buying her first home when we met over tea in a local deli. She snapped her cell phone closed, apologized for repeatedly checking for her realtor's messages, and explained, "If it's a more detailed service that could be screwed up, I do feel more of a concern that I don't know if I would be able to fully surrender to that. [If] I knew they were licensed and working as a licensed plumber that would make a difference." Jill contextualized her expectations of professionalism by placing herself within a specific socioeconomic context. During our talk, she admitted that she had never directly experienced unemployment or financial insecurity. She said she would be happy to receive amateur help "learning how to garden," but that she preferred a guarantee of quality to a low price in the case of "electrical work, plumbing work, home repair, car repair."

Although they believed in the principles underlying time banking, the majority of our participants echoed a sentiment similar to Trish's: "If I'm looking for a very professional job, if it's something that I wouldn't ask my friends to do . . . I don't bring it to Time Trade." Others agreed with this line of logic and grouped their time banking hours together with their other volunteer hours. Many members lamented that the TTC lacked a formal review process like many other connected consumption initiatives. A few years ago the TTC leadership circulated a question to the time bank: "Would you approve of a ratings system for TTC trades?" Many of the younger people did want a rating system, while many of the senior members did not. Online reputation metrics are found on many Web sites where quality control is important, and young adults expect that ratings systems will be attached to peer-to-peer sites. Some of our respondents were like the majority of members who turned down the innovation, saying that a ratings system was "untimebanky." They were afraid of the implications if hierarchical valuations were introduced. Karen feared that the spirit of time banking would fall apart if a rating scheme were implemented. She'd had a negative experience with a time bank member who said he could do something that he actually couldn't, but she was gracious in describing this experience and seemed unconcerned that she had spent hours on something that didn't work out. Karen, however, is highly motivated by connection and is one of the participants who views time banking as a volunteer activity. Others weren't so generous in their discussions of failed trades, with one of our participants sounding a bit scarred by a failed and "creepy" massage experience. Thus there is a structural barrier to ensuring service quality within the time bank because there is no formal way to evaluate the services provided within an exchange. This leaves many young time bankers looking for clues written into offers. Though some time bankers are in favor of a formal rating system, the majority in this time bank sides with the ideals the founders of time banking put forth: the fundamental product of a time bank is increased connections, not services exchanged.

Interviewees' high levels of cultural capital influence their views of other time bankers, their own modes of participation, and their ideals about who should be involved in time banking. While these are understandable and sometimes automatic modes of evaluation, class position set limits on the extent to which time banking can break down inequalities. High-cultural-capital time bankers who profess allegiance to building alternative market relations that do not follow the value judgments of the cash market sometimes falter as they work to build new valuation schemes.

Overall, we find that cultural capital is functioning as a limit on the potential trades available in the time bank. Our respondents have particularly high levels of cultural capital and many come from backgrounds of relative privilege. On the one hand, their habitus is a spur to participation in the bank. They value authenticity, localism, environmentalism, holistic wellness, and self-reliance. They reminisce about being able to rely on a place-based local community while keeping a global and class-conscious outlook on life (Carfagna et al., 2014). However, in practice they sometimes prefer the professionalized services they would expect in the market. For example, market-based thinking was taken for granted by most of our participants. At the same time, they believe in time banking, especially as a way for unemployed people to feel valuable in a culture that defines work as a dominant dimension of identity. However, our findings that are most closely linked to disparities in cultural capital challenge the potential of time banking to alter the dependence of identities on market practice and success. Our participants say they believe in this transformative power, but their accounts were sometimes contradictory. While they expected professionalized and credentialed services from others, many did not offer their own professionalized and credentialed services because they believed that their work was worth more than one hour of someone else's time. This is one example of a larger phenomenon we discovered: time banking can actually enhance differences in cultural capital, as participants use it as a low-cost way to learn new skills and gain experiences that are at the cutting-edge of high-status cultural capital markets. In the most pessimistic interpretation, these authenticating practices and projects are themselves important sources of status, and the time bank comes to serve as a means of cultural reproduction.

CONCLUSION: CAN THE TIME BANK
TRANSFORM MARKET RELATIONS?

Capitalism constructs and normalizes unbalanced economic relations in which those with more access to capital most often control the nature of exchanges. The time bankers featured in this chapter often bristle at these distorted power relations. Discontent or sometimes even hostility to market exchanges whose terms and conditions are set by standard practices have led many to connected market alternatives. In this case study, ideological motives drove economically secure and highly educated participants to try time banking. Participants prefer do-it-yourself exchanges to those set by commercial interests. They seek out connection with others through trades and come together to create a web of connections designed to support local people. The equal valuation of time within the bank sets the conditions for some innovative exchanges to occur. Sometimes these informal exchanges lead to participants' altered standards of professionalism and taste. Often time bankers refer nostalgically to a time in America's history when they believe relations of reciprocity between neighbors and kin were the norm. Though the founders of time banking maintain that the 1:1 ratio is common sense, its potential implications for dismantling the benefits of socioeconomic class, institutional credentials, and professional wage are radical. But as with the constant mental work of learning to speak a new language, participants had to remain mindful of the syntax of informal exchange relations. In many cases, they subconsciously reverted to capitalist logic and evaluated potential trades using the metric of market value. However, the institutional conditions set by time banking overcame the naturalized logic of capitalist exchange when participants actively recalled their initial motivations and ultimate goals. Although the transformational potential of time banking was inhibited when participants reverted to internalized habits of capitalist exchange, the presence of innovative exchange logics suggests the emergence of new economic relations in which interpersonal connection is central.

NOTES

1. The sharing economy also goes by the term *collaborative consumption* (Botsman and Rogers 2010), a designation that emphasizes exchanges or collaborations that do not flow through a middleman or business entity such as a hotel, car rental service, or re-sale shop, and focuses on the consumer rather than the producer side of the market.
2. The paperback edition of *Plenitude,* published in 2011, has the title *True Wealth.*
3. Time banking has been able to move beyond a core of true believers into community-based organizations and mainstream social service groups in areas such as ex-offender reentry (National Homecomers Academy), aging in place (Reach CareBank of Vermont), and the integration of recent immigrants (Visiting Nurses Association of New York Community Connections Time Bank) (Collum 2012).
4. These numbers were generated by a LexisNexis media search detailing the annual English-language press coverage on time banking from 1997 to 2012.

REFERENCES

Aldridge, Theresa, Jane Tooke, Roger Lee, Andrew Leyshon, Nigel Thrift, and Colin Williams. 2001. "Recasting Work: The Example of Local Exchange Trading Schemes." *Work, Employment and Society* 15 (3): 565–79.

Bailis, Daniel S., and Judith G. Chipperfield. 2002. "Compensating for Losses in Perceived Personal Control over Health: A Role for Collective Self-Esteem in Health Aging." *Journal of Gerontology* 57B (6): 531–39.

Becker, Gary S. 1978. *The Economic Approach to Human Behavior.* Chicago: University of Chicago Press.

Belk, Russell W. 2010. "Sharing." *Journal of Consumer Research* 36 (5): 715–34.

Botsman, Rachel, and Roo Rogers. 2010. *What's Mine Is Yours: The Rise of Collaborative Consumption.* New York: Harper-Collins.

Bourdieu, Pierre. 1984. *Distinction: A Social Critique of the Judgement of Taste.* Cambridge: Harvard University Press.

Brown, Keith. 2013. *Buying into Fair Trade: Culture, Morality, and Consumption.* New York: New York University Press.

Cahn, Edgar S. 2000. *No More Throw-away People: The Co-production Imperative.* Washington, DC: Essential Books.

Cahn, Edgar S., and Jonathan Rowe. 1996. *Time Dollars: The New Currency That Enables Americans to Turn Their Hidden Resource—Time—into Personal Security and Community Renewal.* Chicago: Family Resource Coalition of America.

Carfagna, L., E. Dubois, C. Fitzmaurice, T. Laidley, M. Ouimette, J. B. Schor, and M. Willis. 2014. "An Emerging Eco-habitus: The Reconfiguration of High Cultural Capital Practices among Ethical Consumers." *Journal of Consumer Culture.* 14(2): 1–2.

Collom, Ed. 2008. "Engagement of the Elderly in Time Banking: The Potential for Social Capital Generation in an Aging Society." *Journal of Aging and Social Policy* 20 (4): 414–36.

———. 2012. "Key Indicators of Time Bank Participation: Using Transaction Data for Evaluation." *International Journal of Community Currency Research* 6: A18–29.

Collom, Ed, J. N. Lasker, and C. Kyriacou. 2012. *Equal Time, Equal Value: Community Currencies and Time Banking in the US*. Burlington, VT: Ashgate.

Fenton, Anny. 2013. "The Other Embeddedness: How Our Economic Activity and Social Relations Are Embedded in Our Relations with the Goods and Services We Exchange." Unpublished paper, Harvard University, Cambridge, MA.

Folbre, Nancy. 1982. "Exploitation Comes Home: A Critique of the Marxian Theory of Family Labour." *Cambridge Journal of Economics* 6 (4): 317–29.

Frank, Thomas. 2000. *One Market under God: Extreme Capitalism, Market Populism, and the End of Economic Democracy*. New York: Anchor.

Geron, Tomio. 2013. Airbnb and the Unstoppable Rise of the Share Economy. *Forbes,* January 23. http://www.forbes.com/sites/tomiogeron/2013/01/23/airbnb-and-the-un stoppable-rise-of-the-share-economy (accessed March 1, 2013).

Hochschild, Arlie Russell. 2003. *The Commercialization of Intimate Life: Notes from Home and Work*. Berkeley: University of California Press.

———. 2012. *The Outsourced Self: Intimate Life in Market Times*. New York: Metropolitan Books.

North, Peter. 2003. "Time Banks—Learning the Lessons from LETS?" *Local Economy* 18 (3): 267–70.

Schor, Juliet B. 2010. *Plenitude: The New Economics of True Wealth*. New York: Penguin.

Seyfang, Gill. 2003. "With a Little Help from My Friends: Evaluating Time Banks as a Tool for Community Self-Help." *Local Economy* 18 (3): 257–64.

———. 2006. "Harnessing the Potential of the Social Economy? Time Banks and UK Public Policy." *International Journal of Sociology and Social Policy* 26 (9) 430–43.

Seyfang, Gill, and K. Smith. 2002. *The Time of Our Lives: Using Time Banking for Neighbourhood Renewal and Community Capacity Building*. London: New Economics Foundation.

Stack, Carol. 1974. *All Our Kin: Strategies for Survival in a Black Community*. New York: Harper Paperback.

Thompson, Craig J., and G. Coskuner-Balli. 2007. "Enchanting Ethical Consumerism: The Case of Community Supported Agriculture." *Journal of Consumer Culture* 7 (3): 275–303.

Willis, Margaret, and Juliet B. Schor. 2012. "Does Changing a Light Bulb Lead to Changing the World? Civic Engagement and the Ecologically Conscious Consumer." *Annals of the American Academy of Political and Social Science* 644 (1): 160–90.

Zelizer, Viviana. 2005. *The Purchase of Intimacy*. Princeton, NJ: Princeton University Press.

———. 2010. *Economic Lives: How Culture Shapes the Economy*. Princeton, NJ: Princeton University Press.

Chapter 4 How Community-Supported Agriculture Facilitates Reembedding and Reterritorializing Practices of Sustainable Consumption

Craig J. Thompson and Melea Press

Juliet Schor's *Plenitude* (2010) advances an alternative to a long-standing nexus of institutionalized economic policies that aim to increase levels of material prosperity through the resource-intensive engine of incessant economic growth. Schor identifies two critical macro-level constraints that are making the "business-as-usual" (BAU) economy increasingly untenable. BAU is socioeconomically unsustainable because wages are stagnating for most workers, who have been largely unable to benefit from the significant productivity gains of recent years, and because their number of working hours is rising. The combination of productivity gains for corporations and longer hours for employees has reduced the number of workers needed to attain a given level of economic production—a labor market disparity that had been temporarily assuaged through credit, debt, and the ill-fated housing bubble (Stiglitz 2010). As a consequence, the BAU paradigm cannot provide enough well-paying jobs to support the acquisitively oriented middle-class lifestyle that has become the hallmark of the world's developed modern economies. The fossil fuel–driven BAU paradigm is also ecologically unsustainable owing to anthropogenic climate change, the economic complexities of peak oil, water shortages, and ecosystem degradation. Though not due to the contradictions originally anticipated, Marx's famed dictum that industrial capitalism would implode under the weight of its own wealth-producing achievements seems increasingly prophetic (see Roubini 2011).

Schor's *Plenitude* has garnered considerable attention because it directly challenges the conventional cultural view of sustainable lifestyles as impositions of joyless austerity, personal sacrifice, and hardship. Instead, Schor reframes sustainable lifestyles as means to attain an abundance of rewards, including greater economic autonomy, stronger family and communal ties, and more time to invest in gratifying avocational interests. Unlike the BAU economy, the "goods" garnered through *Plenitude*'s four guiding principles also help to lay the foundation for a robust, decentralized, politically empowering, and sustainable economic system of production; it is Mandeville's (1723) *Fable of the Bees* reconstructed as a situation in which private virtues (coupled with requisite degrees of technical know-how and communal solidarity) can provide public benefits.

In this chapter, we wish to address another consequential but less widely recognized aspect of *Plenitude*'s lifestyle prescriptions. We propose that the plenitude paradigm provides a practical means for consumer-citizens to comprehend (and experience) efficacious connections between their localized actions and broader societal problems that are distributed across globally interlinked ecological systems, transnational political and economic organizations, and technological infrastructures (see Heinberg 2011; McKibben 2010). The cultural and practical logic manifest in *Plenitude*'s principles, however, enables these abstract, systemic conditions to be meaningfully understood (and acted upon) in the context of one's immediate social networks and local community: processes we refer to as the social reembedding and reterritorializing of the globally scaled problems emanating from the BAU economy.

In the so-called era of the world risk society (Beck 1999), consumers are reflexively aware that their lives are affected by interconnected ecological and technological systems that transcend national boundaries. In addition, these systems have global reverberations that easily dwarf the scope of individual action, as is shown by the increasingly volatile weather patterns and superstorms generated by anthropogenic climate change (Randall et al. 2007), the BP Gulf Oil disaster, and the tsunami-precipitated nuclear-reactor crisis in Fukushima. As discussed by Giddens (1991) and Beck (1999), such globally diffused problems raise reflexive awareness that omnipresent social-political-technological-cultural systems have effects that are uncontrollable and un-predictable. The flip side of this risk society awareness is that the global scale of the problems can lead to feelings of hopelessness, disempowerment, and futility in trying to combat these issues through personal lifestyle changes (Bauman 2007): why worry about the incremental contribution to climate change made by my daily commute to work when industrializing nations are ramping up their consumption of fossil fuels on a massive scale?

A related, though more subtle problem, is that policy experts often appeal to consumers through discourses that are pitched at a level of abstraction commensurate with the global scale of the problems being cited, as exemplified by the Sierra Club's climate recovery project goals: "For more than a century, we have depended on fossil fuels to run our factories, power our cars and trucks, and heat and cool our homes. Now we are facing the consequences. Six of the last eight years were the hottest on record. Polar ice and glaciers are disappearing, sea levels are rising, coral reefs are suffering, plant and animal species are disappearing. And the wilderness areas and wildlife that the Sierra Club has worked so effectively to protect for more than a century are being threatened and lost" (quoted by Kurt Hochenauer 2012).

At face value, such a narrative may seem like a motivating and compelling statement of the pressing climate change crisis that confronts humanity. However, this moralistic framing—"we" have sinned, biblical disasters are upon us, and now we must all repent—is strangely depersonalizing. The generic "we" refers to no one in particular and does not imply any direct personal accountability. As the old adage goes, when everyone is responsible, no one is responsible. Furthermore, such sweeping entreaties readily lend themselves to a resigned hopelessness (what can I do in the face of all that?) or simple denial. A 2010 survey conducted by the Pew Center found a significant decline in the percentage of Americans who believe there is solid evidence of global warming (Kohut et al. 2010). The survey found an even steeper decline in the percentage of Americans who believe that climate change, if occurring, is related to human activity, and a still steeper decline in those who regard climate change as a serious problem. The survey's bottom-line finding is that in 2010 a slight majority of Americans did *not* believe that climate change has an anthropogenic cause.

Tracking studies of Americans' outlooks on climate change exhibit a noteworthy degree of volatility. A more recent survey of 1,061 voting-age Americans conducted by the Yale Project on Climate Change Communication (Leiserowitz et al. 2012) reports an increase in the percentage of Americans who believe that climate change is both happening and is caused primarily by human activity (54 percent versus 47 percent) and a decline in the percentage of Americans who believe that there is a significant disagreement among scientists regarding the causes of climate change (36 percent versus 44 percent in 2010). While these latest public opinion trends can be seen as encouraging signs for mobilizing public support for carbon-reduction initiatives, they reveal a significant degree of entrenched cultural resistance and/or skepticism toward the preponderance of scientific evidence that anthropogenic climate change is occurring. (Imagine a study reporting as a sign of social progress that only 47 percent of Americans now believe the Earth is flat.) This variability also suggests that many Americans view climate change as an acute concern that is triggered by current-event salience—such as Superstorm Sandy or the wildfires and droughts that plagued the western United States in the summer of 2012—rather than a chronic problem that requires continual attention and effort, whether in the form of lifestyle changes, consumer activism, or political motivation.

Here we note a study by Smith and Leiserowitz (2012) indicating that Americans' views of climate change are highly susceptible to media imagery. From this standpoint, the increased number of Americans who express belief in climate change may reflect news media coverage of the extreme weather events of 2012. Conversely, Smith and Leiserowitz also find that the propagation of "naysayer imagery," such as the conspiracy images invoked by the so-called climategate affair (Inhofe 2012; Pearce 2010), can also generate equally significant increases in self-reports of climate change skepticism and denial. In sum, Americans' views of anthropogenically induced climate change remain far more malleable, volatile, and skeptical than warranted by the available scientific evidence. This volatility can also translate into an attenuated civic and political will to make the necessary transformations in the BAU economy.

This situation seems particularly puzzling given that American consumers have, over the last fifteen years, been inundated with graphic illustrations of climate change's deleterious effects as well as impassioned messages about the absolute necessity of lowering the carbon footprints of their everyday lives. (Al Gore's documentary *An Inconvenient Truth* was a widely viewed example.) However, this circumstance becomes more comprehensible once we take into account that these warnings depict a problem of such global scale and complexity that consumers can easily feel exasperated, overwhelmed, and fundamentally unsure about whether their actions are making a positive change or if they might somehow inadvertently be contributing to another systemic problem or—perhaps more disconcertingly still—be making no substantive difference at all (see Connolly and Prothero 2008). Under such conditions, consumers have psychosocial incentives to find existential solace in scientifically dubious counterexplanations (for example, sunspots are the source of global warming) or an array of conspiratorial tales that link climate change warnings and carbon-reduction initiatives to tyrannical political agendas (for example, Inhofe 2012).

Furthermore, the prevailing discourses of climate change enjoin sovereign consumers to combat these deterritorialized problems by making more socially responsible consumer choices. This individuating ideological frame divorces consumer actions from direct interpersonal ties and communal relationships and subtly reduces collective responsibilities to protect and preserve the commons to the vagaries of personal choice, lifestyle preferences and, somewhat paradoxically, the status value that can be garnered through the conspicuous consumption of green products. In this sense, the commonplace appeal for consumers to make socially responsible choices and to lead sustainable (consumerist) lifestyles has rhetorically reproduced the social disembedding and deterritorializing processes that have led to social fragmentation and retreats from civic life into privatized spheres of consumption (where individuals can at least experience some semblance of personal control) (Bauman 2007; Giddens 1991).

In regard to this latter point, our analysis takes an important cue from Michael Schudson's (1999) historically based argument that early twentieth-century reforms in voting practices and the corresponding rationalization (and privatization) of citizenship also significantly undermined the political sphere's value as a source of social connection and community engagement. According to Schudson, American citizenship in the nineteenth century was a quite different affair from the image of the rational and highly deliberative citizen that became a cultural ideal in the twentieth century. Voting was not a matter of calculated assent expressed by an autonomous citizen; rather, it was a statement of affiliation. As Schudson (2003, 52) aptly describes it, "Drink, dollars, and drama brought people to the polls" and, most important, feelings of social connection were imperative to civic participation. The Progressive reformers of the early twentieth century regarded these Bacchanalian elements as corrupting influences that needed to be excised from the American body politic. While transforming citizenship into a practice of detached information acquisition (which placed a premium on literacy) and the rational evaluation of policy pros and cons, these Progressive reforms also served to distance political discourse from voters' social worlds and their practices of everyday life.

In parallel fashion, much of the discourse on climate change and sustainability encourages consumers to think about these global problems from a detached, rationalizing view-from-above in which they survey a spectrum of systemic complexities and trade-offs. Such a perspective also harbors another reflexive obstacle to practical action: consumers are encouraged to make sustainable choices from a menu of options whose actual effects are invariably clouded in a litany of ambiguous cost-benefit assessments and unintended consequences. Even the environmental consequences of seemingly simple choices—such as the conventional "paper or plastic?" decision at the checkout counter—present an endless array of contingent outcomes. Under these global risk society conditions (Beck 1999), individuals can easily feel disempowered (and perhaps even uninterested) because the effects of their consumer actions on these complex interlinked systems are both hard to gauge (the drop-in-a-bucket dilemma) and prone to reflexive doubt (for example, am I simply trading one bad action for another, or perhaps inadvertently making matters worse?).

Rather than importuning individuated consumers to confront systemic, global problems, Schor's *Plenitude* provides a more practical and human-scaled approach to creating a sustainable new economy from the ground up in a manner that resembles the decentralized yet loosely coordinated approach to collective problem solving and so-called crowd-sourced innovations (Howe 2008; Surowiecki 2004). To fully engage in this mode of praxis, however, consumer-citizens must first reallocate and generally reduce their time investments in the BAU economy. They break from the work-spend cycle of conventional paid employment and mass consumerism and devote their resulting free time to household- and community-based practices of high-productivity self-provision. Such undertakings also require that consumer-citizens cultivate, share, and/or barter for the requisite technical knowledge and skills. As a consequence of these activities, community ties should be strengthened because consumer-citizens are now reliant upon each other for provisioning and economic capital rather than on the market-based BAU economy.

Yet, consumer-citizens can also face significant barriers to reducing their economic reliance on the BAU economy, ranging from needs for employment-based insurance coverage, persistent debt obligations (which are often tied to the costs of treating chronic illnesses), or even the reluctance of other family members to abandon familiar and comfortable lifestyle patterns. A profound sociocultural chasm separates the quintessential practitioners of plenitude— who are growing their own food, building their own homes using low-cost, low-impact natural materials or creating barter-based economies in a self-sufficient eco-community—and members of the proverbial social mainstream, who remain immersed in the BAU economy. Stated conversely, the BAU economy produces not just "goods" and not just the "externalities" of climate change, but also a population of deskilled consumers who are also econom-ically insecure workers: a twin condition that paradoxically fosters structural dependencies on the BAU economy.

The path out of the BAU economy may not directly follow from a paradigm-shifting epiphany and radical lifestyle change. Consumer-citizens may instead pursue principles of plenitude in a more piecemeal, circuitous, and even seren-dipitous manner. In the following analysis, we show how this transformational process is mediated by an alternative market form—community-supported agriculture. For the consumer-citizens in our sample, CSA functions as a tran-sitional institution. Through their participation and social interactions in the CSA market system, they gradually acquire new skills, ideological outlooks, and social relations that, in turn, alter their former status quo outlooks toward the BAU marketplace for groceries, fast food, and processed-foods options. In the course of deploying these new cultural capacities and ideological reference points, these consumer-citizens also begin to incorporate plenitude principles of communal sharing and collaboration into their daily lives, becoming more productive, skilled, and self-providing consumers and investing more time and other personal resources in productive activities that lie outside the prov-inces of the BAU economy.

COMMUNITY-SUPPORTED AGRICULTURE
AS AN ENTRÉE TO PLENITUDE

Community-supported agriculture is one of the more well-established mar-ketplace expressions of the local-food movement, which is generally orga-nized around ideals of enhancing biodiversity, revitalizing local economies and the economic viability of small farms, reclaiming food production from corporate-dominated agribusiness interests, and rekindling communal con-nections that have been weakened by forces of suburbanization, increased geographic mobility, and the privatizing influences of consumer culture (Co-hen, Comrov, and Hoffner 2005; Halweil 2002). CSA farms strive to enact these ideals through their practices of production, distribution, marketing, and the social networks that they foster among consumers and between consumers and farmers. The CSA model has been gaining steady momentum in the consumer marketplace (Press and Arnould 2011b). In 1999, approximately 1,000 farms were operating on the CSA model in the United States (Lass et al. 2003). According to the most recent USDA census of agriculture, in 2007, this number had skyrocketed to 12,540 (http://www.agcensus.usda.gov /Publications/2007/Full_Report/CenV1US1.txt). Notably, CSA did not even appear as a distinct category of farm operation in the preceding 2002 USDA agricultural census.

In a commercial marketplace that venerates consumer choice, breadth of selection, convenience and, above all else, the calculability of what one pays for goods, CSA diverges from models of economic exchange in just about every way imaginable. To participate in a CSA program, a consumer buys a share in a specific farm, with the share price typically ranging from $300 to $800, or becomes a worker member, where labor is substituted for some portion of the share cost. In return for these investments, a CSA member receives a weekly box of organically grown produce for five to seven months (depending on the region) that is delivered to a centralized pickup point. CSA farmers typically invite their members to visit the farm and they host periodic gatherings— potlucks, watermelon-tasting events, farm tours—that are designed to foster a sense of community among members and help them develop a personal relationship with "their" farm. These market-mediated communal connections are also premised on a model of shared risks and rewards in which consumers gain benefits when crops are bountiful and collectively absorb losses when crops are less successful or even fail (Thompson and Coskuner-Balli 2007).

Unlike consumers who support local agriculture through purchases made at farmers' markets, local food co-ops, and now even major chains such as Whole Foods Market—which are seeking to catch the local-food wave in their branding strategies (Warner 2011)—CSA consumers forgo a considerable degree of choice and control over the mix of goods that go into their baskets. This mix is largely determined by farmers' planting decisions and, of course, the climatic factors that affect crop quality and even availability. Furthermore, the CSA model does not allow consumers to easily calculate just what they are paying for any given good in their weekly (or biweekly) basket, nor is it conducive to farm-by-farm price comparisons due to the unspecified and generally unpredictable variations in the volume and type of goods that go into a respective basket.

The CSA movement often claims the ideological mantle of being a much-needed alternative to the "organic-industrial complex" (Pollan 2001) that has adapted, and many argue distorted, the original ideals and practices of organic agriculture to serve the scale and efficiency needs of mass-acreage, monocrop corporate farming (Pollan 2006b; Guthman 2004; Sharp, Imerman, and Peters 2002). Often forgoing the corporate-co-opted term *organic* altogether, CSA farmers and proponents proclaim themselves to be "authentic" growers (Coleman 2002) who are leading sustainable food production into the "postorganic" age. This authenticating claim serves both political and promotional goals by suggesting that CSA is rekindling the original spirit of the organic food movement by enacting small-is-beautiful values in its scale of operation, by tailoring farming practices and planting decisions to local climate and soil conditions and, last but not least, by emphasizing bonds of trust anchored in face-to-face relationships and community connections rather than conformity to abstract regulatory codes and certification standards.

CSA is, therefore, an alternative system of distribution and economic exchange that echoes the core principles of plenitude. Indeed, many of the CSA farmers we interviewed can rightly be considered fully committed practitioners of plenitude. CSA farmers seek to minimize their consumption expenditures by using the barter economy (trading surpluses and skills) to meet household needs; they invest their time and skills in providing sustainably grown food through small-scale, high-productivity, biodynamic farming techniques; and they work to use their farms as a resource for building community connections.

The reflections of our CSA farmers also reveal the importance they attach to the processes we have described as the social reembedding and reterritorialization of globally scaled problems. This ethos is nicely expressed in the following quote from Caitlin, a successful CSA farmer (whose personal history with CSA evolved from member to worker member to apprentice to finally running her own farm):

> Maybe that's a personal thing, maybe that's what it's about. These things that I'm saying feel really small. I don't have this grand idea about the thing as a whole. I try to eat locally, I try to be really conscious about what I eat; it's very personal for me. I just read three articles in the *New Yorker* about global warming and that makes me really worry. But I have a hard time holding those issues present in my daily life. The way I hold them present is by making decisions about how I'm going to live my life and being consistent and thorough with those. What can I do— this is so tired but I'm going to say it—what can I do about Monsanto or Dole? I can choose not to buy food from them, got it, but I'm not in a position where I

can have an effect on that big organization. For me it comes back to weeding the carrots in a timely fashion, that's what I can do about it.

Rather than feeling overwhelmed or disempowered by the enormity of globally dispersed problems, Caitlin invests in her CSA farm (and her share-owners), and this enables her to feel that she can make a tangible difference in the face of a seemingly indeterminate system of global interlinkages and the economic and political power wielded by transnational corporations that are vested in the BAU economy. As the consumer-citizens in our study become more immersed and vested in their respective CSAs, they similarly resonate with this cultural construction of CSA as a means to meaningfully redress globally scaled problems through local actions and to reduce their overall reliance on the BAU economy.

In the following section, we illustrate this transformative process through a set of vignettes drawn from longitudinal interviews with four first-year CSA members. These interviews document each CSA member's experiences and orientations toward the BAU economy (focusing mainly on the food sector) at the beginning, middle, and end of one CSA growing season (see Press and Arnould 2011a for a more complete description of the research methodology). Over the course of their CSA involvement, these consumer-citizens become increasingly sensitized to the personal, communal, and broader social benefits that can accrue from reducing reliance on the BAU economy while also reorienting their food provisioning and cooking practices in ways that directly incorporate plenitude principles into their everyday lives.

HOW CSA FACILITATES
PRACTICES OF PLENITUDE

Tony is a forty-year-old single male with a bachelor's degree in engineering. He works as an engineer in a dark office, smokes, lives alone, and earns about $60,000 per year. Tony's primary reasons for joining a CSA were grounded in largely instrumental and risk-averse concerns over the inflationary effects that petroleum shortages could have on food prices:

You know, it just seems obvious that transportation costs are a big part of food costs, and you know, for the longest time I figured, so what? You know, oil's cheap. But it's not really. I think you know that the rising gas prices last year sort of pointed that out, and if you go into the supermarket it's readily apparent to me that everything is more expensive than it was just a year ago. And so I think reducing the amount of miles your food travels before it gets to you is a great way to reduce the cost of your food. . . . I'd actually talked with people about it beforehand. And my mom said, "Oh, you should join [CSA name]." She looked at it [from] the food will be cheaper and better kind of perspective, but honestly, I looked at it as future-proofing myself. You know, like let's say the price of gas goes through the roof and the price of food goes through the roof—what are you gonna do? And I wanted to know what grew locally, what's available locally. . . . I mean, it's gotten to the point where I've actually entertained the notion of actually trying to learn how to grow food, because that seems like a pretty valuable skill to have now, but you know, I'm not really sure how good at it I would be . . . so I decided to see what was available locally.

Tony expresses a risk society perspective in viewing the production, distribution, and pricing of food as a petroleum-driven system that is not very adaptable to the demanding economic conditions that are emerging in this era of peak oil. While intrigued by the idea of growing his own food, his lack of skills (and confidence) poses a barrier to his enacting plenitude's principle of self-provisioning. By joining a CSA, however, Tony is able to find a practical means to hedge against these peak oil risks and shift his food-provisioning practices away from the BAU economy.

As the CSA season unfolded, Tony's viewpoint broadened from his initial concerns about peak oil and escalating food prices. He became more captivated by the CSA ideas of knowing where his food came from and supporting small-scale local production rather than mass-scale factory farms. Last but not least, his original goal of reducing his expenditures on food was displaced by one of supporting small-scale local production and local farms, even when this disengagement from the BAU system of corporate-controlled agriculture meant paying higher prices: "There is another farmer that comes by the [farm] and she sells prearranged products, you know, beef and pork, and I like buying stuff from her. I don't mind paying a little more for her stuff because it's not factory farmed. It's not coming from Texas or Colorado. . . . I think, like a lot of Americans, if you ask a lot of people, 'Where does your food come from?' they would say a supermarket. They are not growing food in the supermarket, it is coming from somewhere. [The CSA] kind of made me realize the chain involved. I think I'm a lot closer to my food when I buy it from the CSA than buying from the supermarket."

Mary is a married forty-two-year-old mother of two children. She holds multiple advanced degrees, including a PhD, and enjoys a well-paying career as a medical administrator. Her yearly household income is over $200,000. She lives in a new housing development that was built on farmland. She has a gourmet kitchen and takes pride in her knowledge of food, nutrition, and cooking. In keeping with her high level of cultural capital (Bourdieu 1986), Mary is a discriminating food consumer who avidly reads labels, compares prices, and proudly stakes a claim to teaching her children good food values. At the time of our first interview, Mary was also a conflicted consumer who struggled to reconcile her desires to consume in a more sustainable way with lifestyle practices that often stood at odds with this goal. For example, Mary expresses her extreme ambivalence over regularly buying her groceries from those paragons of the BAU economy—Walmart and its subsidiary Sam's Club:

> I think Sam's Club [*laughs*] has a lot of very good produce, although I don't always associate it with the healthiest food practices. I don't know why that is, I think it's just Walmart, my basic mistrust for Walmart, but I think that it tastes pretty good, so I do a considerable amount of my shopping at Walmart or Sam's Club. . . . I have no data to support this, um, feeling, and obviously it's not something that's inhibiting me, or prohibiting me from shopping there, but you know, I do have kind of a, um, a feeling of the fact that these, that Walmart is a big corporate entity that is very much interested in making money, and I certainly don't feel that their labor practices in our country are the best, and for that reason I have an uneasy feeling about, you know, I just don't know what their practices and growing food and meats are like. I never feel *good* about buying my meat at Walmart.

Later in the CSA season, Mary begins to alter her resigned view that there is an inherent trade-off between the convenience and low prices offered by Walmart and shopping in a socially responsible way that she can feel good about. Instead, she gravitates toward the idea that her participation in a CSA offers a practical means to redress larger-scale social and environmental problems while gaining an enhanced (and guilt-assuaging) sense of autonomy from the BAU economy:

> I think CSA to me represents a better way of doing things. I have very little control over better ways of doing a lot of things in the world. I have no control about the fact that my neighbors are going out and buying Hummers and Escalades. I have no control over the fact that 50 percent of my neighborhood doesn't recycle that much. I have no control over people using disposable diapers and they are using landfill space like there is no tomorrow. But this is something like I felt was environmentally sound that allowed me to participate in a sense of community, not like a nonprofit, but participate in a network that was beneficial to the community and allowed me to get something out of it. So I felt that I was participat-

ing in kind of a win-win situation . . . when I joined [the CSA] I joined to be doing something that I considered to be for the community and everything else. And, by the way, I happen to get all of these wonderful vegetables on top of it. That's the way I look at it. . . . I really respect people who farm around here. It makes me feel very good to support these people who I think are so important.

Sarah is a forty-two-year-old single mother of two young children. She has a bachelor's degree and currently works in the human services field. She is very concerned about peak oil and also an ardent believer in seed saving. She grows heirloom tomatoes and takes great personal inspiration from her friends who grow and forage for their own food. On her modest income of $25,000, Sarah struggles to make ends meet for basic needs like housing, food, and medicine, and receives state-sponsored WIC support that provides her with vouchers that can be exchanged for vegetables at the local farmers' market. Sarah is a type II diabetic who now places considerable emphasis on having a healthy diet that includes generous amounts of fresh vegetables.

Sarah joined a CSA in anticipation of no longer qualifying for the WIC program. Looking to stretch her food dollars, Sarah believed that CSA might provide a cost-effective way to maintain her family's supply of fresh vegetables:

> I'm under budget constraints, so, well, I get WIC up until—well, this is my last summer and they give some farmers' vouchers, which is really neat, from the state. So it's not a lot but I've always had those; I've had two kids under five. So I used to get $40 worth of vouchers and I was able to buy things at the farmer markets. But I'm losing that because the kids are gonna be over five [years old]. So that was a consideration too—I thought, jeesh, no more vouchers, and I weighed the costs and how much vegetables we would eat, and it seemed more cost effective. . . . I almost always have vegetables on hand now, which sometimes, you know, if grocery money was low that week, I might not pick up much of a variety. So yeah . . . plus I have type II diabetes so what I really need to be eating is vegetables—you know, it's one of the few things that doesn't take my blood sugar [high]. So that's been great. And right now [because of the CSA], I'm eating half a pound of vegetables a day.

CSA members commonly report that they begin investing more time in meal preparation and developing their culinary skills in response to the wide array of vegetables, often unfamiliar ones, that appear in their weekly boxes: a consequence that also runs counter to the processes of consumer de-skilling that are fostered by the convenience-oriented food culture (see Thompson and Coskuner-Balli 2007). Sarah reports a similar shift in her consumption patterns, with the additional benefit of integrating her children into her family's food-provisioning and food-preparation activities. These changes are also highly consistent with the plenitude principle of using consumption to enliven and strengthen familial and communal ties: "Yeah, the kids have gone with me every time I've gone out [to the farm]. . . . It's neat, they help me weigh everything and pick things out and we learn a lot about new vegetables. Like we never had bok choi before and, um, so I got on the Internet and looked up some recipes and stir-fried it with some other vegetables and chicken. . . . I've had several things that I hadn't had before—Swiss chard, rutabaga—so that's pretty neat. It's forced me to look up new recipes. . . . My son said to me recently—he was eating an apple we got at the grocery store—and he said, 'I like those apples from the farm a lot better.' He was saying he couldn't wait until we got apples again from the farm. That was neat."

As the season progressed, Sarah began to think about local to global connections related to problems posed by the BAU paradigm of corporate farming and extensive supply chains: "So there's not a lot of genetic difference. Like, I read somewhere that the corn crop, like, if some of these major crops that are grown all over the country were affected by some disease of fungus that the entire, you know, it could all be wiped out because they're genetically the same seed . . . so that's interesting to me too, like, I think there should be a wider variety of things that are grown. . . . It's scary. . . . I don't like to lose diversity. Most food is trucked hundreds of miles, so I wanted to prevent that. I wanted things that were fresh. The organic part wasn't so important but that's part of it too. And I thought it was neat that the money goes to the farmer, there's not so many intermediate steps."

As with CSA member Tony, Sarah's participation in CSA has also prompted a shift in her understanding of value. Initially, Sarah regarded CSA as a more affordable way to acquire nutritious vegetables. By the end of the season, she placed more importance on the broader societal value that derives from supporting this alternative to the BAU economy: "Just knowing that the farmer is getting a living wage. I mean, with produce grown in Mexico or whatever, which some stuff sold here is, you don't know. Yes, . . . [being a CSA member] is something you can be proud of, so the feeling you're doing something good for the environment and for your local community and your health. Those are all positive things."

Emily is a recently married twenty-nine-year-old with no children. She holds a master's degree, currently works as a librarian, and is passionate about comic books. Her annual household income is $64,000. Prior to joining a CSA, Emily and her husband's food-provisioning and cooking practices were highly segregated. This culinary division started when Emily's husband went on a strict low-carbohydrate, nonfat diet to lose weight, and Emily was not interested in learning how to prepare such meals, much less eat them. They purchased their food separately; each had designated spaces in the refrigerator; and they prepared and ate their meals separately.

Emily joined her CSA as a means to act upon her budding interest in the local-food movement. Early on, Emily's CSA membership led her to align her cooking practices with plenitude principles. Faced with a weekly abundance of perishable, fresh produce, Emily began to experiment with a variety of new dishes (and build her cooking skills in the process), and she began to take pleasure in cooking at home rather than eating out:

> So it's always in the back of my mind, "Well, I'm not going to go out to eat because I know that I have a pound of Swiss chard sitting in my refrigerator and it will go bad if I don't eat it." I'm eating more vegetables and I think I'm eating out less because I have more things to look forward to at home. I've always been pretty adventurous with food, but I think I've gotten even more so. I've just noticed from the kinds of things I'm cooking that I'm branching out a lot more and changing recipes. I look at the recipe and say, "Well, this is an ingredient I can substitute for this." Then I realize I've made a completely different thing. So I think I've gotten a little more comfortable doing that. . . . I am cooking more. Just going to the farm and seeing what looks good and what they have a lot of. . . . The ingredients are more of a surprise than I'm used to. I think I didn't do that as much when I was just going to the grocery store. I would look at the flyer and see what's on sale and plan what I was going to get. It's a little more fun to just say, "Okay, here's some Swiss chard. I don't know what to do with that, but I'm going to get a ton of it." . . . It's a little more time consuming, but it's a lot more fun too. I've definitely learned a lot. I've tried a lot of things that I've either never heard of before, like celery root, or things that I've heard of but never knew what to do with, like turnips. I didn't even know what a rutabaga was. Now we're having one like every week.

In *Plenitude*, Schor (2010) suggests that consumer-citizens will be able to enrich their familial and communal relationships by engaging in lifestyle practices that diverge from the standard practices of the BAU economy. In Emily's case, this benefit is quite evident. One of the major changes Emily reported over the course of the CSA season was that she and her husband started to share home-prepared meals together on a more routine basis: "I think my favorite thing is my husband and I have actually been eating together more because he's gotten into wanting to try some of the things I'm bringing home. . . . Now that I'm bringing stuff home, we're looking up recipes together and he wants to try more. So I think we're eating more together even if we're not both home to eat at the same time. We're eating [more vegetables] and doing more cooking too. . . . Now he's actually doing more shopping with me. I'll go once at the beginning of the week and then he'll make a trip in the middle of the week for whatever else we need or whatever he wants. Now we're sharing food more than we were . . . he's actually starting to cook some of the stuff that I cook."

By the season's end, Emily became acutely aware of the deleterious effects the BAU food system has on the environment, personal health, and local farm economies, and she now sees local farms as critically important alternatives to support and maintain. Most significant, Emily reports feeling empowered in the face of these daunting systemic problems by the knowledge and experiences she has acquired through her CSA participation. As with our other interviewees, Emily has been fundamentally sensitized to the hidden costs inherent to the low price, chemical-laden foods produced by the BAU economy:

> And it's made me think differently when I go to the supermarket. If they have something that's local I will definitely buy that before I buy something that's from California or Florida, especially with lettuce, which they haven't had lettuce lately. It's not in season anymore. When I get a head of lettuce at the supermarket I almost stop buying it because when I would get it home it would go bad like the next day. It would be all slimy and disgusting. Then when I get the lettuce at [the CSA] it would last like a week in my refrigerator even if I don't touch it. . . . Before I would be like, these are cucumbers and these are cucumbers, so I'm going to buy the ones that are cheaper. Whereas now if they are local [I think] they will probably taste better and they will probably last longer. It's really something that I believe in and it's not using a big truck to get it here. . . . I'm actually spending more money because I'm more interested in food and cooking and I read the labels a lot more closely. You know, the weird things I can't pronounce I find myself, "Well, that's not good to buy." Where before I was, "Chemicals, whatever."

CONCLUSION

Our analysis has highlighted some of the more prominent ways that consumer-citizens can use CSA to reskill their consumption practices, enrich their personal and social lives, and gain a heightened sense of personal efficacy in the face of daunting globally scaled problems. CSA participation can also free consumer-citizens from the paralyzing pangs of reflexive doubt by allowing them to directly experience the farm, form trusting relationships with farmers, and enact plenitude principles of sustainable consumption through the new lifestyle patterns that are implemented and strengthened with every weekly delivery of CSA produce.

CSA farms constitute a decentralized network of localized small-scale operations that encourage consumers to build new capabilities, rethink the exchange logic and environmental consequences of conventional commercial exchanges, and forge new material (and moral) relationships to local farms, farmers, and food. Through their participation in CSA, consumers gain a reflexive awareness of the taken-for-granted preferences and orientations that have perpetuated their dependence on corporate-controlled distribution chains and their alienation from food production, not only on the farm but in their own homes. As CSA consumers begin to alter their food-provisioning and meal preparation practices in ways that are more consistent with the ideals, values, and goals that shape CSA's alternative market system (see Thompson and Coskuner-Balli 2007), they also take consequential first steps down a path that leads away from the BAU economy, with its many hidden externalities. They are not only constructing more skilled consumer identities—thereby countermanding the broader trend toward consumer deskilling that has accompanied the dominance of fast food and convenience food (Jaffe and Gertler 2006)—but also exhibiting greater willingness to make investments of time, effort, and indeed money to support more sustainable marketplace alternatives.

These diachronic transformations are summarized in table 4.1 on the following page. In the initial stages of consumers' participation in CSA, they expressed conventional price-quantity type assessments about whether CSA was good value for the money. Over time, however, members began to adopt another exchange logic that defined value in ways that emphasized environmental sustainability (for example, how food was grown, biodiversity, trustworthiness of organic claims, shipping distances); the moral economy of CSA (fair prices to farmers and fair wages to workers, nontoxic working conditions); the social benefits of CSA (such as sharing excess food with neighbors, cooking and eating meals with family members); and finally, the health benefits that accrued from the changes in their diets and everyday eating habits that their CSA membership precipitated. Plenitude principles are highlighted in CSA exchange logic as shared work, shared risk, and shared reward, anchoring the CSA in community- and human-scale collaborative operations.

In contrast, the BAU economy is singularly predisposed to create tragedies of the commons (Hardin 1968) in which incentives for private profit lead to

Table 4.1. Consumer changes fostered by CSA participation

Consumers' business-as-usual food practices before participating in CSA	Consumers' (plenitude-oriented) food practices after participating in CSA
Taken-for-granted preferences for lowest-cost options and reducing expenditures on food	Viewing food expenditures as investments in local community and the value of supporting sustainable modes of food production
Taken-for-granted priority given to speed and convenience of meal preparation	Taking pleasure in cultivating new culinary skills and the sensory qualities of fresh produce
Experiencing mealtime as a chore and an activity to be fit into the schedule	Having skills, resources, and commitment to treat cooking and mealtime as enriching and rewarding social activities
Feeling that they lacked the skills, knowledge, and resources to create healthful meals	Feeling that they had gained the skills, knowledge, and resources to create healthful (and enjoyable) meals
Feeling alienated from deterritorialized, corporate-controlled distribution channels for food provisioning	Gaining a sense of autonomy and empowerment from direct connections to local farms
Low awareness and/or interest in the social and ecological consequences of the BAU system of food production and distribution	Heightened awareness and interest in the social and ecological consequences of the BAU system of food production and distribution
Feeling overwhelmed and disempowered by the scale of systemic ecological problems	Discovering ways in which personal and collective actions can make tangible differences at the local level

the exploitation and despoiling of shared resources such as wilderness areas, community green spaces, clean water, clean air and, last but not least, smaller, independent farms that play a vital role in maintaining the biodiversity (and hence security) of the world's food shed (see Halweil 2002). In a commercial marketplace dominated by agribusiness oligopolies and globalized supply chains, the tragedy of the commons also becomes a tale of complex global-local interlinkages and socioeconomic interdependencies that help to perpetuate the BAU economy's unsustainable and wealth-concentrating modes of production. In consumer-citizens' everyday lives, these interdependencies are manifest through the colonization of the local by global networks of power, such as the case of Walmart superstores dominating local food markets. On the production side, farmers become entangled in these expansive networks through seemingly mundane choices such as opting to plant Monsanto-patented seeds. Such a decision almost immediately subsumes their production practices and economic viability to the machinations of transnational intellectual property laws, corporate strategies, supplementary technologies linked to GMO production, unintended environmental consequences (including the production of superpests and herbicide-resistant weeds), and the exigencies of global commodity markets.

Unlike the practice of purchasing groceries in the BAU distribution system, membership in CSA does not surreptitiously embed a host of socioeconomic and ecological externalities in an instrumental appeal to an ostensibly low price for a basket of goods. Rather, CSA growers and members are collaboratively seeking to reappropriate localized marketplace relationships and economic practices from globally scaled power structures. To use Saskia Sassen's (2006) triadic framework, this decentralized, reterritorialized market system is organized by an economic and cultural *logic* that values the preservation and restoration of the commons (via a nexus of communal and collaborative practices). It has *capabilities* to enable growers and consumer-citizens to attain greater economic and provisional autonomy from the BAU agribusiness system. And as part of an expanding network of other small-scale entrepreneurial marketplace innovators, CSA can also contribute to a *tipping point* though which a confluence of loosely coordinated localized actions exerts transformative influences on distant and seemingly entrenched global power structures.

CSA narratives and marketplace practices are quite distinct from the standard eco-consumerist imperatives that beseech individuals to act as informed, socially responsible consumer decision makers. Owing to the imperatives of profit seeking and market expansion, these marketing-friendly discourses of consumer-citizenship remain heavily skewed toward the consumerist pole, rendering the citizenship aspects as optional or attainable through symbolic gestures (Johnston 2008). CSA alters this ideological balance by appealing to consumer-citizens as active participants in a collective project that is embedded in their social networks and face-to-face communal ties. Through CSA narratives and practices, consumer-citizens gradually transform their initial preferences for convenience and boundless variety as well as their susceptibility to the allures of commodity fetishism into a marketplace orientation that is steeped in a more pronounced sense of civic responsibilities to protect the (localized) commons and to support alternatives to the corporate-dominated food chain. These concerns are readily linked to other issues of workers' rights, fair wages, biodiversity, and sustainable modes of production.

Consumers' investments and participation in CSA create a pathway for personal transformation that begins with processes of reskilling and becomes gradually immersed in the local movement discourses and sociopolitical goals that are articulated through the CSA market. CSAs also exhibit ideological affinities (in terms of underlying beliefs about the BAU economy and commitments to ideals of sustainability) and social linkages to other alternative market structures that function as plenitude enclaves, including raw milk producers, food co-operatives, artisanal craft enterprises, and other "communities of purpose" (see Schouten and Martin 2011). As consumers forge personal connections to other nodes in the broader network of alternatives to the BAU economy, their market relationships could eventually reach a tipping point where plenitude principles, rather than BAU orthodoxies, organize their lifestyles and identity projects.

At an institutional level, CSA—as a specific expression of the broader local-food movement and the backlash against corporate-dominated agriculture (see Pollan 2006b)—has reached a sufficient cultural mass that it has been able to influence the distribution practices of retail titan Whole Foods (Ness 2006) much in the way that the organic food movement has altered the product line offered by Walmart (Pollan 2006a). More broadly, forging stronger economic and cultural ties among these dispersed, decentralized, small-scale, entrepreneurial, plenitude-oriented enterprises may provide a means through which more peripheral but sustainable sectors of the economy can exert a progressive influence on the corporate-dominated mainstream marketplace. While corporate co-optation of countercultural ideals has long been condemned for debasing the original political values and objectives of these movements, these dynamics of incorporation can also precipitate logistical, production, and product-line changes that result in large BAU firms reducing the environmental and social costs of their operations.

By providing a necessary experiential and indeed pragmatic grounding to this reassembly of capacities, organizing logics, and tipping points, participation in CSA allows consumers to address personal health concerns, build deeper relationships with family members, and assuage guilt for other aspects of their lifestyles that structurally contribute to undesirable environmental or social justice outcomes. Moreover, this aspect of CSA is no mere therapeutic panacea. By enabling consumers to realize that they can incrementally and practically incorporate alternative principles into their lives, CSA helps to overcome not only the disempowering implications of reflexive risk awareness (Beck 1999) but also the "all or nothing" mindsets that can render the embrace of new lifestyle practices daunting or overwhelming.

In sum, CSA is a form of everyday and potentially transformative praxis that enables consumer-citizens to reembed abstract appeals and rationales for sustainable consumption into their social networks and thus to play a more proactive, empowering, and gratifying role in the broad project of creating a new sustainable economy. CSA consumers are able to direct their efforts toward more tangible goals rather than being one of many, relatively anonymous consumers who are seeking to change complex and interdependent systems, like the climate or the global economy, where the consequences of interventions are difficult to calibrate. Instead, CSA consumers maintain a specific plot of land that produces food in an environmentally responsible way. They help to sustain a way of life (the small family farm) that is a clear alternative to the business-as-usual global commodity chains that depersonalize and deterritorialize consumers' relationships to food production.

REFERENCES

Bauman, Zygmunt. 2007. *Liquid Times: Living in an Age of Uncertainty.* Malden, MA: Polity.

Beck, Ulrich. 1999. *World Risk Society.* Cambridge, MA: Polity.

Bourdieu, Pierre. 1986. "The Forms of Capital." In *Handbook of Theory: Research for the Sociology of Education,* ed. John Richardson, 241–58. New York: Greenwood.

Cohen, Maurie, Aaron Comrov, and Brian Hoffner. 2005. "The New Politics of Consumption: Sustainability in the American Marketplace." *Sustainability: Science, Practice, and Policy* 1:58–76.

Coleman, Eliot. 2002. "Beyond Organic." *Mother Earth News,* December–January. http://www.motherearthnews.com/arc/5875 (accessed March 2, 2013).

Connolly, John, and Andrea Prothero. 2008. "Green Consumption: Life-politics, Risk, and Contradictions." *Journal of Consumer Culture* 8 (1): 117–45.

Giddens, Anthony. 1991. *Modernity and Self-Identity: Self and Society in the Late Modern Age.* Stanford, CA: Stanford University Press.

Guthman, Julie. 2004. *Agrarian Dreams: The Paradox of Organic Farming in California.* Berkeley: University of California Press.

Halweil, Brian. 2002. "Home Grown: The Case for Local Food in a Local Market." Ed. Thomas Prugh. Worldwatch Paper 163. Washington, DC: Worldwatch Institute.

Hardin, Garrett. 1968. "The Tragedy of the Commons." *Science,* December 13, 1243–48.

Heinberg, Richard. 2011. *The End of Growth: Adapting to Our New Economic Reality.* Gabriola Island, British Columbia: New Society.

Hochenauer, Kurt. 2012. "Signs of Global Warming: Scorching Temperatures, Fires, Drought, Food Inflation?" *Okie Funk: Notes from the Outback,* July 12. http://okiefunk .com/node/1108 (accessed October 14, 2013).

Howe, Jeff. 2008. *Crowdsourcing: Why the Power of the Crowd Is Driving the Future of Business.* New York: Crown Business.

Inhofe, James. 2012. *The Greatest Hoax: How the Global Warming Conspiracy Threatens Your Future.* Washington, DC: WND Books.

Jaffe, JoAnn, and Michael Gertler. 2006. "Victual Vicissitudes: Consumer Deskilling and the (Gendered) Transformation of Food Systems." *Agriculture and Human Values* 23 (2): 143–62.

Johnston, Josée. 2008. "The Citizen-Consumer Hybrid: Ideological Tensions and the Case of Whole Foods Market." *Theoretical Sociology* 37:229–70.

Kohut, Andrew, Carroll Doherty, Michael Dimock, and Scott Keeter. 2010. "Little Change in Opinions about Global Warming." Washington, DC: Pew Research Center. http://people-press.org/2010/10/27/little-change-in-opinions-about-global-warming / (accessed March 1, 2013).

Lass, D., A. Brevis, G. W. Stevenson, J. Hendrickson, and K. Ruhf. 2003. *Community Supported Agriculture Entering the 21st Century: Results from the 2001 National Survey.* Amherst: Dept. of Resource Economics, University of Massachusetts.

Leiserowitz, Anthony, Edward Maibach, Connie Roser-Renouf, Geoff Feinberg, and Peter Howe. 2012. "Climate Change in the American Mind: Americans' Global Warming Beliefs and Attitudes in September, 2012." New Haven, CT: Yale Project on Climate Change Communication. http://environment.yale.edu/climate/files/Climate -Beliefs-September-2012.pdf (accessed March 2, 2013).

Mandeville, Bernard. 1723. *Selections from Fable of the Bees.* In *The Fable of the Bees and Other Writings,* ed. E. J. Hundert, 1:19–154. Indianapolis: Hackett, 1997.

McKibben, Bill. 2010. *Eaarth: Making a Life on a Tough New Planet.* New York: Henry Holt.

Ness, Carole. 2006. "Whole Foods Taking Flak, Thinks Local." *San Francisco Chronicle,* July 26. http://sfgate.com/cgi-bin/article.cgi?file=/c/a/2006/07/26/FDG3NK2LMV1 .DTL (accessed March 2, 2013).

Pearce, Fred. 2010. "Climate Wars: How the 'Climategate' Scandal Is Bogus and Based on Climate Sceptics' Lies." *Guardian,* 9 February. http://www.guardian.co.uk/environment /2010/feb/09/climategate-bogus-sceptics-lies (accessed March 2, 2013).

Pollan, Michael. 2001. "Behind the Organic-Industrial Complex." *New York Times Magazine,* May 13. http://www.nytimes.com/2001/05/13/magazine/13ORGANIC.html (accessed March 2, 2013).

———. 2006a. "Mass Natural." *New York Times Magazine,* June 4, 15–18.

———. 2006b. *The Omnivore's Dilemma: A Natural History of Four Meals.* New York: Penguin.

Press, Melea, and Eric J. Arnould. 2011a. "How Does Organizational Identification Form? A Consumer Behavior Perspective." *Journal of Consumer Research* 38 (4): 650–66.

———. 2011b. "Legitimating Community Supported Agriculture through American Pastoralist Ideology." *Journal of Consumer Culture* 11 (July): 168–94.

Randall, David A., Richard A. Wood, Sandrine Bony, Robert Colman, Thierry Fichefet, John Fyfe, Vladimir Kattsov, Andrew Pitman, Jagadish Shukla, Jayaraman Srinivasan, Ronald J. Stouffer, Akimasa Sumi, and Karl E. Taylor. 2007. "Climate Models and Their Evaluation." In *Climate Change 2007: The Physical Science Basis. Contribution of Working Group I to the Fourth Assessment Report of the Intergovernmental Panel on Climate Change,* ed. Susan Solomon, Dahe Qin, Martin Manning, Melinda Marquis, Kristen B. Avery, Melinda Tignor, Henry L. Miller, and Zhenlin Chen. New York: Cambridge University Press. http://www.ipcc.ch/publications_and_data/ar4/wg1/en/ch8.html (accessed March 2, 2013).

Roubini, Nouriel. 2011. "Karl Marx Was Right." *Wall Street Journal,* August 12. http://online.wsj.com/video/nouriel-roubini-karl-marx-was-right/68EE8F89-EC24–42F8–9B9D-47B510E473B0.html (accessed March 2, 2013).

Sassen, Saskia. 2006. *Territory, Authority, Rights: From Medieval to Global Assemblages.* Princeton, NJ: Princeton University Press.

Schor, Juliet B. 2010. *Plenitude: The New Economics of True Wealth.* New York: Penguin.

Schouten, John. W., and Diane M. Martin. 2011. "Communities of Purpose." In *Beyond the Consumption Bubble,* ed. Karin M. Ekström and Kay Glans, 125–36. New York: Routledge.

Schudson, Michael. 1999. *The Good Citizen: A History of American Civic Life.* Cambridge, MA; Harvard University Press.

———. 2003. "Click Here for Democracy: A History and Critique of an Information Processing Model of Citizenship." In *Democracy and New Media,* ed. Henry Jenkins and David Thorburn, 49–60. Cambridge, MA: MIT Press.

Sharp, Jeff S., Eric Imerman, and Greg Peters. 2002. "Community Supported Agriculture (CSA): Building Community among Farmers and Non-farmers." *Journal of Extension* 40 (3). http://www.joe.org/joe/2002june/a3.php (accessed October 14, 2013).

Smith, Nicholas, and Anthony Leiserowitz. 2012. "The Rise of Global Warming Skepticism: Exploring Affective Image Associations in the United States over Time." *Risk Analysis* 32 (6), 1021–103.

Stiglitz, George. 2010. *Freefall: America, Free Markets, and the Sinking of the World Economy.* New York: Norton.

Surowiecki, James. 2004. *The Wisdom of Crowds: Why the Many Are Smarter Than the Few and How Collective Wisdom Shapes Business, Economies, Societies and Nations.* New York: Knopf Doubleday.

Thompson, Craig J., and Gokcen Coskuner-Balli. 2007. "Enchanting Ethical Consumerism: The Case of Community Supported Agriculture." *Journal of Consumer Culture* 7 (3): 275–303.

Warner, Melanie. 2011. "How Whole Foods Is Embracing Its Local-Produce Rivals." http://www.bnet.com/blog/food-industry/how-whole-foods-is-embracing-its-local-produce-rivals/2553 (accessed March 2, 2013).

Chapter 5 Raw Milk Underground: Status and Self-Sufficiency in Agro-Food Networks in the United States and Lithuania

Diana Mincyte

I first met Lorie at a cozy coffee shop in New York in the fall of 2011.[1] Confident, articulate, and driven, she worked as a freelancer for a media company while also being actively involved in numerous local-food-procurement movements, including buying and consuming unpasteurized milk (known as raw milk), one of the most controversial products in the United States. What struck me in our conversation was how fundamentally different Lorie was from my informants who were involved in raw milk economies on the other side of the Atlantic. For almost a decade I had been following raw milk markets in postsocialist eastern Europe to examine how semisubsistence farmers and poor consumers were marginalized in the context of European sustainable development agendas (Harboe Knudsen 2012; Mincyte 2012). In Lithuania, where I conducted most of my research, I had recorded scores of interviews with women farmers who did not even define themselves as farmers or as worthy members of society, so low were they ranked in the local social ladder.

Lorie, on the other hand, was an opposite to the image of the peasant. She saw herself as successful, happy, passionate about things she was involved in—someone who lived a deeply meaningful life she'd chosen for herself. It was surprising to see how she had carved out a sense of worth in the context of alternative milk economies in the United States while my informants in Lithuania were fighting against their designation as "backward." At the end of our long conversation, I knew I had to come back and explore the questions of value in the alternative agro-food networks, particularly the ways in which the participants construct their social status.

This chapter addresses that question. Throughout this study I will examine how participants in alternative agro-food economies experience, define, and reproduce their social status, and I will seek to link these issues to broader debates about plenitude and sustainability. Developed in her widely read *Plenitude: The New Economics of True Wealth* (2010), Juliet Schor's concept of plenitude offers a vision of sustainability that recognizes the environmental limits and social costs of economic boom-and-bust cycles while rejecting sacrifice and scarcity as necessary for achieving a more secure future. Schor argues that there are different ways of organizing work, time, and consumption—particularly through self-provisioning, new allocations of time, environmental awareness, and knowledge industries (5–6)—that will serve as sources for wealth and a better quality of life.

Studying social status in relation to plenitude economies is important because it deepens our understanding of conditions, strategies, and practices through which participants in nonconventional food-provisioning networks create such wealth by developing alternative ways of thriving. In the social sciences, there is already a burgeoning literature on alternative agro-food networks exploring the questions of values (Alkon 2008; Johnston, Szabo, and Rodney 2011), ethics (Barnett et al. 2005; Jackson, Ward, and Russell 2008; Jaffee 2007), citizenship (Dubuisson-Quellier, Lamine, and Le Velly 2011; Lockie 2009; Seyfang 2006), and reflexivity (DuPuis and Goodman 2005; Stuart and Worosz 2012). While this research provides insights into the social and ethical dimensions of practicing alternative lifestyles, we still know surprisingly little about the identities and experiences of the participants in these networks, particularly how they construct themselves as successful in the context of the mainstream consumer society. If we approach plenitude economies as a step toward a sustainable future in the United States and beyond, then the question of what factors are at play in creating positive social status becomes crucial for developing appropriate political, social, and economic agendas.

In addition to developing this line of inquiry, I also take seriously the issues of global and local inequalities and experiences of marginalization, subjects that tend to be overlooked in the scholarship on local economies and their middle- and upper-middle-class consumers (see Alkon and Agyeman 2011; Goodman, DuPuis, and Goodman 2011). By focusing on well-heeled consumers in the Global North as the primary subjects in studying sustainability, this scholarship not only devalues other innovative economic practices as potential sites for challenging business as usual but also excludes other people and groups, especially those coming from lower socioeconomic strata or the Global South. This means that these groups are not taken seriously as agents of social and environmental change and are not included in the ongoing debate about what constitutes a sustainable global economy and society (Mincyte 2012). In taking a comparative-historical approach, this chapter is an attempt to fill in this lacuna, and in so doing, rethink plenitude economies outside of the class and geographic bounds of postindustrial consumer culture.

To develop such a comparative study, I present an analysis of two alternative raw milk networks: one in New York and one in Lithuania. Unprocessed, unpasteurized milk is a perfect plenitude commodity. In both New York and Lithuania, raw milk is a local product distributed through short commodity chains that enable its delivery to the consumers before it spoils. In order to mitigate microbial risks associated with raw milk consumption, both consumers and producers participating in raw milk networks tend to develop long-term, trust-based relationships that enable the consumers to know about the farmers, the farms, the land, and the animals. Additionally, most of the participants in these networks are deeply knowledgeable about food, its qualities, and handling techniques. In this sense, these distribution networks function as knowledge economies where participants share information online (in the United States, primarily) or in face-to-face settings (both in the United States and Lithuania), including discussions about milk's quality and taste and about preparation techniques and recipes. Conscious and self-reflexive about their practices, raw milk consumers are often creatively engaged in using milk to make yogurts, flavored buttermilk, kefir, and a wide range of cheeses, deriving not only nutritional but economic value and experiences of fulfillment, meaningfulness, and purpose, key ingredients in their quality of life. The fact that it takes additional time and effort to buy raw milk and creatively use it also speaks to the centrality of slower-paced, experience-rich time for the participants.

Yet it is also important to recognize that raw milk networks cannot be fully understood without taking into account the broader political and economic landscapes in which they function. Raw milk is a highly regulated product in the United States and in Europe. According to the U.S. Centers for

Disease Control and Prevention (Langer et al. 2012, 385), 1,571 people have become sick from drinking raw milk or eating cheese made from raw milk between 1993 and 2006. The organization argues that the product should be banned altogether as a serious public health risk threatening the well-being of society. In the context of lawsuits and steep fines levied against producers, raw milk networks in the United States are significantly different from other local-food-procurement initiatives such as community-supported agriculture, farmers' markets, the homesteading movement, or community gardens.

Additionally, due to the criminalization of raw milk in many locations in the United States, participation in the raw milk economies in New York State and beyond is inevitably a political endeavor, requiring strong commitments and engagement on the part of the consumers. Not surprisingly, participants in informal raw milk–buying clubs are deeply reflexive and articulate about their political agency and their relationship to industrialized food systems and mainstream economies. They draw a clear line between "good" local raw milk and "bad" industrial milk, and in so doing position themselves as advocates of the right cause.

In Europe, on the other hand, raw milk is legal as long as it is sold by authorized producers and distributors in designated places. It is not unusual to see raw milk for sale at farmers' markets as well as in vending machines situated at the entrances to supermarkets, especially in Italy, France, Austria, and postsocialist Europe. Despite the more relaxed regulatory framework surrounding raw milk distribution, participants in raw milk networks in Lithuania have also developed strong political ideas and identities that are rooted in experiences of marginalization and alienation. Unlike their American counterparts, who are pushing against what they see as limits imposed by the "nanny state," Lithuania's small-scale farmers and poor consumers see themselves as abandoned by the state. For example, poor farmers feel that they are forced to the margins of the economy because they cannot take advantage of European and national agricultural development funds that are available to wealthy farmers who can hire expensive expert consultations, access bank loans, and reap higher profits because they are paid twice as much for milk deliveries to the processor than are small producers. Similarly, the poor consumers who have to rely on self-provisioning schemes in order to gain access to nutritionally rich and affordable products often see themselves as losers in the postsocialist era. Not surprisingly, both producers and consumers say that the odds are stacked against them and that they have no future in a rapidly Europeanizing Lithuania.

By developing these insights throughout the chapter, I will highlight the similarities in how participants in these two economic niches define their identities and justify their practices and choices. I will show how, despite their different socioeconomic backgrounds, the New Yorkers and their Lithuanian counterparts share deep reflexivity, acute awareness of state institutions, and values of self-sufficiency that undergird their subjectivities.

What makes these self-perception projects different, however, is their relationship to the state and its institutions. As a discursive vehicle, self-sufficiency is a sign of resistance against the encroachment of the state among well-educated members of raw milk–buying clubs in the United States, who often see their networks as the last bastion pushing against the state's regulatory apparatus. They derive their social status by linking their claims of autonomy to morality, care for others, and responsibility. In Lithuania, on the other hand, self-sufficiency is a sign of social isolation and the disappearance of welfare institutions, exposing the depth of marginalization. This suggests that state institutions play a significant role in shaping identities and status constructions.

The second insight flowing from the comparative analysis is that material practices and performances—not only ideas and political imaginaries—are important in how people build their sense of status. Despite the similarities in how raw milk–procurement systems are organized in the two contexts, there are major differences in how these economies fit into the daily lives of their participants. In the United States, raw milk networks are sites for learning skills, developing tastes, and experiencing creativity in the context of the regimented, mass-produced culture of the mainstream economy. In Lithuania, raw milk economies are an added element in an economy defined by scarcity and frugality that in public debates is often portrayed as a return to peasant lifestyles, devolution, and even feudalism. It is through such lived experiences of global and local inequalities that participants in these alternative networks derive meanings and build identities.

In developing the above themes, the remainder of this chapter is organized into five sections. It opens with an overview of the scholarship on the intersection between social status and participation in alternative, environmentally conscious lifestyles in order to locate my analysis in the larger scholarly debates. A brief background section will cover the historical and political contexts in which raw milk consumption evolved in the United States and Eastern Europe. Two empirical sections—the first focusing on practices and experiences of participation in raw milk markets and the second examining the articulations of autonomy and political agency—follow. The last section presents concluding reflections.

THEORIZING STATUS AND ALTERNATIVE
FOOD NETWORKS

While scholarship on consumption and social status is broad and elaborate, the question of how participation in alternative economies intersects with self-perception and status is relatively new in the field. In a study conducted in the mid-1990s, Sadalla and Krull's (1995) research demonstrated that conservation and other environmentally friendly behaviors such as line-drying clothes, recycling aluminum cans, and using public transportation were often considered low status. This symbolic association has been interpreted as a psychological barrier to conservation that prevents people from participating in these activities (Barr and Gilg 2007; Barr, Gilg, and Ford 2005; Viklund 2004). A recent study by Welte and Anastasio (2010) revisited Sadalla and Krull's analysis to find that the landscape has changed in the last fifteen years and that environmental behaviors are now viewed more favorably.

In fact, researchers are now finding that green behaviors are markers of social status. Griskevicius, Tybur, and Van den Bergh (2010) argue that green consumption practices are cases of "conspicuous conservation," that is, purchases that simultaneously signal altruism and higher status. Merging consumer behavior research and evolutionary psychology approaches, Griskevicius et al. argue that the pro-social behavior, self-sacrifice, and altruism that underlie green consumption increase one's social standing in the group (see also Hardy and Van Vugt 2006) because these values provided evolutionary advantage for our ancestors living in socially integrated groups. In this reading, consumers buying green products are "activating status."

Taking a sociological approach, Carfagna et al. (forthcoming) complicate the conspicuous conservation theory by demonstrating that the link between green behaviors and social status is not hard-wired in our biology but is socially and historically situated. Building on Holt's (1998) taxonomy of values, in which consumers with low cultural capital are defined by their emphasis on physical work, utilitarian interests, and affinity for the local while high-cultural-capital consumers value idealism, cosmopolitanism, and connoisseurship,

Carfagna et al. map a new configuration of values that emerged since Holt completed his study in the mid-1990s. They show that unlike in the 1990s, high-cultural-capital consumers now appreciate opportunities to work with their hands and engage in local communities, characteristics that have historically been attributed to lower socioeconomic status. While the adoption of these sustainability-related values does not erase social inequalities, Carfagna et al. suggest that these shifts in the mainstream consumer culture might be hopeful signs of a new economy in which postconsumerist lifestyles are embraced and valued by the wider public. However, see Holt (chapter 7 in this volume) for a more pessimistic interpretation of the extent to which these new consumer practices will translate into lifestyle changes in labor markets and what their actual ecological impact will be.

The idea that environmental behaviors are not simply motivated by status activation but are related to a wide range of ethical, moral, emotional, and cultural considerations is consistent with scholarship on alternative economies and consumer behavior (Alkon and Agyeman 2011; Starr 2010; Thompson and Coskuner-Balli 2007). In his analysis of shopping patterns in North London, for example, Miller (1998) shows that consumers tend to equate buying "quality" products with love and care for the family and good parenting, framing such practices in terms of family values, morality, and responsibility. This scholarship shows that green practices, including those in the marketplace, are deeply intertwined with affect, definitions of responsibility, and citizenship as well as the values of environmental awareness. (For critiques of this view, see DuPuis and Goodman 2005; Guthman 2004.)

Relying on interviews and ethnographic fieldwork, this chapter extends this line of argument by highlighting the significance of narratives of self-sufficiency and care as key elements in articulations of success, meaning, and fulfillment among members of alternative economies. This means that in addition to the values of manual work and localism that constitute eco-habitus, as argued by Carfagna et al. (forthcoming), ideas of autonomy and self-provisioning are emerging as powerful narrative strategies through which participants claim higher social status and justify their push against mainstream society. Furthermore, I will argue that self-sufficiency itself is constituted through dynamic tension with the larger society and it depends on how participants understand and construct their relationship to the state and its infrastructures. This argument resonates with Georg Simmel's ([1903] 1971) work on identities, which emphasizes the ongoing struggle between the individual and the powers of the society: "[Identity-making projects] flow from the attempt of the individual to maintain the independence and individuality of his existence against the sovereign powers of society" (324).

HISTORICAL BACKGROUND

Known as nature's perfect food in the English-speaking world, fresh milk is, nevertheless, an unusual product requiring a careful orchestration of technological, scientific, animal, and human agents. Today more than ever, the dairy economy relies on technologies and science to produce, process, preserve, and distribute fresh milk. In addition to this finely tuned scientific-technological apparatus, milk consumption is also dependent on the ability of the human body to digest lactose beyond childhood, a rare biological trait that has been acquired by the peoples inhabiting northern Europe, parts of the Mediterranean rim, and in small pockets in Africa and Asia. Due to these biological limits, as Andrea S. Wiley (2011) powerfully argues, popular claims of the "universal goodness" of milk go against the genetic variation in the human population, suggesting that nutritional advice to consume fresh milk is an expression of ethnic discrimination against minority groups in North America and most of the people in Asia, Africa, and South America.

From a historical perspective, milk has been consumed in the form of butter, fermented drinks, or cheese for most of human history. The rise of fresh milk consumption as we take it for granted today can be traced to just the mid-nineteenth century, when ongoing cultural and economic shifts led to a dramatic decrease in breast feeding among working- and upper-class women (DuPuis 2002; Valenze 2011). This trend was accompanied by growing demand for breast milk substitutes, and fresh milk production soared. Yet the first efforts to sell fresh milk to urban consumers as a natural product led to notoriously unsafe milk produced without regard for hygiene or the health of animals. Keeping cows in tight urban spaces—most famously in New York City—and feeding them the by-products of fermentation from distilleries meant that most milk was contaminated and sometimes even deadly. In their efforts to provide healthy milk to young children, numerous social reformers across the United States called for more food-safety regulations and the establishment of public health supervision institutions. In 1873, cows were expelled from New York City and by 1910, all milk sold within the city limits had to be pasteurized.

Despite the tangible success of pasteurization campaigns, the public remained skeptical about pasteurized, or "cooked," milk, which was seen as an overreaction and disproportionate response to the issues of cleanliness (Mendelson 2011, 36–37). Rather than "scorching" all milk through excessive heating, proponents of raw milk consumption called for the establishment of strict raw milk safety certifications as a viable solution to disease prevention. It was suggested that if the cow was healthy, well cared for, and properly milked, and if all the containers through which the milk passed were clean and treated with high heat, then raw milk would be just as safe as pasteurized milk. Such public and institutional views lasted into the 1920s, leaving consumers the option to choose for themselves (Mendelson 2011).

The situation changed rapidly with the economic boom of the late 1920s and especially in the post–Second World War era, which saw the consolidation of agricultural production, driving down food commodity prices and making raw milk production and distribution difficult to automate and therefore quite costly. By the early 1960s, milkmen delivering raw milk to the doors of consumers in the United States had all but disappeared. It is only in the 1990s that raw milk made a comeback among alternative food groups in urban areas, and since then the numbers of consumers buying raw milk have been growing steadily. Reports differ: there are now between half a million to 9 million people involved in raw milk networks across the United States (Mendelson 2011; CDC 2006–7, 2011).[2]

While social reformers were advocating for public health agendas in American urban centers and beyond, Lithuania was still a poor agricultural province on the western edge of the Russian empire. Cows and milk constituted an indispensable part of diverse semisubsistence economies that rested on relationships of reciprocity, exchange, and shared responsibility. These semicommunal forms of animal ownership persisted well into the 1920s when, after gaining independence from Russia, Lithuania implemented a series of agrarian reforms dissolving old villages and distributing land, including pastures, to individual farmers. In this period, fresh milk was consumed directly on the farms, but most of it was still churned into butter or fermented for drinking or cheese making.

World War II was a watershed in Lithuania's history, as it lost its short-lived independence, first to the Soviet Union in 1940, then to Nazi Germany in 1941, eventually going back to the embrace of the Soviet state in 1944. As in the rest of the Soviet Union, Lithuania's agriculture was speedily and violently collectivized, and all the formerly independent farmers became workers and employees in collective and state farms. In contrast to commonly held beliefs that socialist agriculture relied solely on the collective and public sector, the vast majority of products, including milk, were produced on household farms (Hedlund 1989; Mincyte 2009a; Wadekin 1971). Each collective and state farm worker, under socialist law, was not only entitled to a small piece of land and pastures but was required to keep animals and sell their products to the state. In this way, under socialism, two milk economies emerged. The first economy consisted of industrialized and pasteurized milk that looked and tasted similar to its counterpart in the West and was produced on large, state-owned industrialized farms. The second economy involved local raw milk deliveries for sale, gifts, or barter. The milk traveled in large glass jars and buckets covered in thick layers of cream and smelling of cows and countryside. It is this second economy that arguably planted the seeds of the raw milk entrepreneurship that proliferated after the fall of socialism in the late 1980s.

With the restitution of property rights in 1991 and the reestablishment of national independence, Lithuania embarked on a road to globalization and economic liberalization. As a result of the shock therapy advocated by Western experts, who pushed for the immediate privatization of land and industrial enterprises, economic hardships ensued and many farmers and consumers found themselves struggling at the edge of subsistence. In response to the economic and social pressures that accompanied postsocialist reforms, numerous entrepreneur-farmers started traveling to the cities in search of venues to sell their products and generate cash incomes. For many urbanites this milk was a welcome addition to their limited diets. It was considerably cheaper and creamier than dairy products sold in stores and supermarkets. Milk deliveries also opened a new public space for socializing, as consumers often gathered together hours before milk was due to be delivered. In the context of ghettoizing urban environments, these deliveries created new sites for social interaction and learning (Mincyte 2009b). Although the quality of life in Lithuania has improved considerably since the country joined the European Union in 2004, the experience of buying and selling milk has not changed for many consumers (who live on fixed incomes) and small-scale producers (whose livelihood depends on direct sales): both continue to participate in the local-food-provisioning schemes. Today, it is not unusual to see groups of people, usually elders, holding glass containers in their hands as they congregate near Soviet-style apartment buildings waiting for the farmer to bring the coveted milk.

MILK QUALITIES AND PERFORMANCES OF
SELF-SUFFICIENCY IN RAW MILK ECONOMIES

Participants in the U.S. raw milk clubs justify their engagement in alterna-tive food-procurement networks by emphasizing particular material and es-pecially microbial qualities of milk, including its taste, color, biochemical properties, and the presence of microbial cultures. In her article on raw milk cheeses, Heather Paxson (2008) defines the embrace of microbial cultures in alternative food movements as a shift away from Pasteurian definitions of health and well-being that have hinged on cleanliness and hygiene. In the post-Pasteurian worldview, Paxson argues, humans live peacefully with microbes—and by extension with nature—without fear of disease. The emer-gence of a new relationship between people and microbes in the post-Pasteurian modality is also accompanied by a change in biopolitics, or methods for managing the socionatural world. Paxson writes that while "[Pasteurianism] contributes to the production of rational risk-minimizing subjects and to a governmentality devoted to managing public risk" (36), "a post-Pasteurian care of the self goes through the obligatory passage point of caring for the . . . companion species whose bodies and cultures are coproduced with human ones" (40). In other words, the embrace of microbial life in raw milk is not an isolated event but a signal of tectonic shifts in the ethics of human relation-ships to nature.

Among the raw milk consumers in New York, this post-Pasteurian ethic is often expressed in the emotive language of "awe" and wonder about the great-ness of nature. The language consumers use to describe raw milk is reminis-cent of how nature writers such as Rachel Carson describe their encounters with the environment (Sideris 2008). They speak about the importance of sea-sonal change on the pastures, animal and human life cycles, and their impact on the way milk tastes and smells. Sally, a New Yorker in her early thirties, recounts her first experience of tasting raw milk, describing it in terms of "awe," "love," and almost "addiction": "A few years back, a friend of mine . . . gave me to try this amazing, delicious milk. And wow, I had never tasted any-thing like that before. It was so silky and rich in flavor. I loved the color, the smell. . . . I was in total awe. . . . This is what a real natural product tastes like. . . . You can tell the season . . . and literally taste the pastures. I now drink it everyday. . . . We couldn't live without it." In every interview or con-versation with those who consume raw milk in New York, the participants emphasize that they see raw milk not simply as food to be consumed but as "a live matter" to be experimented and played with. Many consumers I encountered in the city tried clabbering milk, an easy procedure in which week-old raw milk is kept at room temperature until it thickens due to the lactic acid bacteria. Clabbered milk tastes a bit tangy, but despite its sourness, many use it instead of yogurt or even sour cream, especially in cooking.

In addition to clabbering milk, some raw milk enthusiasts try their hands at churning butter and making yogurts and cheeses that require knowledge and experience to work with milk's microbial cultures. To produce cheese, for instance, one needs starters (microbes that jump-start fermentation) or rennet (enzymes that can be found in animal stomachs, extracted from certain plants or genetically modified) to enable the coagulation of the milk protein. Online and in daily interactions, there is always a lively debate among milk consumers about what sources are best for procuring starters. Striving for purity and following their ethical commitments, many look for noncommercial options: microbial cultures developed at home are seen as "natural," "diverse," "dynamic," and "indigenous" in contrast to the monocultures harvested by the dairy industry. Not surprisingly, Internet sites are filled with recipes on how to create such homemade starters, some of them using unusual vegetarian fermentation agents such as fig juice, red chili pepper stems, and tamarind. Relying on these online sources, but also on the knowledge shared among the network members and their own experiments, raw milk consumers relish the process of playing with milk's "cultures" and enabling the microbes to transform a "simple glass" of milk into "something more."

The key element in these practices and experiences of engaging with milk is not merely that New York's raw milk consumers enhance their cooking skills and develop a deeper appreciation for food, but also that they are transformed from passive consumers to active participants in the food system. In increasing their knowledge of milk's qualities and by tinkering with it to produce their own cheese, yogurt, or sour milk, they are simultaneously expanding their identities beyond that of the consumer and changing their role in the food economy. This transformation is expressed in their frequent references to play and claims about the pleasure involved in working with milk and producing food. In one case a young professional in her late twenties told me that she and her roommate used most of the milk they bought from the farmer to make cheese. My informant spoke fondly about her experiences of "playing" with the milk and "then seeing what happens," and was deeply knowledgeable about the art of food fermentation. In another instance, a woman in her thirties explained to me that she did not put much advance thought into what to do with the milk she picked up from the farmer every few weeks. She would leave it sitting in the refrigerator for a few days and then on the spot decide what to make from it. In both cases, the women were more interested in the process of cheese making than the results of their work and found this to be a fulfilling experience and an expression of their creativity and skill.

Similarly, an enhanced experience of agency can also be detected in the narratives about health, particularly in the way that participants openly critique "the medical establishment" and use raw milk for healing or preventing diseases. Many proponents believe that raw milk has healing qualities such as preventing asthma, allergies, or even cancer. They cite scores of examples of how people were healed after they switched to raw milk, often arguing that microorganisms and whey proteins that are damaged during pasteurization are natural healers of various ailments, helping the body to build a strong immune system and encouraging the development of balanced gastrointestinal flora. Such arguments are particularly prevalent in the lively online debates surrounding alternative economies.

In the narratives surrounding the issue of health, raw milk is considered nature's perfect food and natural medicine, able to cure a host of chronic conditions and even infectious diseases. Consuming raw milk is believed to be good for one's body and health as well as a sign of care for one's family members. By drinking a natural product that also tastes good and has important preventive and healing qualities, consumers are taking care and responsibility for their own physical health and that of their families. The notions of care and responsibility resonate with the experiences of a woman in her mid-thirties who likes to bike to the farm to pick up fresh produce and sometimes milk and cheese directly from the farmer. Dedicated to buying milk from the same farmer, she not only stops by the house to speak with the members of the farmer's family, she also knows the names of the cows whose milk she consumes. For her, raw milk is a real food that enriches her own life, supports the livelihood of the farmer, and embodies her care for his animals.

The language of care and responsibility is also prevalent among members of local-food-buying clubs, which often include dairy deliveries. To join food clubs in New York, new members are asked to fill out questionnaires explaining their background and why they want to buy raw milk. These are used to judge whether potential consumers know enough about raw food and the risks involved in its consumption. While most of those involved in the networks are avid advocates of the use of raw milk to heal a wide range of digestive, reproductive, and autoimmune issues, I was told that an indication of one's intention to use raw milk as a cure leads to further questioning. In such cases, the coordinator of the network contacts the candidate to speak with him or her directly to make sure he or she has reasonable expectations and understands the risks. From the perspective of the club, the procedures of vetting and clarifying issues surrounding risks constitute care for the well-being of consumers.

These care and morality implications do not, however, stop with one's immediate household members; they extend to distant others. In articulating care for both the human and nonhuman environment, many narratives borrow classical tropes from environmental discourses, such as "interconnectivity," "feedback," or "ecological system," suggesting that New Yorkers consider their food choices as part of a broader, interconnected environment. In one such narrative, consumers argue that raw milk as an element in the larger production system has a far-reaching impact on the environment because it interrupts and challenges industrial agricultural production. The argument goes that pasteurization allows producers to ignore issues of cleanliness and animal health. Counting only on pasteurization to manage health risks, raw milk proponents argue, leads to higher levels of milk contamination, poor treatment of animals, and disregard for environmental health. Paradoxically, rather than solving the issue of milk contamination and ensuring that farms produce the cleanest milk possible, pasteurization enables the production of "dirty" milk. Mark McAffee, the CEO of Organic Pastures Dairy and one of the most outspoken proponents of raw milk consumption and production in the United States, summarizes this argument: "Pasteurization does not create clean milk; it just kills filthy milk" (McAffee 2010).

The use of environmental language and logic is important in the context of raw milk consumption because it marks environmental sensibilities among the consumers. By employing such language, consumers draw strongly on alternative epistemic cultures of environmental movements that place value on relationships, exchanges, and the embeddedness of human life in the natural world. Similar to the analysis of Barnett et al. (2005), which underscores the ways that people link their identities with particular qualities of objects of consumption, the participants in raw milk networks see themselves as caring and deeply moral actors because they buy milk that does the world good.

In emphasizing the values of care for one's body and family as well as by invoking environmental connectedness, these consumers frame their participation in terms of making good and bad choices. While conventional, industrialized, and pasteurized milk is constructed as an abomination of nature and a toxic substance posing risks to human health, raw milk is seen as a moral choice that has far-reaching implications for personal health and the environment. It is through such a stark juxtaposition of what is good and bad that consumers build their case for self-identity as conscious actors who care about themselves and others.

In Lithuania, the material qualities of milk also play an important role in how participants experience and justify their food choices—and by extension their place in the community. Every farmer delivering milk to the city boasts about the taste and color of her milk, and the consumers often comment on the amount of cream that can be skimmed from the milk they buy from a particular producer. Defying the prevalent nutritional advice that suggests consuming fat-free diets, poverty-driven raw milk networks place special value on milk with higher cream content because it yields sour cream, cream, and butter. For this reason, consumers like to use transparent glass and plastic containers for their milk so that they can immediately evaluate the cream line of the milk they buy, a key metric of its goodness and a mark of a "good farmer." When queuing behind milk-delivery cars, consumers are also engaged in a delicate interplay of favors and seniority, as the first few consumers receive more cream than others. Thus the material qualities of milk contribute to reproducing a social order in which notions of seniority, respect, social power, age, and gender are reified.

It is difficult to gauge how many people are involved in the raw milk sector in Lithuania because the official statistic measuring direct sales also encompasses milk that is consumed on the farm, sold in farmers' markets, and delivered to consumers in the village. What is clear is that most of the milk that flows in these economies comes from farms of up to five cows. One farmer usually serves about forty to seventy households, bringing milk to four or five locations every day and alternating deliveries so that each location is visited three times a week. Most consumers buy one to four liters of milk a week, yet it is not uncommon for regulars to buy as many as ten liters (approximately 2.6 gallons) every few days and use it for making cheese, sour cream, and fermented drinks to feed their extended families. In applying themselves to milk processing, they are harnessing the work of microbes, and in so doing, they seem to be working within the bounds of post-Pasteurian ethics and microbiopolitics that define New York's consumers-turned-producers.

The key difference between the raw milk networks in New York and those in Lithuania is that Lithuanian milk enthusiasts do not explicitly use the language of environmental protection, systems thinking, or feedback loops. Environmental issues and acute awareness of nature, however, enter other spheres of their daily life, especially when they grow, process, and store most of the food they consume.

The life stories of some of the consumers and producers are instructive here as they exhibit different ways in which such self-sufficiency projects are practiced. One such story is that of Laima, a sixty-five-year-old woman who grew up in the countryside during the tumultuous years of collectivization and Sovietization after the Second World War. After finishing high school she moved to Kaunas, the second-largest city in the country, to attend a nursing school. In the early 1960s she was assigned to work in the cardiology ward at a major research hospital. After getting married, she and her husband moved into a two-room apartment and acquired a *sodas,* a small (0.15 acre) plot of land on the outskirts of the city issued to urbanites by the Soviet government for the purpose of growing food and engaging in "productive leisure." Their only child, a daughter, works as a middle school teacher and lives in Vilnius, the capital city, with her own family. Laima and her husband both retired in the first decade of the 2000s. The meager life savings they accumulated during socialism were swallowed by the inflation of the 1990s, and they now subsist on a small pension. Like many other urbanites of their generation, their lives revolve around the garden, where they produce a significant proportion of their diet.

Starting in early spring and finishing in late fall, they travel to the sodas every few days to tend their vegetable garden, fruit trees, herbs, and berries. Every spring they plant tomatoes, cucumbers, cabbages, melons, and zucchinis, and they also allocate a large portion of their garden to root vegetables such as potatoes, carrots, and beets. Although they have to take two buses to get to the garden, they do so willingly to spend their time weeding and tending their plants. For Laima, gardening is a way of life and a way of producing good foods for herself and her grandchildren. Throughout summer she is busy making berry and fruit jams, pickling cabbage and cucumbers, drying apples and pears, and picking and preserving wild mushrooms. Their cellar is stocked with the fruits of their hard work.

In the context of this domestic ecology, raw milk is another example of a lifestyle defined by self-sufficiency. By crafting her own yogurt and cheese, Laima uses her knowledge and experience to transform the raw product into the food she proudly puts on her table. Like the raw milk consumers in New York, Laima equates her cooking and gardening with care for her family members and the well-being of the garden ecologies.

Yet, unlike the consumers in New York, who are adamant about consuming milk without pasteurizing it, Laima and her neighbors take a pragmatic approach to the risks that raw milk poses. She argues that nobody "really" knows what happens on the farm and suggests that heating up milk is the way to protect oneself. In her kitchen, she uses a method of slow pasteurization. After picking up the milk from the farmer, she pours it into a pot and slowly heats it up to about seventy-five degrees Celsius. Checking the thermometer every few minutes, she makes sure that the milk is not overheated. She argues that her technique is significantly better than industrial pasteurization, in which milk is boiled under pressure and all the live cultures are eliminated (Mincyte 2009b).

The question of pasteurization is a complicated one, and many raw milk consumers in Lithuania are torn between the health claims for raw milk consumption and the health risks it poses. During the interviews, I was often told the story of a scientist who had run an experiment in which a young calf was fed with pasteurized milk. The story goes that the calf grew weaker and died within weeks because it did not receive the necessary nutrients, enzymes, and "the real stuff" that is eradicated through pasteurization. Despite the lesson expressed in this story, the consumers also noted that they worried about health risks and often, if not always, heated their milk before consuming it.

The issue of health and taking charge of one's body is a recurrent theme in the conversations carried out at the milk-delivery sites in Lithuania. In addition to the common understanding that the milk from the farm is good "to work with" and easily used for various dishes, consumers also emphasize its geography and its connection to nature. Laima says: "Milk from our farmer comes from the real village. . . . It is a real Lithuanian milk from cows raised on pastures." Like other members of her community, Laima sometimes buys milk from other farmers, but she says that she always comes back to the same farmer, Rasa, who has been delivering milk to her neighborhood for over four years. Laima says she feels safe drinking milk from Rasa's farm because she knows somebody who knows Rasa's parents. On every occasion, Laima stresses that trust is the key ingredient in the raw milk economy.

From the farmer's perspective, trust is something to be earned, and this is reinforced every time she delivers milk. Many farmers whom I interviewed in the course of this project are deeply aware that they are judged as much by their own conduct and appearance as by the quality of their milk. Many women farmers, who constitute the majority of semisubsistence producers in Lithuania, put on "better" clothes and apply makeup so as to appear "decent" and "clean" for milk deliveries. They also educate themselves about new recipes and keep up with the news to participate in conversations with their consumers. In emphasizing "decency," they also try to keep their old and often beat-up cars clean, even after taking dirt roads before arriving in the cities. In the end, the line separating carefully choreographed performances of trustworthiness and decency disappears, and these performances meld into farmers' identities and become a source of pride and self-esteem.

Like the New Yorkers engaging with milk's microbial cultures, the participants of raw milk networks in Lithuania are acutely aware of the political and ethical dimensions of raw milk consumption. The material qualities of milk—its microbial cultures, unique tastes, colors, and creaminess—cannot be separated from how people think about decency, self-respect, and even power. This is because milk is never just a biological reality. It is tied to the ways in which ideas about risks, cleanliness, and worthiness are articulated.

RAW MILK BATTLES: RIGHTS, CHOICE, AND
COMMUNITY AS SOURCES OF SOCIAL STATUS

In the same way as half a century ago, when consumers defended their right to have access to raw milk in the United States, today's consumers cast their participation in informal raw milk networks in New York in the language of rights to access and consume foods that are healthy and culturally valued, with choice as the undergirding principle of their arguments. Framing this issue in terms of universal rights, particularly rights to sustenance through nutritious food, participants in raw milk economies imply that raw milk is an indispensable food that everyone should have a right to access. In this context, numerous participants invoke and often even quote the passage from the International Covenant on Economic, Social and Cultural Rights at the United Nations that establishes access to adequate food as a basic human right: "Right to adequate food is a human right, inherent in all people, to have regular, permanent and unrestricted access, either directly or by means of financial purchases, to quantitatively and qualitatively adequate and sufficient food corresponding to the cultural traditions of people to which the consumer belongs, and which ensures a physical and mental, individual and collective fulfilling and dignified life free of fear" (Food and Agriculture Organization of the United Nations 2012).

In the raw milk community in the United States, the right of access to nutritious and culturally valued food is one of the most frequently cited justifications for legalization of raw milk sales across state lines. Such an emphasis on human rights is usually coupled with claims about the freedom of choice, or "food freedom." For example, in his evocatively titled article, "Pasteurization without Representation," Corby Kummer (2010) writes poetically, "'Food Freedom' . . . is reminiscent of the motto on New Hampshire license plates, 'Live Free or Die,'" equating the notion of consumer rights with those of U.S. citizens. This quote also links food freedom with the nation-building project, invoking a patriotic ethos.

Given the appeal of consumer rights to the general public in the United States, the raw milk cause often gets picked up by groups and individuals across the wide political spectrum, ranging from the Far Right to the Far Left. Representative Ron Paul, for one, has repeatedly introduced a bill allowing interstate shipments. The most recent bill, called Raw Milk Freedom Bill, was introduced in 2011. Explaining his motivations for such legislation, Ron Paul asks rhetorically: "How much freedom do we have if we can't even drink unpasteurized milk?" (2011).

In addition to libertarian appeals to freedom, food sovereignty is also frequently invoked among food and environmental activists who challenge current policies that are seen as serving the interests of the agricultural industry rather than consumers and small producers. In one such case recently, the Farm-to-Consumer Defense Fund, which operates as an extension of the Weston A. Price Foundation, an advocacy group that promotes healthy food, including raw milk consumption, filed a lawsuit against the Food and Drug Administration challenging the Pasteurized Milk Ordinance, which prohibits raw milk sales across state lines. The case was dismissed, but the order issued by the federal district judge caught public attention and it was interpreted as a perfect example of "the draconian views of the agency [FDA] on food freedom" (Farm-to-Consumer Defense Fund 2012).

While in the media heated political debates have come to define raw milk networks, participants in networks in New York are taking a much more nuanced approach to autonomy and individual rights. In discussing consumer rights, they simultaneously advance collective agendas, suggesting that the value of raw milk economies lies not only in the advancement of individual rights agendas but also in rich social interactions and lifestyles defined by care for others.

Indeed, although most of the conversations I had with consumers started with common explanations for why raw milk was better than conventional pasteurized milk, every story inevitably ended with references to the social life surrounding raw milk consumption. In one such conversation, a former raw milk producer in Vermont articulated this sentiment particularly poignantly, arguing that what matters in raw milk networks is not only milk but "people" and "relationships." Another informant emphasized the importance of the "broader community."

As such, some raw milk networks are organized as tight communities, where many know not only the names of others but also the history of transactions. In addition to exchanging milk for cash, raw milk networks function as spaces for other sorts of exchanges, including exchanges of knowledge, skills, goods, and services, and as places for finding a sympathetic listener who serves one's emotional needs. One consumer told me that she uses her raw milk club as a site for "freecycling," or swapping household items ranging from furniture to dishes to children's toys. At times, it seems it is almost impossible to disentangle where the raw milk network ends and other socioeconomic arrangements begin.

In addition to the embeddedness of raw milk economies in social relations, participation in these alternative food procurement systems is tied to the broader socialization patterns of consumers and their identities as citizens. For consumers, raw milk fits in their green lifestyles and care for both immediate and distant others. Many participants speak about volunteering, being involved in environmental NGOs, and contributing to what they call their "fair share" of activism by writing posts online, attending events, and organizing local community initiatives.

Louisa's case highlights the range and scale of activities through which members of raw milk clubs participate in the broader public debate. Louisa is trained in environmental sciences, and earlier in her career she was employed at the Environmental Protection Agency. She is now actively involved with an NGO that focuses on water protection, particularly on mobilizing public opinion on hydraulic fracturing in the Northeast. She contributes to the NGO's blog and also helps with writing grants and organizing community initiatives.

Louisa says that growing up on a farm had the greatest influence on her life decisions, and although she stopped consuming raw milk in college because it was difficult to obtain, she went back to it soon after starting her family. She remembers that she did not have to look for raw milk when she and her husband moved to the area. "It all happened naturally," as she was already socializing with the "environmental types" who were members of milk-buying clubs. While she values the connections she makes with people who are like her, she also says she appreciates the opportunity to meet people from different backgrounds, particularly those who have arrived at raw milk clubs through their religion, friendships, education, political beliefs, or out of pure curiosity. Like many other participants in these networks, she emphasizes that alternative-provisioning economies are an expression of care for the nonhuman environment, society as a whole, and the well-being of immediate family and community members. Moral orientation toward others and the sense of active engagement in local and global issues thread through the interviews with Louisa and many others. Through these articulations of care, they find fulfillment and create meaning, justifying their lifestyle choices.

To highlight the significance of care, it may be worthwhile to recall Annemarie Mol's (2008) work on health care (also see Curry 2002; Tronto 1993). Mol has drawn a conceptual distinction between the "logic of care" and the "logic of choice," particularly in relation to sociality. Providing numerous examples from diabetes clinics, Mol suggests that care is oriented toward others, while choice is inherently individualist. In her definition, care is about the entanglements of different social actors: "The logic of care does not start with an individual, but with collectives. A variety of them. Patients who present themselves in the consulting rooms are members of families, colleagues, live in a street, so on. It may be hard to work to disentangle people from their collectives sufficiently for the care that they individually need" (58). Mol's articulation of care as a set of messy, multidirectional social relationships stands in stark contrast to the individualist choices and self-interest-driven behaviors that scholars studying consumer culture have observed. For example, in her analyses of the emergence of industrialized organic dairies in the United States, DuPuis (2000, 2002) contends that health and environmental risk concerns play a key role in consumers' choice to buy organic milk as they refuse the intake of hormones and antibiotics found in milk produced on conventional farms. By seeking to protect one's body against possible pollution by toxins in food, DuPuis (2000) argues, consumers exercise the politics of "not in my body." Similarly, focusing on bottled water consumption, Szasz (2007) defines such practices as "inverted quarantine," suggesting that what consumers achieve when consuming green products is a shield from environmental risks as well as a sense of autonomy.

While it is true that the New Yorkers I interviewed seek to protect their bodies from the chemicals and hormones that are used routinely in industrialized dairy production, their explicit emphasis on care and their immersion in collectivities surrounding raw milk networks suggest that there is more to alternative self-provisioning schemes than policing the boundaries of food intake. And while some consumers join these networks with the goal of protecting their bodies, they also willingly open themselves to the workings of complex microbial cultures and messy social relations, a move that evokes a qualitatively different ethical orientation to nature and society.

As in New York raw milk circles, where consuming raw milk is considered safer than routinely exposing one's body to industrial foods and subjecting oneself to consumer lifestyles, participants in raw milk networks in Lithuania are also challenging biological definitions of risks. From the perspective of poverty-driven economies, the microbial risks associated with raw milk consumption seem insignificant compared with the risks of living on the edge of subsistence, and participants are able to "neutralize" these risks by simply pasteurizing the milk in their homes. In this sense, the dairy markets are operating as economic risk-sharing networks in which the lower profits of dairy sales are outweighed by the stability of social relations ensuring future incomes, however small those incomes may be (Mincyte 2012, 50).

Such an approach to collective risk management is reminiscent of the moral economy of the peasant described in the writings of E. P. Thompson (1971) and James C. Scott (1976, 2005). In their analyses of why poor groups rebel against the established social and economic order, they use the term "moral economy" to explain the methods that people use to spread the risks of falling below the level of subsistence and potentially into famine. Their illuminating examinations of bread riots in England and Southeast Asia show that moral economies operate as systems of sharing risks across social classes and that the breaking of these networks pushes people to protest with all means possible.

Even though economic hardships across Eastern Europe have rarely erupted into the kinds of significant social unrest and protests that Thompson (1971) and Scott (1976) describe, there is a prevailing sense that the moral contract between the Europeanizing Lithuanian state and its poorest citizens has been breached. Indeed, with 20.2 percent of the population at risk of poverty, Lithuania ranks near the top of the list of the most vulnerable countries in Europe, between Greece (20.1 percent) and Spain (20.7 percent) (Eurostat 2013). More important, the most recent data suggest that inequality in the distribution of income in Europe is highest in Lithuania, and it also ranked first in the EU in terms of the depth of poverty.[3] In the context of these structural inequalities, participants in the alternative raw milk economies are painfully aware that they belong to the lowest rungs of this unequal society. It is not surprising that they are constructing themselves not so much as the subjects

I have also argued that raw milk networks emerge as rich sites where various commodities, services, skills, and ideas—not only milk—are traded, gifted, shared, and exchanged, and where new subjectivities are produced. Through participation in raw milk networks, consumers not only gain access to the food they seek, but a wider range of social and economic activities are opened for them as well. In both cases, in New York and Lithuania, raw milk networks operate as the fulcrum for new relationships, exchanges, and subjectivities. More broadly, I have shown that the ways in which consumers justify their actions and define their place in society signal the emergence of particular collectivities in which care for others emerges as the organizing principle for social and economic relations. This emphasis on care and engagement with the material environment constitutes an important break from narratives about consumer choice—and consumer society—as ultimate sites where transformations toward a more sustainable future can take place.

NOTES

1. Names and other identifying information have been changed to protect the identity of the informants.
2. A recent survey by the U.S. Centers for Disease Control and Prevention cites an exceptionally high number of the U.S. population, 3 percent, as raw milk consumers (CDC 2006–7, 14). Because the sample was limited to ten states (California, Colorado, Connecticut, Georgia, Maryland, Minnesota, New Mexico, New York, Oregon, and Tennessee), the reliability of this report is in question, yet these results are suggestive of the prevalence of raw milk consumption in at least these states.
3. In terms of the depth of poverty, the relative median at-risk-of-poverty gap in Lithuania was one of the widest in the European Union, at 28.7 percent (Eurostat 2013).

REFERENCES

Alkon, Alison H. 2008. "From Value to Values: Sustainable Consumption at Urban Farmers Markets." *Agriculture and Human Values* 25 (4): 487–98.

Alkon, Alison H., and Julian Agyeman, eds. 2011. *Cultivating Food Justice: Race, Class, and Sustainability*. Boston: MIT Press.

Barnett, Clive, Paul Cloke, Nick Clarke, and Alice Malpass. 2005. "Consuming Ethics: Articulating the Subjects and Spaces of Ethical Consumption." *Antipode* 37 (1): 23–45.

Barr, Stewart, and Andrew W. Gilg. 2007. "A Conceptual Framework for Understanding and Analyzing Attitudes towards Environmental Behaviour." *Geografiska Annaler* 89 (4): 361–79.

Barr, Stewart, Andrew W. Gilg, and Nicholas Ford. 2005. "The Household Energy Gap: Examining the Divide between Habitual and Purchase-related Conservation Behaviours." *Energy Policy* 33 (July): 1425–44.

Carfagna, Lindsey B., Emilie A. Dubois, Connor Fitzmaurice, Thomas Laidley, Monique Ouimette, Juliet B. Schor. and Margaret Willis. Forthcoming. "An Emerging Eco-habitus: The Reconfiguration of High Cultural Capital Practices among Ethical Consumers." *Journal of Consumer Culture.*

CDC (Centers for Disease Control and Prevention). 2006–7. *Foodborne Active Surveillance Network (FoodNet) Population Survey Atlas of Exposures.* Atlanta: U.S. Department of Health and Human Services, Centers for Disease Control and Prevention. http://www.cdc.gov/foodnet/surveys/FNExpAtlo3022011.pdf (accessed January 20, 2013).

———. 2011. "Questions and Answers." http://www.cdc.gov/foodsafety/rawmilk/raw-milk-questions-and-answers.html (accessed October 11, 2012).

Curry, Janel M. 2002. "Care Theory and Caring Systems of Agriculture." *Agriculture and Human Values* 19 (2): 119–31.

Dubuisson-Quellier, Sophie, Claire Lamine, and Ronan Le Velly. 2011. "Citizenship and Consumption: Mobilisation in Alternative Food Systems in France." *Sociologia Ruralis* 51 (3): 304–23.

DuPuis, E. Melanie. 2000. "'Not in My Body': rBGH and the Rise of Organic Milk." *Agriculture and Human Values* 17 (3): 285–95.

———. 2002. *Nature's Perfect Food.* New York: New York University Press.

DuPuis, E. Melanie, and David Goodman. 2005. "Should We Go 'Home' to Eat? Toward a Reflexive Politics of Localism." *Journal of Rural Studies* 21 (3): 359–71.

Eurostat, European Commission. 2013. "Income Distribution Statistics." http://epp.eurostat.ec.europa.eu/statistics_explained/index.php/Income_distribution_statistics#At-risk-of-poverty_rate_and_threshold (accessed October 27, 2013).

Farm-to-Consumer Defense Fund. 2012. "Press Releases," April 4. http://www.farmtoconsumer.org/press/press-FDA-lawsuit-dismissed.htm (accessed June 27, 2012).

Food and Agriculture Organization of the United Nations. 2012. *The Human Right to Adequate Food,* December 10. http://www.fao.org/righttofood/principles_en.htm (accessed January 14, 2013).

Goodman, David, Melanie E. DuPuis, and Michael K. Goodman. 2011. *Alternative Food Networks: Knowledge, Practice and Politics.* London: Routledge.

Griskevicius, Vladas, Joshua M. Tybur, and Bram Van den Bergh. 2010. "Going Green to Be Seen: Status, Reputation, and Conspicuous Conservation." *Journal of Personality and Social Psychology* 98 (3): 392–404.

Guthman, Julie. 2004. "The Trouble with 'Organic Lite' in California: A Rejoinder to the 'Conventionalisation' Debate." *Sociologia Ruralis* 44 (3): 301–16.

Harboe Knudsen, Ida. 2012. *New Lithuania in Old Hands: Effects and Outcomes of Europeanization in Rural Lithuania.* London: Anthem.

Hardy, Charlie L., and Mark Van Vugt. 2006. "Nice Guys Finish First: The Competitive Altruism Hypothesis." *Personality and Social Psychology Bulletin* 32 (10): 1402–13.

Hedlund, Stefan. 1989. *Private Agriculture in the Soviet Union.* London: Routledge.

Holt, Douglas B. 1998. "Does Cultural Capital Structure American Consumption?" *Journal of Consumer Research* 25 (1): 1–25.

Jackson, Peter, Neil Ward, and Polly Russell. 2008. "Moral Economies of Food and Geographies of Responsibility." *Transactions of the Institute of British Geographers* 34 (1): 12–24.

Jaffee, Daniel. 2007. *Brewing Justice: Fair Trade Coffee, Sustainability, and Survival.* Berkeley: University of California Press.

Johnston, Josée, Michelle Szabo, and Alexandra Rodney. 2011. "Good Food, Good People: Understanding the Cultural Repertoire of Ethical Eating." *Journal of Consumer Culture* 11 (3): 293–318.

Kummer, Corby. 2010. "Pasteurization without Representation." *Atlantic,* May 13. http://www.theatlantic.com/life/archive/2010/05/pasteurization-without-representation/56533/ (accessed October 15, 2011).

Langer, Adam J., Tracy Ayers, Julian Grass, Michael Lynch, Frederick J. Angulo, and Barbara E. Mahon. 2012. "Nonpasteurized Dairy Products, Disease Outbreaks, and State Laws—United States, 1993–2006." *Emerging Infectious Diseases* 18 (2): 385–91.

Lockie, Stewart. 2009. "Responsibility and Agency within Alternative Food Networks: Assembling the 'Citizen Consumer.'" *Agriculture and Human Values* 26 (3): 193–201.

McAfee, Mark. 2010. "The 15 Things That Pasteurization Kills." In *Real Milk.* http://www.realmilk.com/15-things-milk-pasteurization-kills.html (accessed January 14, 2013).

Mendelson, Anne. 2011. "'In Bacteria Land': The Battle over Raw Milk." *Gastronomica* 11 (1): 35–43.

Miller, Daniel. 1998. *A Theory of Shopping.* Ithaca, NY: Cornell University Press.

Mincyte, Diana. 2009a. "Everyday Environmentalism: The Practice, Politics, and Nature of Subsidiary Farming in Stalin's Lithuania." *Slavic Review* 68 (1): 31–49.

———. 2009b. "Self-Made Women: Raw Milk Consumption and Gender Politics in Post-socialist Lithuania." In *Food and Everyday Life in the Post-Social World,* ed. Melissa L. Caldwell, 78–100. Bloomington: Indiana University Press.

———. 2012. "How Milk Does the World Good: Vernacular Sustainability and Alternative Food Systems in Post-socialist Europe." *Agriculture and Human Values* 29 (1): 41–52.

Mol, Annemarie. 2008. *The Logic of Care: Health and the Problem of Patient Choice.* New York: Frances and Taylor.

Paul, Ron. 2011. "How Much Freedom Do We Have If We Can't Even Drink Unpasteurized Milk?" May 16. http://www.ronpaul.com/2011-05-16/how-much-freedom-do-we-have-if-we-cant-even-drink-unpasteurized-milk/ (accessed February 2, 2013).

Paxson, Heather. 2008. "Post-Pasteurian Cultures: The Microbiopolitics of Raw Milk Cheese in the United States." *Cultural Anthropology* 23 (1): 15–47.

Sadalla, Edward K., and Jennifer L. Krull. 1995. "Self-Presentational Barriers to Resource Conservation." *Environment and Behavior* 27 (3): 328–53.

Schor, Juliet B. 2010. *Plenitude: The New Economics of True Wealth.* New York: Penguin.

Schor, Juliet B., Don Slater, Sharon Zukin, and Viviana A. Zelizer. 2010. "Critical and Moral Stances in Consumer Studies." *Journal of Consumer Culture* 10 (2): 274–91.

Scott, James C. 1976. *The Moral Economy of the Peasant: Rebellion and Subsistence in Southeast Asia*. New Haven, CT: Yale University Press.

———. 2005. "Afterword to Moral Economies, State Spaces, and Categorical Violence Export." *American Anthropologist* 107 (3): 395–402.

Seyfang, Gill. 2006. "Ecological Citizenship and Sustainable Consumption: Examining Local Organic Food Networks." *Journal of Rural Studies* 22 (4): 283–305.

Sideris, Lisa. 2008. "Fact and Fiction, Fear and Wonder: The Legacy of Rachel Carson." *Soundings: An Interdisciplinary Journal* 91 (3–4): 335–69.

Simmel, Georg. [1903] 1971. *Georg Simmel on Individuality and Social Forms*. Ed. Donald N. Levine. Chicago: University of Chicago Press.

Starr, Amory. 2010. "Local Food: A Social Movement?" *Cultural Studies/Critical Methodologies* 10 (6): 479–90.

Stuart, Diana, and Michelle R. Worosz. 2012. "Risk, Anti-reflexivity, and Ethical Neutralization in Industrial Food Processing." *Agriculture and Human Values* 29 (3): 287–301.

Szasz, Andrew. 2007. *Shopping Our Way to Safety: How We Changed from Protecting the Environment to Protecting Ourselves*. Minneapolis: University of Minnesota Press.

Thompson, Craig J., and Gokcen Coskuner-Balli. 2007. "Enchanting Ethical Consumerism: The Case of Community Supported Agriculture." *Journal of Consumer Culture* 7 (3): 275–303.

Thompson, E. P. 1971. "The Moral Economy of the English Crowd in the Eighteenth Century." *Past and Present* 50 (1): 76–136.

Tronto, Joan C. 1993. *Moral Boundaries: A Political Argument for an Ethic of Care*. New York: Routledge.

Wadekin, Karl-Eugen. 1971. "Soviet Rural Society." *Soviet Studies* 22 (4): 512–38.

Welte, Teresa H. L., and Phyllis A. Anastasio. 2010. "To Conserve or Not to Conserve: Is Status the Question?" *Environment and Behavior* 42 (6): 845–63.

Wiley, Andrea S. 2011. *Re-imagining Milk*. New York: Routledge.

Valenze, Deborah. 2011. *Milk: A Local and Global History*. New Haven, CT: Yale University Press.

Viklund, Mattias. 2004. "Energy Policy Options—From the Perspective of Public Attitudes and Risk Perceptions." *Energy Policy* 32 (July): 1159–71.

Chapter 6 Sustainable Pleasure and Pleasurable Sustainability at Chicago's Experimental Station

Robert Wengronowitz

OUT OF THE ASHES, AN EXPERIMENT

In 2001, Connie Spreen stood helplessly by, watching as years of labor and resources poured out from the scorched building, much like the water used to extinguish the fire. When the Chicago Fire Department departed from the scene of what was declared an electrical fire, Spreen felt as though the firefighters took with them the coherence of this community space. Still dazed, she noticed Justin, a nine-year-old boy who was a regular at the bike shop, standing beside her. "Boy, Connie," Justin sighed, "I'm sure glad you and Dan [Peterman, Spreen's partner] aren't the kind of people that just pack up and go away."

Ten years later, Spreen now laughs at the memory of her reply: "Geez, Justin, I thought I might be until, like, right now. But if we're not, I guess we're going to have to go in and clean up." Spreen and Peterman would go to court sixteen times after the fire to secure the building's mixed-use status. Citing possible structural instability of the remaining walls, city officials required twenty-four-hour guard at the building throughout the first month of a lengthy clean-up process. The requirement seemed like an additional and potentially impossible burden; however, it became the catalyst for community celebration and affirmation. Neighborhood barbecues became a near-daily occurrence. "People came from all over the place, people we didn't know. At three in the morning, people were playing backgammon out in the street," Spreen explained. "It was a wonderful outpouring of support that fed the desire to rebuild it."

INTRODUCTION

Located on the border of two demographically divergent neighborhoods on the South Side of Chicago, the Experimental Station is a multifaceted, community-oriented venture that aims to repair and construct new social and ecological relationships. The Station seeks to be "a place where people and ideas feel welcome, where individuals matter, and where encounters and conversations are fostered that cannot or are unlikely to happen elsewhere" (Experimental Station 2012a). Re-formed as a nonprofit organization in 2006, Experimental Station's name comes from a Frank Lloyd Wright speech in which he envisioned the productive melding of art and technology under the same roof. The Station creatively sourced construction material—reused bowling alley flooring, for example—to reflect this integrative vision: a blend of the industrial and the organic, with tree trunks rising through its exposed concrete interior to shelter a number of grassroots projects.

Station initiatives range from Blackstone Bicycle Works (BBW), a program in which local girls and boys earn bicycles by accumulating credit hours practicing bicycle mechanics and repair, to reviving local food cultures and increasing food access through the 61st Street Farmers Market. The Station also hosts a team of independent journalists, cooking classes for those with limited financial resources, an on-site wood-fired oven for community bread-baking events, and an assortment of cultural events. Spreen explained the Station's holistic approach: "We seek to build an ecology" through which diverse initiatives function as "inter-related organisms in a living system that, over time, grows richer as it matures" (2010).

The Station "experiments" with cooperative ventures and local forms of provisioning that deviate from business-as-usual (BAU) economics to address social, cultural, and ecological concerns in an interconnected way. Located in Woodlawn—a food desert that ranks seventy-first out of seventy-seven

Chicago community areas in distance residents must travel, on average, to the nearest supermarket (Block 2010)—the Station provides a model of how collective space can be opened to meet social and ecological needs. It unites rural farmers and urban citizens, rich and poor, old and young, black and white, and varied groups such as musicians and journalists as they invest in the quality of their lives outside standard economic paradigms.[1]

Journalist and social activist Jamie Kalven, a longtime Experimental Station fixture, describes the site as "deeply composted in relationships." It derives its richness from people who are brought together by a whole range of interests and who may not have otherwise intersected. "A really important part of the initiatives," Kalven explained, "has to do with the regeneration of public space where neighbors find each other, are visible to each other, share news, engage in conversation, [and] hang out." This reflects the Station's self-described underlying "belief in the singular importance of hospitality as an institutional value" in order to provide "a nourishing habitat that invites inventiveness, creativity, critical thinking, collaboration, resource sharing, and community" (Experimental Station 2012a). The Station provides a powerful example of a multipronged approach that is greater than the sum of its parts. Individual projects matter, but the Station and its participants are deeply rooted and visibly express themselves in their community, city, and beyond. If larger segments of society are to move toward sustainability, the public spaces conducive to cultivating pleasure and the necessary social and ecological relationships will likely be derived from the gathering spaces created by groups like Experimental Station.

In this chapter, I examine the Station through the voices and experiences of those involved. How do participants make sense of their place? What kinds of values guide their actions? How do Station participants' experiences relate to a plenitude-based economy? Is the Station unique to its location, and if so, how? In answering these questions, I pay particular attention to the interconnected social, historical, and geographic contexts. The Station cannot be replicated in cookie-cutter fashion; rather, similar ventures require fine-tuning, attention to context, and willingness to adapt and try novel approaches, even if some projects do not work out.

This essay begins with a note on method, followed by a section on historical context, and then two substantive sections under the theme "Experimenting with Plenitude" discussing the farmers' market and the bike shop. I conclude with lessons and raise the concept of eco-pleasure, especially as a route for those with little economic capital, to help mainstream lifestyles of plenitude. While the Station is particular to its place, this study demonstrates how engaged individuals can renew shared interests in self-provisioning, intergenerational and cross-cultural engagement, and culinary celebration. Experimental Station remains outside of mainstream market channels, opening up an alternative economy alongside the larger complex of industrial manufacture and agricultural production. Yet those involved with the Experimental Station are not dropping out or off the grid; they are digging in more deeply. The ongoing and ever-developing work of Station participants is a reclaiming in this sense—not an act of defiant separatism so much as a celebratory coming together.

NOTE ON METHOD

This project is rooted in three years of multimethod research. Beginning in fall 2009, I collected data via participant observation at the 61st Street Community Garden and the 61st Street Farmers Market. At that point, I conducted eleven semistructured interviews with participants and organizers. A survey completed by gardeners and two surveys carried out at the market supplied respondents' reasons for participating as well as basic demographic information. A more detailed write-up of these methods, including appendices with the surveys, can be found in Wengronowitz 2010. Working with Gavin Van Horn in the fall of 2010, I conducted seven more semistructured interviews with key figures at the Station and participants in the various projects. I also participated at the market, bike shop, and cultural events including a community bread bake. More information on this project can be found in Van Horn 2011.

In addition to formal interviews, I have conducted more than thirty informal interviews with participants in various Station projects. In total, I have visited the market and bike shop approximately fifty times, aiming particularly at witnessing Station happenings in their natural settings. Videos recorded by the Invisible Institute (a journalistic program housed in the Station that seeks to raise issues and give voice to populations made "invisible" by other media), letters to the editor, and online commentary regarding projects at the Station all played a useful role in the analysis. I used an iterative process in the data analysis—listening to interviews, transcribing, coding, discussing with Van Horn and others, recoding, more visits to the site, additional interviews and participation observation, and repeat. Interviewees consented to the use of their names.

CONTEXT: FROM THE BUILDING TO THE EXPERIMENTAL STATION

The physical structure that serves as a hub for Experimental Station's participants and programs has a storied history dating back to the 1960s. Dan Peterman, who cofounded the Station with Spreen, would later say it had "probably the largest fleet of beat-up old VW buses anywhere outside of the Third World" (Wang 2004, 8). The Station's ethos stems largely from a loose-knit group of do-it-yourselfers who inhabited what was then called "the Building." The Building and its creators were products, to some degree, of their temporal, geographic, social, and political context. Therefore, before describing the Building's history, it is useful to consider the general history of Wood-lawn, on whose northern edge the Station is located.

Woodlawn is located approximately seven miles south and slightly east of Chicago's "Loop" (downtown). It began as a small community of mostly Dutch farmers, happily serviced by the Illinois Central Railroad beginning in 1862. It grew slowly until the development boom associated with the 1893 World's Columbian Exposition. Beating out New York City to host the fair, Chicago's elite chose Jackson Park directly east of Woodlawn to develop the "White City"—a moniker rooted in the white neoclassical buildings but one that speaks volumes to then-prevailing attitudes of white superiority. The mile-long Midway Plaisance, directly north of Woodlawn, maintained attractions, including "primitive" civilizations leading to the White City. After the fair, Woodlawn became a relatively quiet residential neighborhood with businesses along Sixty-third Street (the east-west street three blocks south of the Plaisance) and a large racetrack and amusement park in Washington Park to the northwest. Middle-class and University of Chicago–affiliated whites then inhabited the area (Rydell 2004; Seligman 2005).

Contemporary Chicago remains the most segregated of the ten largest metropolitan areas in the United States (Glaeser and Vigdor 2012), but figures on segregation in early twentieth-century Chicago are particularly striking. Prior to 1890, there were scattered settlements of black Chicagoans; however, by 1900 these areas merged into a three-mile-long by quarter-mile-wide area surrounded by railroad tracks (Hirsch 1998, 3). Concentration and expansion of this "black belt" continued and by 1930, fully two-thirds of black Chicagoans lived in areas that were 90 percent black (4). By 1940, almost half of black Chicagoans lived in areas that were 98 percent black, leading sociologist David Wallace to describe the segregation as "very close to being as concentrated as it could get" (cited in Hirsch 1998, 4).

The black belt did not develop naturally. Race itself is a social construct, a fiction that enables power, privilege, and oppression, as it did in Chicago (Slocum 2010). In the 1920s, Woodlawn businesspeople, the Woodlawn Property Owners' League, and University of Chicago officials united in promoting racially restrictive housing covenants that legally enshrined de facto segregation (Drake and Cayton [1945] 1993; Seligman 2005). Washington Park, in the northwest of Woodlawn, was a critical area for these covenants. Drake and Cayton ([1945] 1993, 184) describe it as a "white island" that stood as a "bastion against the Negro influx into areas adjacent to the middle class residential neighborhoods surrounding the University of Chicago." In 1940, the Supreme Court ruled restrictive covenants unenforceable; however, by that time, the Great Depression had already enticed property owners and renters to violate the covenants so that the area was "80 percent Negro. By 1945 there were practically no white families in the area" (187).[2]

Jack Spicer, a well-known area activist and landscaper, explained aspects of this racial turnover. "We had extreme cases of arson going on all over Woodlawn as the neighborhood turned African American. Many of the landowners wanted out and they couldn't sell their property. So there was wholesale arson going on to burn them for insurance money." Confirming this account, Drake and Cayton ([1945] 1993, 188) heard the following from white residents in the late 1930s: "I'm not prejudiced, but I'd burn this building down before I'd sell it to any damned Nigger." By 1970, Spicer explained that Woodlawn "was essentially a wasteland" as the remaining residents were left in isolation from needed material and social resources.[3] Sociologist Loïc Wacquant describes how Woodlawn became filled with poverty and hopelessness. Urban renewal in the 1950s, gang wars in the 1960s, high rates of unemployment, and dwindling resources for social services united to "complete Woodlawn's transformation into an economic desert and a social purgatory" (2003, 19).[4]

This purgatory was the Woodlawn that University of Chicago student activist Ken Dunn found when he arrived in 1967. Dunn had a deep appreciation of the importance of sustainable human-land relationships, an attitude cultivated by his experiences as part of an Amish Mennonite community in Kansas. Dunn explained the community's basic principles as follows. "Care for the soil, care for the plants that grow in the soil, care for the animals that feed off the plants. Then, you care for the community that is built on all of the above." This kind of relational thinking informs Dunn's work and remains foundational to the Station.[5]

When Dunn arrived at the university, he was struck by the inequalities between resource-deprived Woodlawn and resource-rich Hyde Park. Reflecting the idea "that no resource should go to waste," including human resources, he attempted a modest, grassroots-level project to begin addressing these inequities. He approached five men drinking next to a bottle-strewn parking lot and asked if they would help him sort the glass for recycling. They agreed, and Dunn later returned with $2.75 for each man. This was a decent wage for an hour's labor in 1967, a judgment affirmed when the men asked, "Where do we work tomorrow?" Thus the Resource Center (a precursor to Experimental Station) was born. By 1975, operations had grown substantially, requiring a permanent building. Dunn pooled his savings with those of thirty friends and acquaintances involved in the recycling activities. Locating a building occupying the northeast corner of Sixty-first Street and Blackstone Avenue, he offered a third of the asking price. As evidence of the poor real estate and economic conditions, the owners accepted, and the Resource Center moved into the Building.

A variety of programs took root through the 1970s and 1980s. Graduate students who could not afford to repair their cars donated them to the Resource Center. These vehicles helped collect recyclables and soon became the fleet of a car-sharing program in which individuals paid $1 a day to use the repaired vehicles—a prescient program in light of the peer-to-peer car-rental schemes of the 2000s. Multiplying volunteers added a community garden, while other collaborative activities included a food cooperative, a woodworking shop, and a collection of mechanical tools for basic repairs. A steady supply of donated and salvaged materials developed into the Resource Center's "creative reuse" enterprise, which allowed participants to trade in three bags of anything they possessed for one bag of Resource Center materials. Roger Hughes, an art student at the University of Chicago in the early 1980s, explained, "It was people who needed stuff. People who needed a window: 'Oh, let's go look in the windows and doors room.' It was like a hardware store that was off the map, and if you were lucky you could get something that would perfectly suit your needs."

Activities at the Building flourished; however, this growth, the open-ended structure, and a lack of steady supervision eventually led to problems. Dunn explained how the car-sharing program became attractive to people outside of the community who did not understand that "these were old vehicles and had to be treated gently." Building organizers decided to discontinue the program. A reluctance to turn away those in need in the creative reuse program soon led to a large supply of undesirable items. Hughes elaborated on some of these issues: "Sometimes these rooms would get so full that they would spill into the room next to it. Sometimes the rooms would get a little scary and you didn't know what might jump out at you." Meanwhile, Mr. Wong, the auto repair expert, found himself nudged out into an adjacent alley because of the growing inventory of parts and tools.

Art student Dan Peterman, attracted to the creative reuse program but recognizing its problems, stepped up his involvement and began working for the Resource Center. Hughes explained that Peterman and Dunn "operate in the same kind of sphere. . . . That relationship went on for a long time, and it was a mutual one too, because Dan was salvaging, really, the building that was falling apart." Dunn sold the Building around 1996, "when it was clear [Peterman] had the same vision we had, and if he owned the Building he would spend all day and all night working on it instead of just the day!" Peterman and partner Connie Spreen took ownership of the Building, with many of the mixed-use activities continuing as interested individuals took the initiative to improve their own and others' quality of life. Early tenants included artist collectives, a custom furniture business, a group of independent social journalists and cultural critics who put together the *Baffler* magazine (currently seeing a rebirth at MIT Press) and other media, the Neighborhood Conservation Corps, and a bicycle shop that would later become Blackstone Bicycle Works.

EXPERIMENTING WITH PLENITUDE

Two facets of the Station are especially important, as they draw upon local talents and resources to meet unmet needs: investment in personal relationships at the 61st Street Farmers Market and the microentrepreneurial venture Blackstone Bicycle Works.[6] People participate in these projects with pleasure and joy. Such projects evolve organically, enriched by lessons accumulated over time at the Station. Participants come to the Station for one thing and discover something else. For example Gabrielle, founder of the raw vegan deli B'Gabs Goodies, which the Station recently began hosting, now teaches weekly cooking classes to adults and youth from the bike shop. They learn how to prepare healthy, regionally grown fruits and vegetables, often using foods purchased at the 61st Street Market. The web of relationships at Experimental

Station grows, weaving new patterns as lines of interest intersect with one another. These relationships, Spreen observed, "lead to a rich civic life" by connecting people to place and to one another.

61st Street Farmers Market

Corey Chatman, a staff member at the Station who grew up in the area, likened finding decent food in Woodlawn to trying to find the Loch Ness Monster: "Just to the north of us we have one of the top twenty schools in the nation. Just to the south, we have a major food desert in Woodlawn. We have vacant lots. If there's any store, there's a liquor store on one corner, then there's a currency exchange, and then there's another liquor store." The market directly increases food access while it also helps bridge difference by providing space for Woodlawn and Hyde Park residents to come together in a positive environment. Spreen explained, "It's literally bringing those two neighborhoods together. [When] you're in the middle of the market, you are connecting those two neighborhoods." As residents "overcome anonymity" at the market, they celebrate difference while they improve diets and support a more sustainable agriculture.

Reviewing research on food access, Larson, Story, and Nelson (2009) found that individuals with greater access to supermarkets and lesser access to corner stores tend to have healthier diets and lower levels of obesity. Supermarkets abandoned areas such as Woodlawn long ago in a process McClintock (2011) calls "demarcated devaluation," which is tangled in the racist mortgage practices, planning, development, industrialization, and deindustrialization that occurred in Woodlawn, West Oakland (McClintock's case), and other urban centers. Compounding the challenge of food access is the issue of food knowledge. As Spreen observed, in this area of the city "you can't just set up a market. You have to rebuild a food culture. You can't sell the stuff if people don't know what to do with it." Chatman put it more bluntly: "It's one thing to buy some great product at the market, but you take it home and you think, 'What the hell am I going to do with it?'"

Developing a food culture is one way of figuring out what to do with the food. The term is shorthand for an understanding of food that recognizes its powerful cultural, symbolic, and social elements. The market's motto, "Connect with your food," expresses the goal of fostering food cultures that can also be useful in bringing different kinds of people together. Barbara Kingsolver describes how food cultures distill the collective wisdom regarding the many ways people consume various combinations of plants and animals. "Living without such a culture," she adds, "would seem dangerous" (Kingsolver, Kingsolver, and Hopp 2007, 16). Similarly the Station asks, "Can a culture be healthy if its food is not?" and replies with "an emphatic 'no'" (Experimental Station 2012b). On any given Saturday from May to November, one may find lively conversations between neighbors, an exchange of garden knowledge between vendors and buyers, a dance workshop, live music, cooking classes and demonstrations, and education-oriented programs such as worm-composting ("vermiculture") workshops and dietician consultations. These programs underscore how developing a food culture—"connecting to food"—can act as a catalyst for healthy social reconnection.

Reflecting on his own experiences growing up in an Italian neighborhood that transitioned from local artisan foods to a food desert, market manager Dennis Ryan explained, "I don't think you can have culture without food . . . [because] one determines the other." Ryan's culinary experience helped shape this understanding. During his time in one of Chicago's premier culinary schools, he first encountered the notion of sustainable agriculture. For Ryan, this prompted a reorientation in his professional aspirations. His thoughts became increasingly dominated by the ways in which food cultures shape communities. These concerns have served as inspiration for his work at the market, which now includes expanding the "healthy farmers market workshop" at area schools. In 2012, six hundred elementary students took part in this free workshop, while seventy adults and children in Woodlawn took part in free healthy-cooking classes.

Through these workshops, the market itself, and other developing relationships, market participants are developing their local "foodshed," a conceptual term based on the watershed that helps connect the "physical, biological, social, and intellectual components of the multidimensional space in which we live and eat" (Kloppenburg, Hendrickson, and Stevenson 1996, 41). Some market goers have found work as vendors for farmers, others lead cooking classes, and some are now finding ways to pursue careers in agriculture or culinary arts. For the farmers and vendors, the market has been a way to introduce new customers to their products. As participants engage socially at the market, they create a feedback loop between farmers struggling to keep land out of conventional agriculture and customers learning how their food choices influence the larger bioregion.

Market organizers knew that developing their local foodshed called for meticulous and inclusive planning. While most projects at the Station succeed or fail based on their own momentum, staff conducted feasibility studies to determine if a market was viable or whether some other option, perhaps a brick-and-mortar store, might be preferable. They chose the market because of its relatively low start-up costs and the opportunity to connect consumers with one another as well as with producers. Organizers hoped these connections would help lead to long-term viability. Community residents, Woodlawn Buying Club members (the organization has been in operation since 1998), community gardeners, and cooking and baking participants contributed to the planning process, which eventually resulted in postponing the launch for a year to allow for more networking. Since farmers depend on a reliable site with clientele willing to purchase their food, and patrons depend on access to high-quality, affordable, and culturally appropriate food, the extra year allowed for a better match between the two groups. For example, market organizers recruited two separate vendors to provide high-quality, pasture-raised lamb, goat, pork, poultry, and beef products. Meat is an especially important product in the consumption habits of low-income women (Wiig and Smith 2009, especially 1731–32).

Other factors may also be aiding the market's success. Crocket and Wallendorf (2004, 511) examined how normative political ideologies of African Americans function in "a large racially segregated Midwestern city." The authors find that, especially at a time when individuals are less active in the political arena itself, consumption takes on increasing importance as a site where consumers can demonstrate their political ideologies. The 61st Street Market is composed of roughly 65 percent European Americans, 25 percent African Americans, and 5 percent for both Latino Americans and Asian Americans. These data, however, are from 2009, and the market continues to attract an increasingly diverse customer base. Almost 37 percent of market patrons are men, a figure more than double that for self-identified food purchasers in another study (Beardsworth et al. 2002, 482). The market provides an option other than the "dominated alternatives" Crocket and Wallendorf (2004, 525) found, "symbolized by rotting fruit, green meat, and shelves without unit pricing in ghetto stores." One African American shopper pointed out that she especially appreciated the "more affordable" options provided by Growing Power, Will Allen's Milwaukee-based program that has operations in Chicago. The market provides an alternative space to purchase fresh, healthy foods, but it also opens an outlet for expression.

Kate Miller, who helps with market outreach, emphasizes the changes she has seen in the community. Whereas before the area was better known for its lack of food access, "drive-by shootings . . . and gambling in the alley," the market now provides a safe space for neighborly commingling, because "people are much more at ease with each other in a public space. They sit down and watch chef demonstrations together. Otherwise, they might not have contact with each other. It leads to conversation; people's kids interact." In this way—bringing different kinds of people together—the market provides a counterexample to the racism and classism long associated with farmers' markets and alternative-food outlets in general (Alkon and Agyeman 2011; Alkon 2012).

For market organizers, improving food availability in a low-income African American neighborhood has always been interdependent with food affordability. They took special effort to ensure the market accepted LINK to provide low-income patrons with increased access (Illinois LINK is the state's Supplemental Nutrition Assistance Program, SNAP, colloquially known as food stamps). The market has been a leader in this area, piloting Illinois' first "Double Value" program in 2009, which doubles LINK purchases up to $25 per week. Market organizers find that some two-thirds of customers discover the market via word of mouth, a process that seems to be working. Between 2008 and 2010, the market had a 1,000 percent increase in LINK-related purchases. In 2010, this translated to $10,000 worth of sales plus an additional $7,000 from the Double Value program. In 2012, the market made it possible for low-income residents to purchase $23,000 worth of food through LINK and the Double Value program.

Because of their success in increasing food access, market organizers joined Wholesome Wave Foundation and the Illinois Farmers Market Network to organize LINK Up Illinois. Beginning in 2011, LINK Up provided technical expertise (LINK uses a card that requires infrastructure many farmers' markets do not possess) and funding for Double Value to twenty markets. By 2012, LINK Up made it possible for low-income residents to purchase $220,000 worth of foods at thirty-seven markets throughout Illinois, and there are plans for further expansion to seventy-five markets by 2014. "Food should not be a class thing, but unfortunately because everything is so tied to the dollar it's hard not to be," Ryan observed. From his perspective, LINK "levels the playing field," as reflected in the number of patrons from Hyde Park and Woodlawn, now nearly evenly divided. Ryan explained his current outlook this way: "The shoppers are happy. The farmers are happy. And people stay all day; they don't want to go. Whether you have a six-figure salary or you're on LINK, you can still enjoy these types of things. It's not just for the foodie world. It's for everybody."

The market may be influencing the community more broadly as well, with volunteer-led community gardens emerging nearby on abandoned lots. Kate Miller believes it offers opportunities for interaction, because the "cohesive, welcoming social atmosphere" has nurtured a strong and committed group of volunteers who help "develop the ecology" of different parts of the community. "We really wanted to create that kind of a place for farmers as well as for customers," Miller noted. "I think at a lot of other markets it's treated more like business as usual." Operating outside of the BAU paradigm makes the market much more than a place to buy and sell good food. As Spreen observed, "There's nothing anonymous about that market—that's why it works."

Blackstone Bicycle Works

Visiting the market, one may encounter a group of youths negotiating selling prices on refurbished bicycles. These bikes are the handiwork of Blackstone Bicycle Works, a program that in many ways exemplifies the Station's holistic mission. Through the "Earn a Bike" program, youth receive an ecologically sensitive means of transportation (and a new helmet and lock) while they learn the craft of bicycle maintenance and repair. This after-school and summer program provides valuable lessons and support beyond bicycle repair. Two parallel economies function at BBW—one based on credit hours and apprenticeship, the other on cash and bicycle repair and retail—allowing youth to take part in and understand different kinds of economic relationships. As nonfunctional bicycles are reborn and sold at reasonable prices, community residents can access an affordable form of transport that works to decrease ecological footprints. These activities weave into the fabric of the community as youth ride, repair, trade, and sell bicycles in the area. BBW provides children and young adults a supportive and pleasurable social ecology to develop relationships, learn practical skills, and enjoy material benefits.

Jamie Kalven understands bicycling as a better-founded form of environmentalism than one motivated by doing "your part to save a dying planet." In his view, bicycling itself is a constructive activity that "makes a community of resistance *visible to itself*":

> As more and more people are on the streets . . . it becomes easier and easier to see your way into something that might have initially been very hard to conceive even days or weeks before. And I think it's how social change works—both having these practical, concrete avenues for action that aren't grandiose, that are one step

at a time, that don't require you to leave your family and take a vow and throw everything aside, but on the other hand have a dynamic process that take[s] you down a path [so] that as you proceed you take on more and more. I've always thought there's a feedback loop between action and perception. . . . The more that you're able to act, the more that you're able to see; the more you're able to see, the more that you're compelled to act.

Station participants experience the kind of feedback loop that Kalven mentions. In the context of the bike shop, for example, one small part of the world changes as more youth take part, as more residents purchase refurbished bicycles and take them in for repair, and as more people come to know one another as fellow bicyclists, mechanics, and friends.

Youth at BBW learn bicycle repair, but experience this training as a broader means of empowerment. It leads sometimes to school projects and other times to cooking classes. According to Spreen, "They've developed a group mentality around kale." BBW participants perform bike tricks for their float at the famous Bud Biliken Parade, visibly expressing their prowess to the South Side community. Along with the public workshops and the Major Taylor Racing Club, BBW has no problem attracting youth. Spreen watches as these experiences form "the basis for them of a sense of civic life." Youth come to understand a mutual reciprocity between their work and the larger "rhythms" of the building, the people, and the events—they belong to the Station and the Station belongs to them.

The original motivation for a bike shop came in the early 1990s, when the Resource Center faced the practical challenge of making use of the scores of rundown bicycles collected through recycling operations. Dunn noticed that many children, especially boys who were less interested in gardening, had an affinity with danger and speed and imagined bicycles as an attractive alternative to gang life. In a place where few have their own reliable automobile and many regularly use public transportation, BBW provides people with the means to extend their mobility and, perhaps more important, empowers neighborhood youth with skills applicable beyond the bike shop, opening otherwise unavailable pathways. In this way, the bike shop represents another deeply practical deployment of extant yet underutilized resources for individual and community benefit.

Aaron Swanton became a BBW manager because he wanted to give young people the same kind of freedom he experiences as a cyclist. He noted that repairing bikes teaches kids to prevent waste: "You don't just throw something

Figure 6.1: Woodlawn youth with bicycle (© Andy Gregg / MQTphoto.com)

away . . . you can definitely make it better. . . . Enjoyment and pride comes from that." This creative reuse builds skills locally and reduces environmental impacts while also creating "our own kind of economy." BBW works like other bicycle shops in that it charges customers for labor and parts, but nearly everything else is different.

Individuals, community groups, and institutions donate approximately 150 to 200 bicycles a year, and BBW takes over from there. Youth can exchange two hours of work for a bike tire; twenty-five hours earn any available bike in the shop. As youth accumulate hours, parts, and bikes, they begin trading in and outside the shop. Some youngsters have started side businesses, selling bikes and accessories they accumulate. Informal nonmonetary forms of trade are organized under formal rules that control the beginning and end of the cycle so that one hour of work equals one credit hour, and credit hours can be exchanged for various items. These activities can have great significance in cash-constrained places such as Woodlawn. As BBW youth repair and up-grade bicycles "on the side," they often sell them, which highlights how this nonmonetary exchange system can result in a net cash flow into the community. In these ways, BBW provides an alternative economic space that otherwise might be filled by the drug trade.

Much of what happens at BBW relates directly to Dunn's idea that no resource should go to waste. Beyond using materials that otherwise would be discarded or remain idle, BBW provides a safe and stimulating environment for youth who also might otherwise be discarded by society. This safe structure is not school, which has a negative connotation to many of these youth (see Horton 2006, 144–45). BBW is shared public space with collective goals including completing school projects, catching up on bicycle back orders, and "tricking out someone's ride" (accessorizing or otherwise upgrading one's bicycle). Spreen highlighted just how important these simple activities can be: "When you know the story of a lot of kids who are at the shop . . . kids who don't have a bed, who sleep on the floor. . . . Grandparents taking care of them, barely . . . parents in jail, parents on drugs. . . . It's not all of them, but it's a lot. Here they can find a way into a place and carve out a space for themselves. They are known entities here."

One hundred eighty young people participated in the BBW program in 2010, with definite social ripples. One relationship developed with the University of Chicago's Office of Sustainability and its "recycles" bicycle-share program. Based on its reputation for quality work, nearby location, and use of refurbished bicycles, BBW collaborated with the university in the planning process and now maintains thirty-five bicycles on its behalf. This partnership led to the university hiring Kevin Applewhite to manage the program.

Kevin grew up close to the shop. After seeing friends bicycling and learning about BBW, Kevin said he picked up the paperwork, got his mom to sign it, and began at the shop the *same* day. Although he initially just wanted his own bicycle, he instantly "fell in love with the place" and remembers his first bike as "one of the biggest accomplishments" because "I did it with my own hands." Quickly becoming a regular at the shop, he "earned so many bikes that it was ridiculous, I didn't know what to do with them all." Kevin became a "youth apprentice" in a program started in 2009 that pays a handful of individuals to mentor other youth. By his junior year of high school, BBW offered him a full-time position. Thanks in part to the support he received at BBW, Kevin became the first male high school graduate in his family, and has now been with the university bike program for two years.

Kevin's story underscores how informal shop activities are just as important as its credit-hour economy. BBW currently provides after-school tutoring and there are plans to strengthen relationships with University of Chicago student tutors. That Kevin describes the group at BBW "like my other home, it's just like family," reveals that the benefits of involvement are not reducible to money management or mechanical expertise. He sees such an atmosphere as critical to his own journey and those of many of the neighborhood kids he knows:

> I wasn't with the right crowds before I came to the shop, which is the case with most of the kids that come to the shop. Most of the neighborhoods that we live in, there's a lot of gang activity, and because we see it every day, that's what we grow up to know. But coming here, you see that you don't have to do that. You can do anything. . . . I literally didn't know if I was gonna live to see eighteen, and I'm about to be twenty in twenty-one days. I'm ecstatic. Bringing kids to the shop, it does a lot for them, and the people here do a lot for them. You learn skills, not just being a mechanic on a bike—life skills. Kids look up to us. . . . I see kids—eight, nine years old—outside in the morning with gangbangers. Because they came to the shop, they turned around. . . . They have a childhood here.

In addition to bestowing the unquantifiable value of having a childhood, BBW functions as an integrated learning environment for the "lesson nobody learns by being told" (Jacobs 1961, 82). The lesson Jane Jacobs had in mind—essential to the social health of any community—is the experience of being cared for when no one is obligated to do so. The shop was described as a "safe space where you're gonna be treated well, with kindness" and a place "where people really care." During the summer months, the bike shop often has young people who stay all day because they enjoy the collegiality. BBW manager Chris Willard observed, "It's little things like being able to take a bike that's broken and do something simple. . . . That can completely change the way a kid looks at the world." I agree with Szerszynski (2006, 95–96), who usefully contrasts abstract learning with the "slow, steady development of craft skills and tacit knowledge" we see at BBW.

JT, another early participant in the apprenticeship program, explained how he "could tell what was wrong with a bike just by turning it a little bit and wiggling a couple things and turning the wheel." JT accumulated enough credit hours to "probably bankrupt the shop." He explained, "So I was just doing it because I liked it, simple as that, simple as that." JT appreciates hands-on work because he has been "knee-deep in grease" since he could talk, when his dad began teaching him mechanics. JT is, rightfully, one of the most celebrated individuals at the shop. However, his supportive relationship with his father and the benefits of a caring family equip him with resources unavailable to many of the other youth. Since Station activities build relationally, the different forms of capital possessed by some can open possibilities for others. This is why the Station works with local institutions—Chicago Public Schools, the university, local aldermen, community gardens—and this is why, with each passing year, the Station seems to affect more people in and beyond the community.

TyJuan Edwards embraced mentorship when he became a BBW employee in 2008. The bike shop has been open to some of his "crazy ideas," including rewarding youth with strong report cards. He sees his position as celebrating youth who "may never have been celebrated before." Not knowing his own father influenced his desire to be a positive male role model. Once youth know he cares, TyJuan sometimes works with their families and supplies his cell phone number for emergencies. He says this is the only reason he pays the phone bill. The lessons he tries to impart to kids in the shop is "to always play up," to be the bigger person, to have integrity, and to return negatives with positives and meanness with kindness.[7]

Bicycling connects youth to other Station programs, but it also provides a way for young people to connect directly and visibly to each other and the community. Swanton said he enjoys "mechanic-ing" because it provides kids with "that same kind of freedom" he experiences while bicycling. He finds greater possibilities for interaction when bicycling, relative to the car or public transit. Being "connected to the place where you are" makes bicycling fun "even in shitty weather." The shift in perspective achieved on a bicycle can lead to a new vision of one's surroundings. As Kevin notes, "[Nature's] not just about how big the forest is, it can be inside your neighborhood." The Station nurtures these ways of thinking that are simultaneously pleasurable and instrumental.

CONCLUSION

Four decades ago, counterculturalists had to remind themselves that simple living was to be "light, carefree, neat, and loving—not a self-punishing ascetic trip" (Belasco [1989] 2007, 66, quoting Gary Snyder). This point is just as important today, when the national discourse offers the same idea that sustainable lifestyles require sacrifice and austerity and are generally less enjoyable than more commercialized living. The Station shows how one need not defer gratification to practice plenitude; change can come in a deeply practical and practicable way. The Station presents a model of "eco-pleasure"—a paradigm of social change built on pragmatic, ecologically sensitive, pleasurable practices.

The Station increases community wealth in ways that are only loosely associated with money. Cultural knowledge, mechanical skills, gardening prowess, and culinary competence all blend to cultivate the eco-pleasures that can help mainstream plenitude. The Station hosts dramatic performances, musical productions, and public forums on wide-ranging issues that bring people together for public discourse. Events have included appearances by musician Gil Scott-Heron, the Hyde Park Community Players, energy scientist Rick Knight on the necessity for climate action, Ladies Ring Shout on the (mis)representation of black females, and scores more. Semiregular though well-established and well-attended community bread bakes draw a mix of people, from professional chefs to home amateurs, with the wood-fired oven serving as a common hearth for learning, conversation, and enjoyment.

In all of these ways, the Station serves an integrative function, reclaiming a healthy space for social and ecological engagement in an area long marked by tension. "Integrative and community activities should be driven by pleasure," explained Kalven. "One of the ways we think of Experimental Station is: put pleasure at the center of it. People come to a garden not as a project, but because they like to be outside, they like fresh food, they find the work interesting. People come into a space and meet other people because they want to hear the music, because they find the topic of conversation interesting and compelling; that is what urban life at its best offers and is driven by. . . . It solves some problems in [people's] lives, it enlarges things, and above all it brings pleasure and a greater sense of agency."

Kalven finds that environmental advocates' "crisis rhetoric" "deepens people's sense of paralysis." Sociologist Kari Norgaard (2006, 2011) examined this paralysis in the context of climate change, describing the "social organization of denial," a process that involves people understanding anthropogenic climate change but not wanting to contemplate the effect we are having on the planet. Practicing eco-pleasure resonates with Norgaard's findings: people like pleasure, not pain, and they will organize their thoughts and lives around that model. Such a basis for environmental concern (and for the possibility of its cultivation) is therefore not a "cause" to which one subscribes in competition with other concerns, but rather is embedded within the pleasures of self-provisioning, neighborhood celebration, do-it-yourself mechanics, and social engagement. Roger Hughes described his time at the Building: "Activities were happening with an air of just ordinariness and common sense. There was a lot of joy in it too; everybody did their part and it really worked." The Station has changed mentalities and daily practices so that sharing a ride with friends or bicycling has become the default approach.

In stark contrast to the "individualization of responsibility" (Maniates 2001, 33) prevalent in environmental discourse and what sociologist Andrew Szasz (2007) calls "inverted quarantine," the Station motivates collective solutions to problems. Inverted quarantine is an individual consumer solution to avoid contaminated water, toxins, pesticides, or other environmental dangers. Since one must possess the economic capital to purchase quarantine, this option is exclusionary. The Station chose to create the 61st Street Market because it addresses food access in a collective and public way. Yes, individuals purchase foods, but the Station has worked diligently to make foods affordable. The bike shop offers another collective solution available to low-income youth, who learn skills that have multiplier effects for the common good.

Perhaps the greatest tribute to the Station's effectiveness in cultivating eco-pleasure embedded in the neighborhood is the many people who tell Spreen that "this place feels like home." Indeed, the community bread bake I took part in stirred memories of family gatherings. We made (mostly) delicious bread in a process that would have seemed more taxing alone in our kitchens. The perception that Experimental Station is a second home, an extension of domestic space, draws people into its activities as participants instead of paying customers. (The bread bakes and nearly all the cultural offerings are free.) It provides a nurturing environment, a home place, for people to dwell richly in and connect socially, culturally, and ecologically with one another.

The 61st Street Garden represents a striking example of nurturing eco-pleasures; however, it also lucidly shows the disproportional power between BAU and plenitude. Various gardening activities began in the 1980s, but the 61st Street Garden itself began in 1999. Over the next decade, the garden flowered from 25 to approximately 145 ten-by-ten-foot plots cultivated by some 130 households. In early 2009, university officials announced they required the area to stage construction equipment for a new building. Gardeners united with writers and videographers from the Invisible Institute in a comprehensive campaign to highlight the garden's importance.

Throughout 2009, garden supporters took a pragmatic, inspired, but ultimately unsuccessful approach. They wrote letters in local newspapers, engaged with university administrators, worked with the local alderman, and talked with friends and neighbors to garner additional support. Although the university has itself deployed the rhetoric of civic and community engagement while it ramps up sustainability initiatives, it proceeded to destroy the garden, which had grown to be a community fixture working wonders on those same issues of sustainability. It was a sad irony when the university replaced the garden to build a LEED-Silver building (Silver is the third-highest ranking used by the U.S. Green Building Council's Leadership in Energy and Environmental Design program, which certifies buildings across a suite of environmental indicators). No one questioned the university's right to do what it pleased with land it owned; they questioned the university on its own values and mission. The university did offer to help move the garden, but Jack Spicer said this only showed its misunderstanding: "The soil *is not* a commodity in bales that can easily be picked up and moved." Writing in early spring, Kalven (2009) explained: "It takes a sustained act of imagination to comprehend how deeply *cultivated* [the garden] is. To see the density and intensity of attention invested in every square foot. The quiet drama of natural vitality given form by human care. The tangled roots of history, custom, and identity that make a particular place on the earth distinctive, nourishing, [and] a means by which people know who they are."

These kinds of sentiments, together with a video collection of gardeners' stories, did not change the university's plans. This story reminds us that sometimes even committed groups cannot overcome the growth paradigm. Kalven believes that the garden represented a case in which supporters did not possess a language to communicate accurately the garden's meaning. Perhaps further lessons, then, are the need to better understand why we value what we value and to improve our ability to express those understandings. Those who view land as commodity or, more generally, think under a BAU paradigm, do so for what seem to them sound reasons. Improved language will be necessary but might not be sufficient. In addition to collective solutions that celebrate eco-pleasure, the Station teaches us another lesson—we must articulate and demonstrate to ourselves and those not familiar with eco-pleasures that alternatives exist, they are being practiced, and they work.

Andrew Leyshon and colleagues (2010, 122) write, "By thinking the economy differently, we can see that what on the surface may appear to be a series of inconsequential small acts . . . actually draws attention to the real limits to capital. So while resistance may be hard work, may suffer as many retreats as advances, it is by no means futile." Indeed, the only way to recruit more individuals into a different way of thinking is by engaging with them. This can be difficult, if for no other reason than people seem busier than ever. This is why showing can be more effective than telling. Effective articulation and demonstration require a clear understanding of one's own values. Therefore, reflexivity is important in understanding how historical, sociocultural, political-economic, and ecological context all influence the ways people think and act, for these are conditions not entirely self-chosen, to paraphrase Marx.

Kate Miller explained, "I see the Experimental Station as an alternative in a heavily industrialized landscape—an alternative in relationships to each other, in relationships to land, in relationships to developing communities." Miller believes the Station "really provides people a way to envisioning and developing an alternative future to the one we're headed toward." As participants take root and mature in the Station, we see "community development and ecological development going hand in hand." The Station teaches us that we are social beings bound to come into conflict sometimes; different projects commence and conclude, usually not as envisioned. It takes time for people to find the benefits of eco-pleasures, of practicing plenitude. And since we are short on time, we had better get showing—and telling—everyone we can about a more rewarding, ecologically sane lifestyle within our grasp.

With the fire that threatened the integrity of Experimental Station now a receding memory, Spreen occasionally muses on the dynamics of change. If the Station ceases to be vibrant and fails to live up to its "experimental" name in responding to the needs and interests of the community, then it should not continue. "Nothing should go on forever just because it's been created"; however, Spreen emphasized, neither would she "want it to die a premature death." She has great hopes for the bike shop replicating itself as the kids grow up. The market will find new ways to thrive and help other markets across the state in meeting the needs of low-income people. This is all part of the constant evolution of Experimental Station. As a hub of innovation and a gathering space for diverse groups of people, the Station is a marketplace—not, I hasten to add, in the truncated and abstracted sense of the rise and fall of the Dow Jones Industrial Average but as a grounded gathering place where food, ideas, skills, music, and knowledge are the mediums of exchange for the eco-pleasures of plenitude and a verdant future.

NOTES

1. In uniting rural farmers with urban dwellers, the Station is following a similar alliance that helped create Chicago's first railroads, central to the city's development. See environmental historian William Cronon's impressive work on Chicago, including his discussion of the railroad's importance in "opening a corridor between two worlds [city and country] that would remake each other" (1991, 97).

2. Lorraine Hansberry's play *A Raisin in the Sun* is based on her family's experience moving into Washington Park, which resulted in the 1940 Supreme Court case *Lee v. Hansberry.* Writing on the twenty-fifth anniversary of *Raisin,* Weber (2011) averred that it "changed American theatre forever." *Hansberry* preceded the 1948 *Shelley v. Kraemer,* in which the Supreme Court unanimously held that judicial enforcement of racially restrictive covenants violated the Equal Protection Clause of the Fourteenth Amendment; however, the Court maintained that restrictive covenants themselves were legal (Rosen 2007).

3. Woodlawn was home to over eight hundred industrial and commercial establishments in the 1950s. By the mid-1990s, however, only approximately one hundred of these sites remained active (Wilson 1997, 129). At its peak in the early 1960s, Woodlawn had a population of eighty-one thousand. By 1990, the population stood at twenty-seven thousand and was among the poorest in Chicago, with a median family income at 59 percent of the median family income for the city as a whole (S. B. Friedman and Company 1998, 5).

4. For further analysis of Chicago's black ghetto see, for example, Wacquant 1994 and Wilson et al. 1988. See Mary Pattillo's *Black on the Block* (2007) for a masterful account of gentrification in a South Side Chicago neighborhood.

5. See Redekop 2000 for essays on Mennonite ecological thought and issues with sustainability in practice and Walbert 2002 for a more positive account of Mennonite environmental sensibility.

6. There is an abundant literature on social capital. See Bourdieu 1984 and Coleman 1988 for influential early work, though Jacobs 1961 might be the first use. See Putnam 1995, 2000 and Portes 1998 for a review of the literature.

7. "Playing up" is a borrowed sports phrase referring to playing in a game beyond one's age and/or ability.

REFERENCES

Alkon, Alison Hope. 2012. *Black, White, and Green: Farmers Markets, Race, and the Green Economy.* Athens: University of Georgia Press.

Alkon, Alison Hope, and Julian Agyeman. 2011. "Cultivating the Fertile Field of Food Justice." In *Cultivating Food Justice: Race, Class, and Sustainability,* ed. Alison Hope Alkon and Julian Agyeman, 331–47. Cambridge, MA: MIT Press.

Beardsworth, Alan, Alan Bryman, Teresa Keil, Jackie Goode, Cheryl Haslam, and Emma Lancashire. 2002. "Women, Men and Food: The Significance of Gender for Nutritional Attitudes and Choices." *British Food Journal* 104 (7): 470–91.

Belasco, Warren J. [1989] 2007. *Appetite for Change: How the Counterculture Took on the Food Industry.* Ithaca, NY: Cornell University Press.

Block, Daniel. 2010. Personal e-mail correspondence with author, April 13.

Bourdieu, Pierre. 1984. *Distinction: A Social Critique of the Judgement of Taste.* 11th ed. Trans. Richard Nice. Cambridge, MA: Harvard University Press.

Coleman, James. 1988. "Social Capital in the Creation of Human Capital." *American Journal of Sociology* 94 (supplement): S95–S120.

Crocket, David, and Melanie Wallendorf. 2004. "The Role of Normative Political Ideology in Consumer Behavior." *Journal of Consumer Research* 31 (3): 511–28.

Cronon, William. 1991. *Nature's Metropolis: Chicago and the Great West.* New York: Norton.

Drake, St. Clair, and Horace R. Cayton. [1945] 1993. *Black Metropolis: A Study of Negro Life in a Northern City.* Chicago: University of Chicago Press.

Experimental Station. 2012a. "About the Experimental Station." http://experimentalstation .org/about (accessed March 8, 2012).

———. 2012b. "What Is Food Culture?" http://www.experimentalstation.org/food-culture (accessed October 1, 2012).

Glaeser, Edward, and Jacob L. Vigdor. 2012. "The End of the Segregated Century: Racial Separation in America's Neighborhoods, 1890–2010." *Manhattan Institute for Policy Research* 66 (January). http://www.manhattan-institute.org/pdf/cr_66.pdf (accessed August 29, 2012).

Hirsch, Arnold R. 1998. *Making the Second Ghetto: Race and Housing in Chicago, 1940–1960.* Chicago: University of Chicago Press.

Horton, Dave. 2006. "Demonstrating Environmental Citizenship? A Study of Everyday Life among Green Activists." In *Environmental Citizenship,* ed. Derek Bell and Andrew Dobson, 127–50. Cambridge: MIT Press.

Jacobs, Jane. 1961. *The Death and Life of Great American Cities.* New York: Vintage Books.

Kalven, Jamie. 2009. "61st Street Community Garden at Risk." *The Invisible Institute,* March 30. http://www.invisibleinstitute.com/node/70/author (accessed October 27, 2013).

Kingsolver, Barbara, Camille Kingsolver, and Steven L. Hopp. 2007. *Animal, Vegetable, Miracle.* New York: HarperCollins.

Kloppenburg, Jack, Jr., John Hendrickson, and G. W. Stevenson. 1996. "Coming in to the Foodshed." *Agriculture and Human Values* 13 (3): 33–42.

Larson, Nicole, Mary Story, and Melissa Nelson. 2009. "Neighborhood Environments: Disparities in Access to Healthy Foods in the U.S." *American Journal of Preventive Medicine* 36 (1): 74–81.

Leyshon, A., R. Lee, and C. Williams. 2010. "Commentary 2." *Progress in Human Geography* 34 (1): 117–27.

Maniates, Michael F. 2001. "Individualization: Plant a Tree, Buy a Bike, Save the World?" *Global Environmental Politics* 1 (3): 31–52.

McClintock, Nathan. 2011. "From Industrial Garden to Food Desert: Demarcated Devaluation in the Flatlands of Oakland, California." In *Cultivating Food Justice: Race, Class, and Sustainability,* ed. Alison Hope Alkon and Julian Agyeman, 89–120. Cambridge, MA: MIT Press.

Norgaard, Kari M. 2006. "'People Want to Protect Themselves a Little Bit': Emotions, Denial, and Social Movement Nonparticipation." *Sociological Inquiry* 76 (3): 372–96.

———. 2011. *Living in Denial: Climate Change, Emotions, and Everyday Life.* Cambridge, MA: MIT Press.

Pattillo, Mary. 2007. *Black on the Block: The Politics of Race and Class in the City.* Chicago: University of Chicago Press.

Portes, Alejandro. 1998. "Social Capital: Its Origins and Applications in Modern Sociology." *Annual Review of Sociology* 24 (August): 1–24.

Putnam, Robert. 1995. "Bowling Alone: America's Declining Social Capital." *Journal of Democracy* 6 (1): 65–78.

———. 2000. *Bowling Alone: The Collapse and Revival of American Community.* New York: Simon and Schuster.

Redekop, Calvin, ed. 2000. *Creation and the Environment: An Anabaptist Perspective on a Sustainable World.* Baltimore: Johns Hopkins University Press.

Rosen, Mark D. 2007. "Was *Shelley v. Kraemer* Incorrectly Decided—Some New Answers." *California Law Review* 95 (2): 451–512.

Rydell, Robert W. 2004. "World's Columbian Exposition." In *The Encyclopedia of Chicago.* http://encyclopedia.chicagohistory.org/pages/1386.html (accessed August 28, 2012).

S. B. Friedman and Company. 1998. "Woodlawn Redevelopment Project Area: Tax Increment Financing Eligibility Study, Redevelopment Plan, and Project." City of Chicago, Department of Planning and Development. http://www.cityofchicago.org/content/dam/city/depts/dcd/tif/plans/T_065_WoodlawnRDP.pdf (accessed September 30, 2011).

Seligman, Amanda. 2005. "Woodlawn." In *The Encyclopedia of Chicago.* http://www.encyclopedia.chicagohistory.org/pages/1378.html (accessed August 28, 2012).

Slocum, Rachel. 2010. "Race in the Study of Food." *Progress in Human Geography* 35 (3): 303–27.

Spreen, Connie. 2010. "Letter from the Executive Director." *Experimental Station Newsletter* (Fall): 2.

Szasz, Andrew. 2007. *Shopping Our Way to Safety: How We Changed from Protecting the Environment to Protecting Ourselves.* Minneapolis: University of Minnesota Press.

Szerszynski, Bronislaw. 2006. "Local Landscapes and Global Belonging: Toward a Situated Citizenship of the Environment." In *Environmental Citizenship,* ed. Derek Bell and Andrew Dobson, 75–100. Cambridge, MA: MIT Press.

Van Horn, Gavin. 2011. "Civic Agriculture in Chicago." *Minding Nature* 4 (3): 26–44.

Wacquant, Loïc. 1994. "The New Urban Color Line: The State and Fate of the Ghetto in Postfordist America." In *Social Theory and the Politics of Identity,* ed. Craig J. Calhoun, 231–76. Cambridge: Blackwell.

———. 2003. *Body and Soul: Notebooks of an Apprentice Boxer.* New York: Oxford University Press.

Walbert, David. 2002. *Garden Spot: Lancaster County, the Old Order Amish and the Selling of Rural America.* New York: Oxford University Press.

Wang, Dan S. 2004. "Downtime at the Experimental Station: A Conversation with Dan Peterman." *Temporary Services* (September). http://www.temporaryservices.org/downtime.pdf (accessed September 26, 2011).

Weber, Bruce. 2011. "Philip Rose, *Raisin* and *Purlie* Producer, Dies at 89." *New York Times,* June 1. http://www.nytimes.com/2011/06/02/theater/philip-rose-broadway-producer -dies-at-89.html (accessed August 29, 2012).

Wengronowitz, Robert J. 2010. "Connecting with Your Food: The Social Impact of Community Based Agriculture." MA thesis, University of Chicago. Available from author.

Wiig, Kristen, and Chery Smith. 2009. "The Art of Grocery Shopping on a Food Stamp Budget: Factors Influencing the Food Choices of Low-Income Women as They Try to Make Ends Meet." *Public Health Nutrition* 12 (10): 1726–34.

Wilson, William Julius. 1997. "Towards a Broader Vision of Inner-City Poverty." In *Sociological Visions,* ed. Kai Erickson, 123–52. Lanham, MA: Rowman and Littlefield.

Wilson, William J., Robert Aponte, Joleen Kirschenman, and Loïc Wacquant. 1988. "The Ghetto Underclass and the Changing Structure of Urban Poverty." In *Quiet Riots: Race and Poverty in the United States,* ed. Fred R. Harris and Roger W. Wilkins, 123–54. New York: Pantheon Books.

Chapter 7 Why the Sustainable Economy Movement Hasn't Scaled: Toward a Strategy That Empowers Main Street

Douglas B. Holt

In *Plenitude*, Juliet Schor (2010) maps the twin breakdowns caused by the business-as-usual (BAU) economy: the acute ecological over-shoot problems created by an economy concerned only with eco-nomic growth and purposely ignorant of market failures, and what she predicts will be a growing problem of labor market dislocations and declining incomes. In response, she offers a call to arms pushing for socioeconomic transformation toward an alternative sustain-able economy. She develops particular rhetoric to do so, which she calls *plenitude.* Schor's goal in constructing the idea of plenitude is to make sustainable lifestyles a desirable alternative, directly challenging the notion that sustainability requires personal sacrifice. More broadly, her goal is to encourage the "bottom-up" diffusion of an alternative sustainable economy across the country, supplanting BAU.

I will use *Plenitude* as a prominent recent example of what I will call *sustainable economy movement strategy. Plenitude* joins similar calls by other leading activists in the sustainable economy movement (for example, Jackson 2009; McKibben 2007; Speth 2009), which have sought to frame sustainable economy in a way that will encourage citizens to give it a try. Considered within this campaigning literature, Schor's argument has a number of distinctive and notable aspects. But from the strategic viewpoint that I will argue here, what these campaigners have in common is more significant than their differences. These academics and activists illuminate the ecologically destructive contradictions of BAU and then call on citizens to consume less, work less, enjoy social life and build local community, pursue creative leisure time, and engage in self-provisioning. They write from within a taken-for-granted strategy paradigm that I find widely shared across the sustainable economy movement. This paradigm centers on the assumption that the best way to build the movement is to communicate leading examples of people enacting sustainable economy to inspire nonactivists to sign up to the movement's ideology and practices. This approach is very common too in environmental sustainability media: on Web sites like grist.org, in magazines like *Orion* and the *Utne Reader*, and in progressive newspapers like the *Guardian*. This book is another good example of this conventional strategy.

My concern is that sustainable economy movement strategy is not working. Over the past four years, the United States has experienced the most acute economic crisis since the Depression. Most Americans are very disenchanted with our economic system and are questioning deeply ingrained assumptions. It is hard to imagine a better opportunity to launch an alternative economy movement. Yet sustainable economy has not caught on. Arguably, the BAU economic ideology dominates the country in a more hegemonic manner today than it did a decade ago. And this lack of diffusion is not for lack of effort. A devoted contingent of activists and subculturalists has worked industriously to build the movement throughout this period. Rather, I will argue that the movement is applying the wrong strategy.

My goal in this chapter is to constructively critique this strategy, point out why it isn't working, and provide a framework and some suggestions for building a more effective approach. I build my argument by applying a marketing perspective to movements: What is the most opportune target for the movement? What is this target's worldview and life experience with respect to the movement's issues? What movement strategy will resonate powerfully with the target and compel its members to action? My hope is to instigate a new strategic conversation among activists who are committed to the sort of transformation that Schor envisions.[1]

In contrast to other chapters in this book, which consist of case studies of plenitude in practice, I want to step back and examine the central big-picture question raised by this book: What is the best strategy for diffusing sustainable economy at a scale that actually tips the balance away from BAU? While the cases provide valuable clues regarding the cultural, social, and phenomenological drivers of sustainable economy participation among activists, they do not provide evidence that the scaling of plenitude has been a success. One can find numerous small, local examples of sustainable economy throughout North America and Europe, but this has been true for at least four decades, as I outline below.

I argue that the sustainable economy movement has made a classic marketing mistake: it has (implicitly) chosen the wrong target and, therefore, has put most of its resources behind the wrong strategy. I place "implicit" in parentheses because, while I have no direct evidence, my reading of the movement's texts suggests that there has been little explicit strategizing, and so this strategic miscue is an unintended consequence of activists doing their best to diffuse the movement by trying to make their ideology attractive to others. My argument is multifaceted. So I begin with an outline to provide the reader with a road map for the analysis to come:

The movement today consists of a subculture of sustainable economy practitioners, some of whom are active campaigners. These countercultural activists pursue sustainable lives (in work, consumption, provisioning) to enact a global ecological ethos (sometimes expanded to include global social justice) similar to what is advocated in the sustainable economy literature mentioned above. This book contains a number of excellent case studies of this subculture.

The movement's sustainable economy ideology has resonated powerfully with members of modern bohemian subcultures (many of whom have joined the movement) and has become an increasingly important plank in bohemian ideology over the past four decades. By the late 1990s, the two subcultures had substantially merged (imagine two heavily overlapping circles in a Venn diagram) into what I will call *sustainable bohemia*. Participants in this sustainable bohemian subculture have been prolific entrepreneurs, launching many businesses grounded in sustainable bohemian ideology. These sustainable bohemia marketplace offerings have been immensely attractive to a significant fraction of America's upper middle class—the bourgeois-bohemians—which finds great symbolic value in them (here I adopt David Brooks's [2000] parodic but accurate term for this class fraction). So the market for sustainable bohemia ideology has exploded, largely driven by bourgeois-bohemian (bobo) consumption.

If bobos truly embraced sustainable economy, this would be a great result— precisely the mass diffusion of the movement that activists are trying to promote. After all, bobos are a significant percentage of the population on their own (perhaps 8 percent) and, more important, they are very influential both culturally and politically. So if bobos truly embraced sustainable economy, they would likely drive the transformation of the BAU economy. However, my research suggests that this is not the case. Most bobos embrace sustainable economy superficially, as consumption symbolism. They are unlikely to adopt sustainable lifestyles in significant percentages because they gain so much now from BAU. Likewise, they are unlikely to push for political and institutional challenges to BAU, since this would undermine their status and incomes. So from a strategic perspective, they are a dead end. The wrong target.

Yet because the sustainable economy movement strategy is premised upon showcasing great examples of sustainable living within the subculture, movement campaigning (such as in the books cited above) tends to replicate sustainable bohemia. This campaigning appeals to bobos as another mode of symbolic consumption, but it won't convert them.

Meanwhile, the movement's best prospects—the segment of Americans most likely to adopt sustainable economy—are members of a different socioeconomic class, what I will call the new "Main Street" class. Main Street lives are very different from those of bobos; they pursue different ideals and struggle with different problems. And so the sustainable bohemia rhetoric that resonates so powerfully with bobos doesn't connect at all with Main Street. This is a marketing problem I call a *cultural chasm:* the strategy that works best to win converts within the subcultural/activist population fails when applied to nonactivist citizens. The way to overcome this chasm, diffusing sustainable economy to Main Street, is to build a new campaign strategy that identifies with and is responsive to the everyday understandings and aspirations of Main Street. I offer one such example at the end of the chapter.

THEORY, DATA, AND METHODS

To make my argument, I adapt ideas from my prior work on what I term *cultural branding* (Holt 2004; Holt and Cameron 2010), which I have also applied to social movements (Holt 2012). My model draws from various sociocultural traditions in the social sciences and humanities, including cultural history, cultural sociology, cultural studies, and the cultural tradition in marketing called consumer culture theory (Arnould and Thompson 2005). The basic application of the model runs as follows. For the sustainable economy movement to resonate deeply and motivate collective action, it must: (1) target a group of citizens sharing the same socioeconomic circumstances; (2) address an acute cultural contradiction that is disrupting the target's identity projects; and then (3) propose an alternative that offers a compelling path to the substantial resolution of these collective tensions and anxieties.

My analysis focuses on social class–based segments, for reasons that will become apparent as the argument progresses. How Americans perceive the benefits of pursuing a sustainable economy, and thus how they respond to campaigning, varies dramatically by social class. The American population is demographically very diverse, and the sample in the qualitative research I report below reflects that diversity (across ethnicity, politics, religion, and sexual preference). However, in seeking out the most opportune target for sustainable economy strategy, these aspects of identity are far less important than their common social class thread.

For these purposes, it is useful to divide Americans into four segments (to which I've added rough percentages). I ignore the upper class as a direct target, since it constitutes such a small percentage of the total population—usually somewhere between .1 percent and 1 percent—while acknowledging its profound influence on consumerism (Schor 1999).

I. Professional-managerial class (20 percent)
    A. Materialist lifestyle (12 percent)

Upper-middle-class citizens whose lifestyle lines up closely with the usual critiques of American consumerism—conflating the American Dream with the pursuit of more and better stuff.

B. Bourgeois-bohemian lifestyle (8 percent)

Upper middle class also but high in cultural capital, well educated, living in urban metro areas and college towns and tend to be professionals (see Holt 1998; Holt and Cameron 2010). Bobos tend to be socially liberal, aligning with progressive social issues and environmentalism. Not all bobos are in the top economic quintile, and so they do not always fit intuitive portrayals of the "upper middle class." For instance, teachers, social service workers, and managers in the not-for-profit sector all tend to be bobos, yet they earn less than the national average for work requiring a college degree. However, their economic life chances are much more similar to their fellow four-year-college graduates than to the Main Street class below them: they work in secure occupations, usually with good benefits, within a competitive labor market, earning salaries significantly above the American average.

II. Main Street class (60 percent)

What I will term the new Main Street class combines social class groupings often separated into class fractions such as lower middle class, working class, and working poor. I rely upon recent socioeconomic portraits of class in the United States to forge this single metaclass grouping. Political and economic shifts over the past thirty years have organized society into two increasingly divergent classes: the professional-managerial class at the top and everyone else. As I briefly review below, the economic lives of people within this otherwise heterogeneous spectrum are increasingly alike, a tectonic shift that Paul Krugman (2007) calls "the great divergence." This characterization aligns with Schor's predictions as well. Main Street consists of households in which adults work outside the professions and management. The large majority of Main Street adults do not have a four-year college degree, though Main Street also increasingly includes a percentage of young adults who have earned bachelor's degrees but have not been able to land a job in management or the professions. Main Street work includes services, clerical, retail, and various types of manual labor. Main Street also includes adults working in the public sector, skilled trades, and union jobs that have historically been secure, with better pay and benefits. These economic remnants of the postwar economy are quickly disappearing, today representing a minority of the Main Street economy. For that reason, my analysis focuses on the "new" Main Street economy.

III. Long-term poor (20 percent)

This segment consists of the long-term unemployed, the permanently disabled, seniors living only on Social Security, and prisoners. Official government statistics estimate that about 15 percent of Americans live in poverty, but many experts think this statistic underestimates the true number. Structurally, the long-term poor already live very modestly and are not embedded in the BAU economy. Arguably, they are already living sustainable lifestyles, though this is not how they would characterize their lives. As a result, I bracket out the long-term poor in my analysis.

I draw upon two empirical sources for my analysis. For my arguments concerning bobos, I rely upon extensive academic and professional research that I have conducted on this population over the last decade. Space limits prevent me from reviewing the academic research here, and so I encourage the interested reader to read the relevant chapters in Holt and Cameron 2010 (case studies on Starbucks, Ben & Jerry's, and Patagonia). For the Main Street portion of the analysis, I rely on a set of thirty ethnographic interviews, which I conducted with my colleague Douglas Cameron in Boston, Dallas, Denver, and Greeley, Colorado. We assembled a random sample of adults who did not have a four-year college degree and whose household incomes fell between $30,000 and $80,000. (The median U.S. household income is around $50,000.) Our sample includes seven African Americans and seven Hispanic Americans.

SUSTAINABLE BOHEMIA AS SUBCULTURE
AND THE BOBO CONSUMER MYTH

The Rise of Sustainable Bohemia

Schor's *Plenitude* (2010) engages a historic countercultural intellectual tradition. By other names, and with modest variations in content, the idea of plenitude has been the central ideological rebuttal to the contradictions produced by the American economy since the rise of modern capitalism stretching back to the late nineteenth century. These calls for personal and economic transformation have ebbed and flowed ever since, led by the likes of Edward Bellamy, the "Agrarians" of the South, Lewis Mumford, Ralph Borsodi, Scott and Helen Nearing, Kirkpatrick Sale, E. F Schumacher, and many others. Early critics often promoted an antimodern agenda, calling for a revival of a Jeffersonian pastoral society dominated by local economies, small businesses, and small farms, with an emphasis on a vital social life and community rather than acquisition and materialism. It is useful to recall that Franklin Roosevelt promoted a very similar ideology in response to the Great Depression, launching the Civilian Conservation Corps (CCC) as a massive effort to get young men out of the cities and to indoctrinate them into work based upon Jeffersonian principles (Shi 2007).

Today, with the explosion of small-scale sustainable businesses that leverage all sorts of new technologies (IT, CAD, prosumer media production, and so on), this antitechnological bias has largely been set aside. Indeed, Schor celebrates the use of such technology in *Plenitude*. However, the rest of the premodern utopian ideal remains: sustainable economy involves reviving organic local community—with meaningful work, community provisioning, artisan craft, and indigenous culture replacing the BAU society dominated by impersonal globalization, technocracy, brute standardization, never-ending status games, possessive individualism, and media simulacra. I will employ this slightly broader construction of plenitude as movement ideology for the remainder of the chapter, specifically referencing Schor's version where appropriate.

For the past forty years, the plenitude ideology of the sustainable economy movement has increasingly merged with the bohemian ideology advanced by various bohemian subcultures to forge a discourse that I will call *sustainable bohemia*—by far the most powerful cultural force promoting sustainable economy today. While the original bohemian subcultures of the nineteenth century organized to challenge social norms regarding sexuality and the family, bohemian challenges of the past forty years have been organized largely as an antidote to the hyperindustrialization of culture and the hyperrationalization of work. Modern bohemians are equally allergic to both the rationalized commodification of everyday life and culture and the rote work, psychological management principles, and heavy surveillance of contemporary corporations. Bohemians source their countercultural codes from the margins of society, from history, and from preindustrial societies that haven't been captured by modern industrial norms. Bohemians' sustainable utopias take their cues largely from an imagined preindustrial society: a world of handmade, local, artisanal goods centered around an agrarian ideal of the country.

This sustainable bohemian challenge to BAU first peaked during the "back-to-the-land" movement of the early 1970s, in which millions of young Americans migrated to rural enclaves to engage in the kind of DIY crafting and self-provisioning that Schor imagines. Using *The Whole Earth Catalog* and various Rodale publications as their bibles, they learned a wide variety of practical household skills such as how to harvest water, build a teepee, and farm biodynamically. Their aspiration was to reinvent society in microcosm. As this social experiment eventually crumbled, it splintered into a number of interesting directions: grocery cooperatives, a new epicurean food scene centered in Berkeley featuring a return to artisanal production and local organic livestock and produce (Chez Panisse, Peet's coffee, Anchor Steam beer), and new businesses organized around social missions (Ben & Jerry's, Patagonia, Tom's of Maine, Burt's Bees, and the like). In this era, for the first time sustainable economy activism and bohemian lifestyles blended into a single counterculture, which has continued to evolve to the present day. While these businesses devised popular "social missions" that promised to transform business toward sustainability, none of them threatened to subvert the BAU economy.

A very aestheticized version of sustainable bohemia has expanded recently as demand has soared among bobos for sustainable bohemian consumer myths, as I develop below. For the last fifteen years or so, sustainable bohemian pockets have exploded all over the United States, embracing precisely the kinds of sustainable economy initiatives that Schor advocates, combining DIY artisanal collaborative provisioning and work: from farm-to-table restaurants, snout-to-tail meats, the tiny-house movement, the "makers" movement, knitters' circles gathering weekly at bars, the urban revival of back to the land (raising chickens, rooftop gardens), the rise of craft hobbyists via Etsy, and many others. However—as with the back-to-the-land movement—this new incarnation of sustainable bohemia poses no systemic threat to BAU. Rather, it has been readily incorporated as valued new cultural source material for many thousands of new businesses.

Bobos and the Sustainable Bohemia Myth

Many members of the bobo fraction of the professional-managerial class also embrace plenitude, but in a highly attenuated symbolic fashion as a key component of a consumer myth that largely rejects the movement's transformational socioeconomic ideals. As plenitude migrates from the lived experience of sustainable economy activists and participants in the sustainable bohemian subculture to bobo consumption, it becomes transformed into myth. I have conceptualized these cultural mechanics in the cultural branding model that I developed in prior research (Holt 2004; Holt and Cameron 2010).

Beginning in the late 1980s, the United States encountered a demographic shift, accelerating to the present, in which a huge new cohort of young adults whose parents were college educated came of age, creating what I call the *cultural capital cohort* (Holt and Cameron 2010). Socialized to desire more culturally sophisticated and aestheticized goods than prior generations, they faced a consumer culture in which the mass industrialized and increasingly anonymous goods of the BAU economy dominated, just the opposite of what these new tastes demanded. Entrepreneurs responded by developing a vast array of goods and services that pushed against this dominant consumer ideology to promote what we may term the *artisanal-cosmopolitan ideology* of the bohemian counterculture. While food and drink are core categories for the aestheticization of consumer culture, the same holds true for clothing, interior decor, travel, autos, appliances, bicycles, and many other goods.

Since the 1990s, competition across these categories has led to what we call *cultural code inflation:* businesses seek to outdo their competitors on the key cultural codes that best express this ideology. For instance, in the 1980s restaurants pioneered "California cuisine," emphasizing fresh, locally sourced ingredients, but these codes had become table stakes for bobo food by the late 1990s. So leading-edge restaurants pushed ever farther on these codes, developing "farm-to-table" cuisine, "snout-to-tail" butchering of animals, and advancing underdeveloped artisanal categories such as pickles, tea, whiskey, and charcuterie. The latest push to advance bohemian codes in food is to challenge the formal business organization of the restaurant itself in the form of pop-up restaurants and underground restaurants that bohemian types run out of their own homes in whimsically creative and intensively foodie fashion.

Likewise, this same cultural code inflation process pushed entrepreneurs responding to bobo market demand to ally with the sustainable economy movement (a pivotal shift that I analyze in the Starbucks chapter in Holt and Cameron 2010). Hence, plenitude became an important component of sustainable bohemia, not because of activist pressure but because culturally savvy entrepreneurs understood that the ideology was just what the market demanded. The incorporation of the sustainable economy movement added an earnest dose of environmentalist credibility to the subculture's market offerings.

Bobos are not interested in joining a subculture or movement. Rather, they imbibe sustainable bohemia as consumer myth—as an idealized narrative that one aspires to because its ideology is appealing, though it is "lived" only through occasional consumer rituals rather than embraced comprehensively. Bobos demand goods saturated with the sustainable bohemia myth because the myth resonates so powerfully with their identity project. For adults who work non-stop at symbolic analysis as instrumental "free agents" in a national and often global labor market for large corporations, plenitude promises a return to a small scale, crafting with one's hands, local community, solidarity, living viscerally with nature.

Marketers excel at creating these sorts of consumer myths, as I explain in my prior writings (Holt 2004; Holt and Cameron 2010). As a consultant, I have helped to create such myths for a wide variety of brands. Conventional multinational companies often market myths that have little to do with their products—consider, for example, Coca-Cola, Nike, or Harley-Davidson. Thus the popular meaning of *myth* (that it is fictitious and perhaps even deceitful) is closer to the truth. But what about social enterprises that make products according to social missions that seem to align so well with the sustainable economy movement?

While social enterprises are often founded by movement activists and have earned a loyal base of activist customers, my research has revealed that for the most successful of these brands, most customers use the products to ritually consume myth. Social mission brands help bobos to imagine that they are living a sustainable, ethical, progressive life—even if most of their choices and activities violate this identity ideal. Bobos are hangers-on of sustainable bohemia, drawing from it selectively to construct their identities. In our research on and consulting for a number of well-known sustainable brands (Patagonia, Ben & Jerry's, New Belgium, and Starbucks, reported in Holt and Cameron 2010), we find that bobos love the stories and images of sustainable bohemia. And so they place a high value on culturally charged rituals that allow them to participate meaningfully in this world: eating a farm-to-table meal at an actual farm, taking an eco-vacation, or wearing a Patagonia jacket. However, they aren't willing to pursue sustainable economy comprehensively in their consumption, nor are they willing to take the leap in their work and provisioning, despite its symbolic attractions.

Bobos find the DIY creative collaborative work of plenitude to be very attractive in principle. They often experience contradictions in contemporary white-collar work. While they desire work that allows them creative expression and individual idiosyncratic pursuits—the imagined work of bohemians injected into professional life by Steve Jobs and fellow Silicon Valley enthusiasts during the dot-com era—few are able to find such work today. The rationalized technocratic workplace, once aimed squarely at blue-collar jobs, has trickled up into the professions and middle management. The sustainable bohemian alternative provides the perfect antidote: bohemian work rejects overscheduled, overly pressured, overly demanding, ladder-climbing work in favor of the intrinsically rewarding work that exists in America's nooks and crannies. Bohemians thrive on work that they would do even if they weren't paid: work that is humane, improvised, unpredictable, thought provoking.

However, bobos do very well in the BAU economy. For them, BAU operates as golden handcuffs: they are well paid, enjoy many perks, and have committed themselves to a lifestyle that requires this level of income. They are also committed to sustaining their social class position and ensuring that their children can do so as well, which requires the right social networks, school districts, and colleges. Hence, bobos routinely experience what we call "the ache of the bobo": they evince a deep desire to jump ship and pursue work that fits the plenitude model, yet they are unable to do so because they are locked into the financial commitments and social networks demanded by their current occupations.

Paradoxically, the segment that today enthusiastically embraces plenitude in symbolic terms is the least likely to embrace the actual transformation in work and lifestyle required to shift out of BAU. Bobos consume the packaged myths of sustainable bohemia to embellish their identities while remaining firmly anchored in the BAU economy. They readily bracket out the political and institution-building aspects of plenitude in favor of "political consumption"—voicing their identity politics through their purchases. It is a have-your-cake-and-eat-it-too lifestyle that is not easily disrupted. While some bobos dream of leaving the BAU economy, very few are willing to endure the economic sacrifices and status insecurities that are required.

In sum, sustainable bohemia is a valued ideology that is now governed by the mechanics of market commodification in modern consumer culture. The sustainable economy movement, especially its vision of plenitude, has been co-opted as an important pillar of this ideology. The market is extremely adept at circulating and amplifying the valued symbolism of plenitude—imparting to consumers the cosmopolitan outlook and moral higher ground that comes from engaging the Earth's environmental problems through consumption choices—while trivializing its underlying sociopolitical goals.

Within the sustainable bohemia subculture, ever more impressive sustainable businesses constantly emerge, offering innovations that have potent sociopolitical potential. However, because bobos evince little interest in the sociopolitical side of these innovations, neither does the market. The businesses that succeed in scaling sustainable bohemia offerings typically grab the valued symbolism for their brands while discarding much of the potential to advance the movement. Both bobos and corporations have a vested interest in stripping out the more radical sociopolitical ramifications of sustainable innovations. The cumulative result is small incremental gains in sustainability bundled with ever more valuable symbolism. Consider two iconic bobo brands: Whole Foods brilliantly showcases its small percentage of industrial organic offerings to bathe the brand in a halo of environmental enlightenment so that we bobo shoppers believe that everything we buy from Whole Foods is somehow good for the planet. Starbucks works the same branding magic. The company's Estima Fair Trade coffee, Ethos bottled water, and Shared Planet retail campaigning leaves customers feeling like every cup of Starbucks coffee they drink is doing its part to sustain farmers in Africa.

As hard as movement activists try, these market mechanics remain stubbornly in place. As long as bobos are locked into BAU for its economic and status benefits, they will consume plenitude primarily as myth. So, strategically, bobos are a poor target for the movement. If the movement is to have any chance of success, it must shift its targeting to a segment that is more likely to take up sustainable economy as workers, families, and community members, not just as consumer symbolism.

MAIN STREET AS MOVEMENT TARGET

My research on market transformations, along with what I've learned from histories of social movements, suggests that the kind of tectonic shift aimed for by the sustainable economy movement can arise only in response to an acute cultural contradiction. The target population must collectively experience a socioeconomic disruption that challenges the taken-for-granted assumptions of its current lifestyle and creates latent demand for an alternative. Movements do not spread beyond their activist base without such a contradiction to motivate diffusion. From the standpoint of cultural strategy, Americans who constitute the "Main Street" social class are the only viable target to diffuse sustainable economy because they have endured acute contradictions of the BAU economy for years.

Today, despite tremendous efforts by environmental activists to construct this sort of collective tension, leveraging extreme weather events like Katrina and Sandy, Americans do not yet view environmental issues as crises that demand a personal (much less a political) response. The reasons for this relative lack of concern have been much discussed, including the impact of the climate denialism industry and the particular characteristics of global environmental problems. Regardless of the cause, climate change and other global environmental problems remain toward the bottom of the list of Americans' rankings of problems that concern them, a consistent finding for the past twenty years in Gallup polls. And relative to other social classes, Main Street is most susceptible to pushing environment to the margins; Main Streeters view the environment as a luxury good that they can't afford.

Rather than trying to amplify the environmental crisis, shifting the focus to the ongoing economic disruption offers a much more promising path. Unlike the case with those in the professional-managerial factions, for whom BAU continues to provide a very desirable living standard, Main Street life suffers from economic trauma, which shows no signs of abating. Today we must look for opportunities where economic dislocations are challenging the dominant growth-at-all-costs consumerist ideologies and practices of the past sixty years, creating a cultural opportunity for the sustainable economy movement.

To devise a sustainable economy strategy that will resonate with Main Streeters requires entering their lives, understanding their dreams and anxieties—their collective identity projects and the obstacles that the BAU economy throws in their path. The thirty informants we interviewed provided a redundant data set: every interview we conducted fit the general pattern described below. Interestingly, in addition to the thirty informants, we mistakenly included two college students in the interview set. Their identity projects fit nicely with sustainable bohemia and so provided a sharply drawn antithesis to the Main Street interviews we were conducting.

Let's first sketch a social landscape of this class, culling highlights from the burgeoning literature describing recent shifts in American social class structure (Bartels 2008; Hacker and Pierson 2010; Haskins, Isaacs, and Sawhill 2008; Krugman 2007; Noah 2012; Stiglitz 2012). Since the late 1970s, a series of political-economic shifts (including the demise of unions, regressive tax policies, and the liberalization of labor and capital markets) has had a devastating impact on Americans who are not part of the professional-managerial class. Economic life in Main Street America has fallen apart: well-paid and secure jobs have disappeared at a rapid rate and been replaced with jobs that pay much less and offer only skimpy benefits. Retirement benefits have been retracted, medical costs have skyrocketed, and college education costs have risen dramatically. Main Street pay has been pushed downward toward a "$10 an hour economy." The explosion of consumer debt and bankruptcies is a symptom of the economic trauma. Economic conditions have further deteriorated since 2008: real incomes have declined 10 percent and are now at a lower level than in the early 1970s, despite the fact that corporations have enjoyed substantial productivity gains in this period. While unemployment for the professional-managerial class hovers around 3–4 percent, real unemployment (including Americans who've given up looking for full-time employment or are severely underemployed) on Main Street exceeds 15 percent. Nearly two-thirds of Main Street workers have suffered a job loss, pay cut, or reduction in hours since 2008. Perhaps most damning for a country that has long been willing to trade off economic inequality for mobility, class mobility in the United States is now lower than in Europe, including all of the

Scandinavian countries, which have always served for neoliberal proponents as case studies for lack of personal initiative and industry.

Among our informants, personal crises begot by these economic conditions are the norm, not the exception. One after another reported falling into economic crisis (foreclosure, bankruptcy, even homelessness) as the result of job loss, divorce, a medical condition, or a family emergency. The macro statistics reflect this on-the-ground reality: 75% percent of Main Street will spend at least one year in poverty, 75 percent worry about having enough money to pay their bills, 50 percent suffer from chronic financial problems. One in seven American families declared bankruptcy over the last decade. More people will go bankrupt this year than graduate from college.

Daniel is a single white male in his twenties. He grew up in a secure middle-class Boston-area household, in which his father earned $30 an hour as a skilled electrician and his mother was a waitress. After high school, he apprenticed as an electrician for $19 an hour, but when the recession hit, there was a huge decline in demand for construction-oriented trades. The biggest Boston electrical company, which had ninety electricians in 2007, was down to five employees. Everyone he knew from the trade is now out of a job, and even his father struggles to find work. So he went to college, the University of Massachusetts–Boston, where he majored in philosophy as a prelaw degree: "I thought I could make good money as a lawyer, might be something I'm good at." But after two years he pulled out, as he was accumulating debt and becoming increasingly skeptical that there would be good jobs for lawyers once he got out of school. So he's now a bartender at a country club, working side by side with a college grad in finance who was laid off two months after starting his first job out of college. He's given up on his big career dreams and stays focused instead on enjoying "simple stuff": hanging out with his girlfriend (whom he lives with), going out to eat, and playing pool. He wants to have a family and own a home someday—"nothing extravagant, three bedrooms so everyone isn't crammed in"—and so knows he needs to move on to a better job but has no idea what that will be.

Kasha grew up in a small town in Mississippi, one of eleven siblings. She is African American, in her thirties, and currently lives in Dallas. Her mother and father never worked, except for an occasional mowing job. She dreamed of having kids and being an airline stewardess and traveling the world, a fantasy she picked up from television. Her mother died in her senior year of high school. Kasha went straight to college, first out of state, then back home to Alcorn State, and then Mississippi Valley State for two years. In each case, she "burned out." "I should have taken a break. College is for some and not for others. I couldn't concentrate and was sick of school, so I didn't go back." She vowed not to have kids but ended up having two children immediately after she quit college. "Kids are a blessing, I would never give them up, but you can get more accomplished without kids." Her first kids are now young adults, and she has a three-year-old daughter also. She has worked in data entry and customer service her entire adult life. She tried call center work briefly, but found it too boring. She hates living in Dallas ("the economy sucks and it's hot as hell") and imagines that New York would be better. "There are companies that are hiring, but they pay you $9.50 or $10.00 an hour and they want you to run the full office." For her, happiness is freedom from financial stress. Her happiest moments are simple things like going to the state fair with her kids or lazing around on Sundays all day watching football. Her dreams for her kids are very modest: she just wants them to have decent secure jobs that they enjoy.

Angelica is an Italian immigrant, married and in her forties, whose parents came to the country to live the American Dream. Her father always told her, "America is a place you could come and make your fortune." She and her husband lived for decades in the highest tier of Main Street with a successful small business. They pushed their kids to advance up the social class ladder by graduating from college. But her husband's business remanufacturing brake parts was gradually "snuffed out" by Chinese competition. When his business finally went under, the economy was so bad that there was no related work for him to move to. So they were forced to downsize, selling their big home in a "hoity-toity" neighborhood and moving into a small rental house in a working-class neighborhood. (She emphasizes the one great benefit of moving from a professional-managerial class neighborhood to a Main Street neighborhood: people are more friendly and neighborly.) The family stopped going out to eat. They sold their newer cars that had loans and bought old cars for cash. Even with four kids, she went back to work, doing contract work in elder care. Her husband was stressed out, searching for work for almost a year without success, finally creating a new small business as an "auto concierge," taking care of the cars of wealthy clients.

The experiences of the last five years have totally reshaped her identity project. Her primary goal today is financial security—"There is no better feeling than money in the bank." She is very apprehensive about her kids falling into debt from college and struggling to find work. She advises her daughter in college not to "study something crazy like women's studies. Study something that might get you a job. It's sad but you can't study what you're interested in." She is counseling her remaining son at home to avoid college altogether and instead "use your hands to fix something" because "you rack up $200,000 in loans and there are no jobs."

In the United States, Main Street enclaves are everywhere (urban, suburban, and exurban Main Streets abound) but are particularly pronounced in midsize cities that have been hollowed out economically: cities in California's Central Valley dominated by big agriculture, cities in Texas dominated by dirty petrochemical industries, midwestern cities that have never been able to replace union jobs previously tied to major industries like autos and steel, cities in the Deep South that have never developed an industrial base. These are cities where the labor market contradictions inherent in the BAU economy play out in the most dramatic and "pure" fashion. They present Main Street life in stark relief.

Greeley, Colorado, is one such city dominated by Main Street economics. I claim no great ethnographic expertise on Greeley: I spent five days there conducting interviews. But even this small snapshot provides a window into Main Street life that we can use productively. The Greeley economy is held in place by JBS Swift, a huge beef- and pork-processing plant on the east side of the city. The plant was originally owned by Swift & Company, one of the first national meatpackers. Jobs at the plant were always physically taxing and dangerous, but like other blue-collar jobs at large companies in the mid-twentieth century, cutting meat paid reasonably well and offered good benefits and job security, and so they were highly valued. Swift grew into a typical postwar conglomerate, venturing into a variety of unrelated businesses, including insurance, oil, brassieres, and even Avis Rent-a-Car. In the 1980s, Wall Street began attacking conglomerates, with wealthy "raiders" aiming to break them up to generate higher profits. Swift was forced to sell off all its businesses, and the meatpacking business was bought by the huge packaged goods company Conagra. In turn, Conagra sold out to a private equity firm in 2002, at which point intensive cost cutting began, requiring workers to speed up work on their lines while accepting lower wages. The company relied heavily on the labor of illegal immigrants from Mexico, Central America, South America, and Africa, which eventually led to a raid by U.S. Immigration and Customs Enforcement (ICE) and the deportation of over a thousand workers at six plants, including Greeley. In 2007, having enhanced the company's profitability through these aggressive measures, the private equity firm sold the business for $225 million to the Brazilian multinational

JBS S.A., the largest meat processor in the world. Today, the plant's economics are driven by the hard-line profit goals of a multinational company competing in what is now a global market for meat. So JBS pushes pay as low as it can for grueling repetitive manual labor in slaughter rooms where the temperature hovers around fifty degrees. Yet, at around $13–$14 an hour, jobs at JBS are still prized as the best-paying work in town for Main Street citizens. Because the work is so hard and dangerous, meat cutting tends to attract immigrants despite the ICE crackdown. Greeley is now 30 percent Mexican American. Additionally, when the U.S. government needed a place to relocate thousands of Somalis seeking asylum, it chose Greeley because they could enter this labor pool as well, which caused considerable ethnic turmoil locally. My white informants freely spouted damning racist slurs against both Mexicans and Somalis.

The only other significant private-sector employers in Greeley are two huge call centers—a common work destination for women and less-fit men who don't have the physical stamina to work at the slaughterhouse. Startek and AFNI provide outsourced customer service for companies such as Verizon. Like JBS, these businesses compete in a global market to help multinationals drive down their costs. (Startek also has centers in the Philippines, Costa Rica, and Honduras.) So wages are set at poverty levels: pay is $9.50–$10 an hour with minimal benefits and no job security. Other Main Street jobs—such as administrative work at the University of Northern Colorado and service work at the local hospitals—rarely become available because these positions are so desirable. So many Greeley Main Street workers bounce around retail and call center jobs that pay just above minimum wage.

Greeley's Main Street citizens live in cheaply constructed apartments and rundown bungalows, which dominate the east side of the city near the JBS plant. The smells wafting from the plant on the weekly slaughter day fill the entire city but are particularly pungent nearby, so only Main Street citizens live there; the professional-managerial class resides on the city's western fringes. Nearby retail is dominated by dollar stores, pawnshops, payday loan operations, and bail bond shops. Walmart is viewed as the premium high-end of the retail spectrum.

On Main Street, economic turmoil is the central fact of life. Families live a paycheck-to-paycheck existence, in which everyday decisions always begin with questions of affordability. This everyday financial stress is punctuated by serial household crises that are directly related to economic trauma: layoffs, bankruptcy, poverty wages, and medical emergencies run hand in hand with divorce, prison, and drug addictions. Single mothers, in particular, struggle to keep their households afloat.

Tammy is a single mother in her forties with a teenage son. She grew up with a single mother, a nurse who became a devout follower of televangelists. Her mother viewed her as a heretic because she believed the Bible was fiction and hung out with gay men. Tammy was caught committing petty theft at age twelve, and her mother put her in a group home. She now works at one of the call centers for $10 an hour. Her identity project is constructed around parenting, correcting for the mistakes her mother made with her. Her life is centered on keeping her son focused on school, safe, and out of trouble. She tries to keep him entertained but is financially limited, so this usually means watching a movie together on television.

Before moving to Greeley, she lived in Las Vegas, a constant point of comparison in our conversation. She dislikes Greeley because it is so boring. For leisure, she relies heavily on free public spaces and events, which were far better in Vegas. She can't afford a car so they live on the bus route; she's angry that Greeley has no bus service on Sundays so she has to walk seventeen blocks to work. She spends lots of time in the public library as it's nearby and free. She dreams that she will move with her son to Denver sometime soon. Call center jobs there often pay $11 an hour, and there's far more free events and entertainment. It is her land of opportunity—if only she can get together enough money to afford the seventy-mile move.

Sally is a white woman in her thirties living with her partner. She grew up in rural Nebraska on her grandparents' farm. Her father was a long-haul trucker who often took Sally along for the ride when she was young. She loved it. She followed other family members to Greeley, where she got into lots of trouble as a "rebel" in high school. She was expelled from school when she got pregnant. She credits her kids with pulling her out of her teenage life of drugs and petty crime. She now lives in an apartment with her three kids (from two former relationships) and "my old man"—her partner, who works cleaning up oil rigs in rural Colorado and Wyoming. He recently got out of jail and has two kids of his own; their mother, his former partner, is now in jail. Sally has done manual labor her entire life— waiting tables for many years and more recently working as a nursing assistant at a nursing home where she spent most of her time lifting elderly people. She developed carpal tunnel syndrome as a result and recently had surgery. She can't go back to lifting so will probably wait tables again once she recovers.

Sally has no hobbies or avocations. Neither she nor her partner likes Greeley because the general poverty leads to a high incidence of crime, gangs, and drugs. They live a purposely isolated life, trying to avoid other people in their apartment complex and beyond because such interactions often lead to "too much drama." They fill their leisure time with simple, safe, and cheap outings: either barbequing in the local park or taking the kids to the Boys and Girls Club to play in a safe environment. There is no money for leisure apart from watching movies and playing video games at home. Like other mothers we talked to, Sally spends much of her energies worrying about how to keep her kids safe and out of trouble. Her and her partner's short-term dream is to rent a house with a yard so their kids will have a place to play that is separated from neighbors. Their long-term dream is to move back to rural Nebraska and live on the farm with her grandparents: physically isolating themselves from the problems and despair of the Main Street economy.

CROSSING PLENITUDE'S CULTURAL CHASM

The Main Street citizens we interviewed are oblivious to the idea of sustainable economy and are unlikely to respond to the rhetoric of plenitude. This lack of resonance is an example of what I term a *cultural chasm* (Holt and Cameron 2010). I adapt the term from the diffusion of innovations literature in high-technology categories, in which Geoffrey Moore (2002) extended Everett Rodgers's original formulation to describe the diffusion barrier that new technologies often face in "crossing the chasm." New technologies are vigorously adopted early on by those who like to be on the cutting edge of new technologies and who do not encounter increased risk by adopting them. But the marketing that works so well to attract early adopters often fails in attracting the mass market because the preferences of the latter are so different. They perceive the innovation through a very different lens, and they are often reluctant to embrace the new technology because the existing technology it seeks to replace plays a crucial role in their business. For companies selling innovations to "cross the chasm," they must entirely reformulate their marketing to address this broader target.

Many social movements hit an analogous diffusion problem. Movements often adopt strategies that echo the ideology of their own activists. These strategies fail because they resonate primarily with fellow activists rather than with potential converts to the movement. To attract prospects outside the activist community requires a different strategy.

Main Street today is living with acute everyday contradictions due to the breakdown of the BAU labor market. So, unlike bobos, Main Street citizens are potentially very receptive to an alternative as long as they can be convinced that it offers a plausible path to leapfrog the economic problems they face. But sustainable economy campaigning speaks in a language attuned to the cultural tensions faced by bobos rather than those on Main Street. So we need to significantly revise the current strategy in order for it to resonate with Main Street.

Focus on pragmatic improvements in Main Street lives rather than appeal to cosmopolitan ethical commitment. Sustainable economy campaigning appeals to citizens to gather together to address massive environmental and economic problems. The scale of these problems is such that taking them on requires a cosmopolitan worldview, a confident and ambitious idea of one's ability to change the world on such a broad scale, and a significant level of economic security. This sort of rhetoric is the coin of the realm in places like Boulder, Berkeley, Brooklyn, and Cambridge, but it is alien to Main Street. Main Street citizens have no choice but to devote their energy to immediate household problems. The thought of grappling with global problems or problems of future generations rarely crosses their minds, as they are contending with the challenges the BAU economy presents their household today.

While they are deeply concerned about the American economy, those on Main Street view it at a distance as passive observers. They don't believe they could ever have an impact. They are not at all engaged in global sustainability issues. The rhetoric of plenitude and all other sustainable economy campaigning begins with the assumption that prospects are concerned about global problems and eager to contribute to societal transformation if only they could be convinced of the right solution. For Main Street, this is not the case. Rather, the movement will succeed only if it alters its rhetoric to focus intensively on the locally relevant concerns of Main Street communities.

Respond to today's economic crisis rather than project environmental crises in the future. The sustainable economy movement is focused primarily on how to avoid global environmental collapse, sometimes making linkages to the economy (as Schor does) and to global social justice issues. So if you're not concerned about the environment, it's unlikely you will engage with the movement. Main Street Americans are suffering the economic traumas of the BAU economy, exacerbated by American political policies. As yet these economic problems have no perceived connection to the environment, so the basic argument is a disconnect for them. Our Main Street informants view such issues as tangential compared to the personal issues they must overcome. This is a foundational aspect of the cultural chasm that the movement strategy must address: while environmental issues are central to the movement, this doesn't mean that environmental arguments are the most compelling pathway to attract nonactivists. Rather than trying to convince Main Street that environmental overshoot is indeed worth acting on, strategy must instead seek an alternative path to the same result. Main Street's pathway into sustainable economy is through the promise of grappling with the acute personal economic problems caused by BAU.

Create credible work alternatives rather than promote working less. Like other sustainable economy tracts (including Schor's prior work), *Plenitude* (2010) advocates working less and creating more time for family, play, and social life. For the professional-managerial class, which works long hours and is paid high salaries, such that cutting back is entirely plausible, this idea of working less can really resonate. But for Main Street, the idea of working less is fraught with problems. Main Streeters live with tremendous economic insecurity. Many have lost their jobs in the recession and have struggled to find work at decent pay. Everyone has family members and friends who have been out of work for many months. They work long hours because they desperately need the money. Several informants talked about moving to a different city for a better job, based upon wage differences as small as $0.50 an hour. Janet, a Mexican American woman living in Denver with three children, described how her husband, an electrician for the City of Denver, had been forced to take three weeks of furlough in 2008 and the days had not yet been added back. As a result, the family would likely have to pull their children out of parochial school and send them back into the public school system. To avoid this, she had been trying to go back to work after nearly two decades being out of the workforce raising her children, with no luck.

We spoke to a woman in Boston whose husband was fired without warning from Filene's department store when the company went into bankruptcy after he'd worked there for over three decades. The woman immediately went to work although she had two school-age kids. The only work she could find at first was with a small outsourcing firm that did "shelf sets" for grocery stores: her job entailed stocking shelves in the middle of the night when there were no customers. Starting work at 8 p.m., she and other workers were driven in a minibus to grocery stores around the county, often an hour away, where they spent the night cutting open boxes and loading up shelves—she was bussed back home just in time to get her children breakfast and see them off to school. She moved on to a job at UPS sorting packages, working in a fifty-degree warehouse that kept her fingers numb all day long. She shares with other Main Street informants a fundamental economic desperation: she would take any additional hours working any decent job. Her dream, like that of other Main Street adults, is to work in a secure job with decent pay where she is treated well. This ideal, not working less, needs to be the focus of sustainable economy campaigning to Main Street.

Focus on consumption equity rather than consuming less. Another core sustainable economy message—buy less—suffers from the same problem. The idea is entirely sensible for members of the professional-managerial class— most of whom are deeply ensconced in the culture of consumerism—but it comes off as incoherent for Main Streeters. They live in relatively small apartments or bungalows. They are careful with their energy use due to the cost. They seldom take vacations out of state, and they can't afford air travel. They buy used cars. They rely heavily on Craigslist (their favorite business, beating out the likes of Google and Apple) for cheap used goods if they need a baby crib or a television. They shop only sale and coupon items at the grocery store, and they buy meat only when it's marked down. They rely extensively on public space for their leisure—spending time with their families in the parks was the most popular activity among our informants. The exceptions we encountered were three families that had enjoyed relatively high incomes as small-business owners, only to have these once-reliable incomes fall apart in the recession. These families all describe chasing a materialist good life. But the shock of the country's financial implosion and their own corresponding personal economic problems led them to renounce their old ways and embrace financial autonomy and security instead. Main Street denizens are intensely concerned with providing the goods and services that their households require at a basic level of quality—a constant struggle for them. Sustainable economy movement strategy needs to shift its rhetoric away from consuming less (a message focused on the upper middle class) and instead focus on the social justice angle, what we might call *consumption equity:* the idea that a sustainable economy requires that everyone should receive a basic level of household goods and services.

Build resilient local economic institutions rather than champion entrepreneurial communities. Sustainable economy campaigners want to rejuvenate local social and civic life as a means to generate more life satisfaction than that produced by participating in the BAU economy. Our informants vary widely in their current communal engagement: some live a "circle-the-wagons" life within their households, while others are already very much engaged in their local communities. The dominant community institutions among our informants are the church and the military (the one economic sanctuary that still exists for Main Street, with many community extensions as well).

In *Plenitude* (2010), Schor advises citizens to participate in sustainable economy via myriad small-business opportunities that are now thriving using new technologies. (She also mentions that community economic initiatives can be effective in the transformation, but that is not her main focus.) While many of our informants have struggled to find good work, most could not pursue this kind of entrepreneurial alternative simply because they do not have the working capital to start up such a business. Even if they did, most would consider such an endeavor far too risky, as the recession has made them highly risk averse. Finally, because they are not concerned with global environmental issues, they would have no particular interest in pursuing businesses that delivered environmental sustainability.

Two of our thirty informants did pursue an entrepreneurial path. When Angelica's husband lost his custom auto parts fabrication business to severe Chinese price competition, he searched for any sort of job in which he could use his skills, with no luck. Out of options after a year, in the end he invented his own job: helping well-to-do executives get their cars serviced and repaired. His new venture has him joining the service economy for those who have become very wealthy in the BAU economy (a new member of the class of service workers for the upper middle class found in all global cities, as described by Saskia Sassen). The fact that he was working on servicing very expensive new autos—the antithesis of a sustainable business—would never cross his mind as a problem. He was thankful to have finally come up with a business that paid the bills.

Judy lost her first husband when he slipped and fell into a canyon while hiking in the Rocky Mountains. She used the life insurance money to renovate her home in order to obscure for her children the emotional challenges of living with memories of life with their father. But she didn't have enough money remaining for the mortgage and soon lost the house to foreclosure. She met her current husband playing online poker; he moved from Ohio to Colorado to be with her. Neither of them had work, and they became desperate to bring in money. Her deceased husband had been a house painter and had supplies in the garage. So they placed an ad on Craigslist as painters and began to get work. Eventually they met a man who "flipped" houses (bought dilapidated houses, fixed them up, and then sold them for a profit). They earned his trust and he promoted them to act as contractors for his renovations, overseeing all the tradespeople working on the project. Now they work very long and unpredictable hours, spending extended periods overseeing construction sites and driving their truck all over the city to track down materials. That their work involves one of the hotspots of the BAU economy—the speculative end of the real estate market, in which they rip out functional kitchens and bathrooms and replace them with new ones in order to attract sales—never crosses their minds as a problematic way to make a living.

Main Street citizens, desperate for any secure job that pays well, pursue whatever opportunities they come across, as these cases indicate. The vast majority of such opportunities will be deeply embedded in the BAU economy. Main Street does not have the risk-taking capacity to pursue the less economically viable and more speculative opportunities at the fringes of sustainable economy. They will pursue such opportunities only if the movement creates them. So it is up to the sustainable economy movement to inflect the creation of local labor markets toward sustainability.

CONSTRUCTING A COMMUNITY-CENTERED
SUSTAINABLE JOBS AND SERVICES PROGRAM

Given that everyday economic insecurities tightly coupled with the BAU economy are the dominant tensions in Main Street lives, the sustainable economy movement will resonate only if it offers an economic alternative that helps Main Streeters grapple with these problems. To engage sustainability on Main Street requires retooling conventional campaigning: in the midst of a structural economic crisis with no end in sight, communication that calls on Americans to personally address environmental issues, especially with such a global and long-term perspective, is a nonstarter. Sustainability must be construed in economic terms, with the desired environmental impact treated as an unintended consequence.

Further, Main Streeters do not have the resources to pursue economic alternatives on their own, as entrepreneurs. So the movement must offer tangible local economic models that Main Street families view as a desirable alternative to their current situation. This requires launching innovative new programs—social innovations rather than campaigns. In particular, I want to think through this problem through the lens of cultural branding, exploring ideas that respond to Main Street's identity desires caused by the contradictions of their engagement with the BAU economy.

The idea needs to center on how the community can create sustainable work for its Main Street citizens, not how Main Street individuals can transform their lives. We need to consider how to develop models of the new economy in microcosm, invite Main Street citizens to join up, and then use these lead successes to diffuse the model to other communities. American cities spend exorbitant sums in tax breaks to court businesses in the quixotic pursuit of new employers. But the grand promise of new jobs rarely pays out, as the companies move on to the next bidder or relocate overseas. Even when they stay, the cost per incremental job is extraordinary. So, what if cities instead decided to invest this money to build their own local alternative economy?

Let me briefly sketch a speculative idea, which I will call Main Street Community Corps (MSCC), to illustrate the direction I believe the sustainable economy movement must go. MSCC is a local community corps of young adults, a new spin on the community service model of Vista and AmeriCorps (a model which, in turn, borrows from the Depression-era Civilian Conservation Corps). MSCC is a social innovation designed to simultaneously address a number of issues: to provide an economic pathway toward a local workplace autonomous from the BAU economy, to make material improvements in the lives of Main Street households now traumatized by the BAU labor market, to build community networks of economic security for members of a population now forced to struggle for self-reliance as free agents, and to introduce indigenous environmental sustainability initiatives for a population that does not need to consume less as individuals.

The central concern of Main Street families is that there is no pathway today for their children to become productive adults with respectable jobs that pay well enough for them to start their own families. Main Street adults have gone down the path that the dominant discourse has pushed them to embrace—do whatever it takes to get you and your kids through college and your worries are over. In case after case, my informants discovered that they had been sold a false bill of goods. Most can afford only community colleges, and there is no pipeline of jobs available for those with associate degrees. Others have tried to make four-year college work, but the costs overwhelmed them (forcing most to work full-time in addition to schoolwork), so none of them made it. They dropped out with big debts and no job opportunities. Their children, many now in high school, are entirely cynical about the rewards that come from education and so have no interest in working hard at school. An innovation that provides real opportunities for their children would be hugely valued. If we can make these opportunities deliver on sustainable economy, then we will have a way to diffuse the ideology through practice rather than continue to fail at the unwinnable battle to persuade through communication.

MSCC is a job corps of young adults (last two years of high school and two years after graduation) who enter a business apprenticeship program that provides needed services to their Main Street community. MSCC members are selected based upon recommendations from their teachers, community organizations (religious organizations, Boys and Girls Clubs, and so on), and interviews. They enter into a business that serves Main Street at subsidized rates, mentored by adults with expertise, as a springboard into the permanent workforce. The MSCC is promoted to local businesses as a training program that provides a credential and training pipeline into local jobs. These local businesses become vested in the program as well and volunteer to help develop MSCC services.

The huge gap in public services for Main Street citizens provides the opportunity to create important local work that the community will relish. The neoliberal era of stripped-down public goods affords a chance to create a jobs program that is directly responsive to Main Street's local needs for these services. In practice, I envision that the choice of community services would be crowdsourced, with local Main Street communities developing and then voting on sustainable community services that they would most value. We can also devise these ideas through market research, which we've started to do. As part of the research, we interviewed twenty-five social service workers who spoke to us about the service gaps that impact Main Street citizens most acutely. From these gaps, I have inferred a variety of MSCC services that also align with environmental sustainability concerns.

Home energy conservation. Main Street families often struggle to pay high utility bills because they live in poorly insulated homes, yet don't have the money to pay for the needed repairs. This is a "low-hanging fruit" sustainability initiative that a community jobs corps can effectively deliver. Main Streeters don't have the time to work their way through the paperwork and contractors or the financing to do it themselves. Government initiatives are woefully underfunded despite efforts by the Obama administration. MSCC can provide a simple standardized weatherization service, which can be offered door-to-door. The cost can then be added to utility bills over the following year.

Parks daycare. For Main Street, public parks are the most important oases for leisure. MSCC can offer outdoor daycare at low subsidized rates to provide kids with healthy and safe outdoor play and parents with a convenient way to further enjoy parks.

Work shuttles. Main Street workers rely on older cars, often neglecting maintenance, and so consistently have car trouble, which keeps them from getting to work and adds big expenses to their lives. Bus services in Main Street neighborhoods are seldom organized to efficiently transport workers to their jobs. MSCC provides shuttle services to the major businesses in the community (for example, JBS and the two call centers in Greeley) at inexpensive subsidized rates.

Convenient healthy food shops. Main Streeters suffer from high rates of obesity and diabetes because they live on a diet of artificially cheap, heavily processed carbohydrates. MSCC runs a network of small retail stores, located in Main Street neighborhoods, that offers healthy prepared meals at subsidized rates (further subsidized by sourcing from various food banks).

Social innovation concepts like MSCC can provide a concrete pathway for Main Street families to pursue the sort of self-reliance and economic security that they dream of, while building local community around desperately needed services. Along the way, they become immersed in the sustainable economy and learn its value firsthand. Imagine walking through the neighborhood seeing crews of workers wearing MSCC uniforms who are insulating homes, providing recreation for children in the parks, preparing meals, and driving shuttles for workers. By launching businesses that deliver on environmental sustainability, the MSCC could provide a visceral lived example of the kind of alternative economy that sustainability campaigners wish to promote. If the movement successfully launched a handful of MSCCs around the country as "showcase" projects, and then promoted the successes, other communities would quickly join the scheme, and we would see the sustainable economy concept grow much more quickly than is possible with the communication-centered campaigning approach that the movement now relies upon.

CONCLUSION

I argue that the sustainable economy movement is inadvertently pursuing a dead-end strategy. The movement shines a light on the subcultural pockets of what I call *sustainable bohemia* as microcosmic models for the societal transformation we need. Activists work tirelessly to bring citizens from outside the movement into this fold, proclaiming that this life is better, people are happier, social life is more pleasant. While, given the focus of this edited volume, I use Juliet Schor's *Plenitude* as an exemplar, her book is by no means exceptional in this respect. Schor's arguments and calls to action are situated within a strategy paradigm that has long been taken for granted by the major actors in the space, from the foundations and NGOs that promote sustainable economy to major academic bodies that organize knowledge on the subject (for example, SCORE and SCORAI) to other movement leaders such as Bill McKibben and Gus Speth.

Narrating the movement's successes certainly plays a valuable role, as such narration does in all movements: it builds solidarity, identity, and focus within the movement. However, such rhetoric is necessarily inwardly focused: the stories activists tell each other are not necessarily the best campaigning tools to diffuse the movement to a broader public. Rather, this approach often leads to a cultural chasm. Successful campaigns must be crafted to identify with the worldview of the most opportune prospects, in this case Main Street. Because the movement does not even try to engage Main Street's most pressing life issues, it is perceived as irrelevant.

Even more problematic from a strategic viewpoint is the fact that the movement's rhetoric has been wedded to a wide variety of sustainable bohemia-branded goods and services favored by bobos for their identity symbolism. Bobos embrace sustainable bohemia ideology to demonstrate that they are deeply concerned about the Earth's problems and that they take seriously their role as virtuous worldly citizens. But their superficial embrace through consumer rituals is ecologically meaningless and politically detrimental. They are locked into BAU because they benefit enormously both in economic and status terms and so will not give it up. Hence, this alignment is a strategic dead end.

Moreover, this unintended connection between the movement and bobos has led to a problematic cultural consequence: it has forged a class divide that alienates Main Street, pushing it away from movement ideology. To the extent that elites use sustainable economy ideology to claim moral superiority while continuing to be happily ensconced in the BAU economy, they are badly damaging the sustainable economy brand. They provide rhetorical ammunition to Main Street to see it as something frivolous that people who are "full of themselves" pursue—what "the people in Boulder do," as one of my Denver informants dismissively proclaimed. The movement must repudiate the use of its ideology as empty status symbolism and instead focus singlemindedly on improving Main Street lives.

To do so, the movement must take seriously Main Street concerns and shape its "offering" accordingly. If it is to be viable, the movement must take leadership in launching community-level social innovations that create sustainable economy jobs by offering sustainable services that the community really needs. The MSCC is merely a speculative idea, and perhaps the wrong one. But imagine how Main Street would react if all the sustainable economy movement's community organizing, cultural influence, financial resources, and political power were focused squarely on a strategy that builds this sort of sustainable economy initiative in the localities that most desperately need them.

NOTE

1. Useful Main Street sustainability projects do exist today: there are dozens of impressive small, local initiatives around the country. The problem is that these projects are narrowly conceived and receive little of the elite attention and financial resources they need to succeed. This is because such projects are tangential to the movement's primary strategy, which I outline here. The one notable exception has been Van Jones's success in garnering elite participation in his "green jobs" initiative. So it's not surprising that most existing initiatives focus on residential weatherization programs (for example, Clean Energy Works Oregon and WeatherizeDC). This is an important service, to be sure, but it addresses only one service deficit in Main Street life and does so on such a small scale that it can never have a collective impact on the local Main Street economy. Main Street residents will not join the sustainable economy movement until we launch more ambitious interventions that provide more robust solutions to the problems they face and make a material difference in the local jobs market. Main Street can lead the transformation to a sustainable economy, but only when elite political capital, media, and financial resources are singularly focused on this strategy.

REFERENCES

Arnould, Eric J., and Craig J. Thompson. 2005. "Consumer Culture Theory (CCT): Twenty Years of Research." *Journal of Consumer Research* 31 (4): 868–82.

Bartels, Larry M. 2008. *Unequal Democracy: The Political Economy of the New Gilded Age.* Princeton, NJ: Princeton University Press.

Brooks, David. 2000. *Bobos in Paradise: The New Upper Class and How They Got There.* New York: Simon and Schuster.

Hacker, Jacob, and Paul Pierson. 2010. *Winner-Take-All Politics: How Washington Made the Rich Richer and Turned Its Back on the Middle Class.* New York: Simon and Schuster.

Haskins, Ron, Julia B. Isaacs, and Isabel V. Sawhill. 2008. "Getting Ahead or Losing Ground: Economic Mobility in America." Washington, DC: Brookings Institute. http://www.brookings.edu/research/reports/2008/02/economic-mobility-sawhill (accessed March 1, 2013).

Holt, Douglas B. 1998. "Does Cultural Capital Structure American Consumption?" *Journal of Consumer Research* 25 (1):1–25.

———. 2004. *How Brands Become Icons: The Principles of Cultural Branding.* Cambridge, MA: Harvard Business School Press.

———. 2012. "Constructing Sustainable Consumption: From Ethical Values to the Cultural Transformation of Unsustainable Markets." *Annals of the American Academy of Political and Social Science* 644 (1): 236–55.

Holt, Douglas B., and Douglas Cameron. 2010. *Cultural Strategy: Using Innovative Ideologies to Build Breakthrough Brands.* Oxford: University of Oxford Press.

Jackson, Tim. 2009. *Prosperity without Growth: Economics for a Finite Planet.* London: Earthscan.

Krugman, Paul. 2007. *The Conscience of a Liberal.* New York: Norton.

McKibben, Bill. 2007. *Deep Economy: The Wealth of Communities and the Durable Future.* New York: Times Books.

Moore, Geoffrey A. 2002. *Crossing the Chasm: Marketing and Selling Disruptive Products to Mainstream Customers.* New York: HarperBusiness.

Noah, Timothy. 2012. *The Great Divergence: America's Growing Inequality Crisis and What We Can Do About It.* New York: Bloomsbury.

Sassen, Saskia. 1991. *The Global City: New York, London, Tokyo.* Princeton, NJ: Princeton University Press.

Schor, Juliet. 1999. *The Overspent American: Why We Want What We Don't Need.* New York: Harper Perennial.

———. 2010. *Plenitude: The New Economics of True Wealth.* New York: Penguin.

Shi, David. 2007. *The Simple Life: Plain Living and High Thinking in American Culture.* Athens: University of Georgia Press.

Speth, James Gustave. 2009. *The Bridge at the Edge of the World: Capitalism, the Environment, and Crossing from Crisis to Sustainability.* New Haven, CT: Yale University Press.

Stiglitz, Joseph E. 2012. *The Price of Inequality: How Today's Divided Society Endangers Our Future.* New York: Norton.

Chapter 8 Cooperative Networks, Participatory Markets, and Rhizomatic Resistance: Situating Plenitude within Contemporary Political Economy Debates

Craig J. Thompson and Juliet B. Schor

> I think we have gone through a period when too many children and people have been given to understand "I have a problem, it is the Government's job to cope with it!" or "I have a problem, I will go and get a grant to cope with it!" "I am homeless, the Government must house me!" And so they are casting their problems on society and who is society? There is no such thing! There are individual men and women and there are families and no government can do anything except through people and people look to themselves first. It is our duty to look after ourselves and then also to help look after our neighbor.
> *(Margaret Thatcher)*

To preface the summary chapter of this volume with a quote from Margaret Thatcher—the iconic and, in many left-leaning political circles, reviled neoliberal warrior—may strike readers as discordant. The alternative economies that constitute the plenitude universe are premised on ideas and ideals that are widely regarded as being antithetical to neoliberalism's defining maxims of continual economic growth, the radical discounting of environmental externalities, and the canonization of privatized markets (see Harvey 2005; Peck and Tickell 2002). However, plenitude-oriented alternatives to the BAU economy often exhibit points of tangency with neoliberalism and its market-centric approach (see Hamilton 2001; Ryder 2002).

Rather than looking to top-down government solutions, the plenitude paradigm suggests that at the current moment, the diversified actions of entrepreneurial agents generating new assemblages of technology, human capital, lifestyle practices, and market-mediated social relationships are the more likely impetuses for a more sustainable and emotionally rewarding economy. This is hardly surprising, as market relations and market exchanges have emerged as key ordering principles of modern societies (Slater and Tonkiss 2001, 2). But what kind of market? According to Slater and Tonkiss, "To certain thinkers, market relations exemplify the competitive struggle between atomized individuals; to others, market mechanisms work to secure social harmony between diverse social interests" (3).

The latter position, highlighted by Slater and Tonkiss (2001), captures a central proposition of Austrian School economists such as Friedrich Hayek and Ludwig von Mises, whose ideas have exerted a significant influence on contemporary neoliberal thought and constitute the intellectual subtext to Thatcher's polemical "no society" proclamation. The former position finds expression in many critical views of plenitude-oriented economies. From this standpoint, practices of plenitude do not challenge the BAU economy so much as place a socially responsible gloss upon a subset of market relations and individuated consumer practices that subtly reproduce class distinctions (Guthman 2008b) or function as placating substitutes for organized collective action (Littler 2009; Szasz 2007; Johnston 2008). In this chapter, we more closely interrogate this critical view by showing that it conflates the neoliberal vision of markets with the alternative logic of plenitude-oriented economies.

Family resemblances do exist between the neoliberal valorization of competitive markets and the market practices that characterize plenitude-oriented economies, but they are embedded in very different ideological systems. To begin with the points of commonality, the case studies presented in this volume address localized (and hence, decentralized) entrepreneurial activities, which imply a structural reliance upon private market-mediated exchanges, even when embedded in communal and anticommercial discourses. They also represent lifestyle choices as a potent medium for effecting social change, an argument that seems, at first blush, to align with neoliberal celebrations of sovereign consumer choice and the innovative spirit unleashed through the power of free enterprise. Furthermore, practitioners of plenitude seek varying degrees of DIY and self-provisioning autonomy from the BAU economy, a socioeconomic goal that can readily be aligned with neoliberal veneration of personal responsibility and entrepreneurial skill development. Last but not least, an underlying premise of many plenitude-oriented alternative economies is that political institutions are too constrained by bureaucratic entanglements and forces of institutional inertia to function as primary drivers of social innovation, much less transformative social change, an orientation that is quite compatible with neoliberalism's antipathy toward top-down government interventions.

Numerous critics and commentators view these points of tangency as damning evidence that models of social change based on market-mediated solutions and lifestyle choices are ideological Trojan horses that place a progressive and humanizing face on the neoliberal logics of marketplace discipline, privatized solutions, and personal choice at the expense of collective organization and class-based political mobilization. From this standpoint, practitioners of plenitude may be enacting different choices and modes of life politics than those readily available in the BAU economy, but they are nonetheless operating within a framework that further naturalizes beliefs in the economic logic of the market, market-oriented governmentality (that is, discourses and practices that channel social actors toward individuated, economic cost-benefit calculations rather than toward collective political action and higher-order civic virtues), and the socioeconomic inequities and exclusions that have emerged from the neoliberal era (Allen and Guthman 2006; Blue 2010; Guthman 2008a, 2008b, 2011; Lamont and Molnár 2000; Lavin 2010; Littler 2009; Szasz 2007).[1] Hence, plenitude-oriented alternatives to BAU are accommodations to prevailing power structures and neoliberal hegemony, rather than critically transformative practices.

Lurking in these critical accounts is a noteworthy conceptual and realpolitik conundrum: neoliberalism is a nebulous and increasingly conflated constellation of principles, ideals, and goals (Mudge 2008). Critics routinely confound neoliberalism with market fundamentalism (the belief that unregulated markets are self-correcting systems that result in optimal societal outcomes), libertarianism, Straussian-inspired neoconservativism (see Amable 2011; Brown 2006), and techno-globalist visions of economic utopias created by liberating powers of technology and free trade (Edgerton 2007). The use of such sweeping and undifferentiated treatments of neoliberal precepts means that any kind of social movement that seeks to effect societal changes through marketplace alternatives and lifestyle choices will have some discernible characteristics that can be interpreted as perpetuating the neoliberal BAU economy by assuaging consumers' guilt and anxieties over its deleterious social and ecological consequences.

Our counterproposal is that practices of consumer sovereignty and market-mediated activism are not inherent manifestations of neoliberal governmentality. To make this point, we need to revisit some of the core tenets of neoliberalism, particularly the philosophical rationales underlying its emphasis on marketplace competition, social hierarchies, and individual self-interests as societal ordering principles. This analytic strategy brings us back to Margaret Thatcher's signature statement. For commentators on the political Left, her privileging of individuals and families over the idea of society is a naive and destructive denial of the social influences, structures, and interdependencies that organize everyday life. However, Thatcher's "no society" pronouncement did not express so much a monumental failure of the sociological imagination as it did the profound influence that the writings of Friedrich Austin Hayek, and most particularly his 1944 *Road to Serfdom* (see Berlinski 2008), exerted on her political philosophy.

Hayek is widely regarded as the intellectual progenitor of contemporary neoliberalism (Harvey 2005). While some of Hayek's signature ideas are now criticized in contemporary neoliberal circles for their modulated view of laissez-faire principles,[2] his writings have remained an important theoretical touchstone for the intellectual and moral justification of neoliberal policies. For our purposes, his viewpoints and policy prescriptions remain distinct from other ideological forces—corporatism, market fundamentalism, monetarist economic policies, neoconservativism, and the "world-is-flat" ideology of corporatist global capital—that have so muddied contemporary understandings of the neoliberal intellectual tradition (Barnett 2010).

Writing in the historical shadows of World War II and Stalinism, Hayek revamped numerous ideas from classical economists to contend that top-down government interventions in market processes, whether in the form of centrally planned economies or Keynesian efforts to moderate business cycles, would inevitably yield not only disastrous economic inefficiencies but also create a slippery slope toward totalitarian rule (Wapshott 2011). Seen in this light, Thatcher was reiterating Hayek's argument that no single institution or political body can effectively speak for the economic interests of "society" and thereby enact programs that serve or enhance those interests. Predating more contemporary postmodern accounts of socioeconomic fragmentation (Holt 2002; Jameson 1991), Hayek (1945) argued that in complex industrial societies, economic conditions and interests vary significantly across local contexts. Owing to this diversity, top-down policies that impose restrictions on competitive market dynamics are pernicious conceits that codify incomplete knowledge and erroneous market calculations, which in turn create pricing distortions. In Hayek's vision of an optimal socioeconomic order, economic decisions are best made in a decentralized fashion by autonomous actors who assess local conditions as they pursue their own interests and let themselves be guided by supply and demand in the market.

At face value, there are similarities between plenitude-oriented alternative economies and Hayek's endorsement of decentralized decision making and localized market knowledge. Plenitude's high-tech and localized self-provisioning ethos, the consumer sovereignty expressed by raw milk producers and consumers revolting against constraining regulations, and CSA farmers eschewing the bureaucratic demands of organic certification are examples of the importance of local information and markets. And a core plenitude idea is that unplanned actions at a local level lead to bottom-up social transformations that enhance personal autonomy and quality of life, a proposition with a superficial similarity to Adam Smith's invisible hand or Hayek's emphasis on decentralization. By focusing on these points of tangency, critics could connect the rhetorical dots to argue that the plenitude economy is a cosmetic gloss on the neoliberal regime and its counterproductive narrowing of social life to the vagaries of privatized choices, market-oriented modes of governmentality, and economic reductionism. A worry may be that plenitude does not alter (and may even exacerbate) neoliberalism's oft-noted corrosive effects on collective political engagement and civic solidarity (see Harvey 2005).

Such comparisons fail to consider divergent meanings and implications that stem from stark ideological differences between plenitude-style economies and neoliberal prescriptions. These differences can be traced to the core assumptions underlying Hayek's belief that competitive markets are essential to free and economically dynamic societies. By teasing out these underlying assumptions, we can show that plenitude-oriented alternative economies present an approach to social change that transcends what have become paralyzing dichotomies between individual choice and collective action and between civic virtues and market logics.

HAYEK: ALIGNING SOCIAL AND INDIVIDUAL INTERESTS THROUGH COMPETITIVE MARKETS

Hayek's neoliberalism echoed Tönnies's (1887) classic distinction between *Gemeinschaft* and *Gesellschaft*. Gemeinschaft (community) refers to social aggregations that display an organic unity constituted by geographic proximity, regular face-to-face interactions, strong social ties, shared core beliefs, fidelity to tradition, and governing norms of trust and reciprocity. In contrast, Gesellschaft (society) refers to social aggregations that display a mechanical (or, more accurately, contractual) solidarity constituted by geographically dispersed membership, weak social ties, heterogeneous belief systems, contingent social actions that are no longer bound by traditional constraints, and codified rules and laws designed to overcome distrust and reduce the risks of exploitative opportunism.

While the sociological adequacy of Tönnies's dichotomy has often been called into question (see Brint 2001), its tenets have served to organize the philosophical debate between classical liberalism (which views tradition-bound communities as bastions of authoritarianism, foregone personal liberty, and crippling social stagnation) and communitarianism (which celebrates the Gemeinschaft ideal as a model of fraternal equity, social solidarity, and deep commitments to collective values that defy commodification and reductions to economic rationality). Hayek's position aligned more closely with the liberal suspicion of community, but this moral-normative argument was not particularly central to his economic vision. Rather, he assumed that contemporary life in the industrialized world had irrevocably become a sphere of Gesellschaft relations which, in turn, suggested four fundamental principles for organizing economic life in ways that Hayek (1945, 1948) believed would produce the greatest social benefits and the maximization of personal freedom.

First, individuals are de facto economic free agents whose interests are best served by efficiently allocating their resources according to the laws of supply and demand. Second, economic information is widely dispersed across individual actors and local contexts such that allocation decisions are always made under conditions of imperfect and uncertain knowledge. Third, the incentives for individuals to use their contextually nuanced informational advantages hail from their ownership of private property (and rights thereof protected by the rule of law). Fourth, price stands as the most informative and effective market signal for helping economic agents to accurately gauge prevailing supply-demand conditions: "The mere fact that there is one price for any commodity—or rather that local prices are connected in a manner determined by the cost of transport, etc.—brings about the solution which (it is just conceptually possible) might have been arrived at by one single mind possessing all the information which is in fact dispersed among all the people involved in the process" (Hayek 1945, 526).[3] Drawing inspiration from Adam Smith's economic and social philosophy, Hayek also posited that any mechanisms or interventions that distort the signal value of price (for example, price controls, tariffs, subsidies, monopolies, legally or contractually enforced wage standards) lead to misallocations of resources, lowered standards of living and, most significant, coercive actions to repress public dissatisfaction over these suboptimal conditions (1948).

In further affirmation of views of human nature espoused by Adam Smith and Bernard Mandeville, Hayek further contended that competition was the grand organizing principle that adaptively guides widely dispersed individual decision makers—with different assemblages of knowledge, skill, and goals (as well as incomplete market knowledge)—to produce goods and services that are demanded by consumers at a given time, at the lowest possible costs (and to pass those savings onto customers):

> The practical lesson of all this, I think, is that we should worry much less about whether competition in a given case is perfect and worry much more whether there is competition at all. . . . Competition is essentially a process of the formation of opinion: by spreading information, it creates that unity and coherence of the economic system which we presuppose when we think of it as one market. It creates the views people have about what is best and cheapest, and it is because of it that people know at least as much about possibilities and opportunities as they in fact do. It is thus a process which involves a continuous change in the data and whose significance must therefore be completely missed by any theory which treats these data as constant. (1948, 105–6)

Absent the optimizing pressures of competition, Hayek held that individuals would unduly profit from localized monopolies in which their resources could be perpetually allocated in inefficient ways, with few incentives for adaptation to prevailing market conditions thereby resulting in a dismal nexus of higher costs, lower product quality, and unmet customer demand. Lurking in the background of Hayek's beatific vision of free-market competition is the cautionary tale of dreadfully understocked retail shelves, frustration-inducing paucities of product variety, and woeful-quality goods produced by the command economies of the Soviet Union and East Germany.

In sum, Hayek's neoliberalism asserted the necessity of market competition among geographically dispersed sovereign producers (supply side) who are free to respond adaptively to the localized demands of equally sovereign consumers (demand side)—as guided by the market signal of price—in a system in which societal good is defined as meeting consumer demand for goods and services at the lowest overall cost and most efficient market price. The most salient commonality between Hayek's neoliberalism and plenitude economies is the emphasis on the sovereignty of economic actors, who are free to create local solutions to socioeconomic problems that are not being addressed by the BAU economy. However, the respective logics of neoliberalism and plenitude position the ideal of sovereignty in very different networks of assumptions and ideological meanings. Whereas neoliberalism assumes that a functional economy must be governed by the disciplining forces of market competition, plenitude-oriented economies are premised on an ethos of cooperation and seek to leverage the benefits that can emerge from co-operative networks. In contrast to neoliberal economic visions, plenitude draws on new research showing that complex systems do not converge to efficient self-correcting equilibria, as in stylized but unrealistic neoliberal models (Mitchell 2009). Rather, complex systems retain their robustness by continually adapting to micro-level or localized changes. These bottom-up sources of dynamism now underlie popular proposals for leveraging spatiotemporally dispersed and contextually nuanced knowledge, such as the "wisdom of crowds" (Surowiecki 2005), collective intelligence (Malone and Klein 2007; Malone, Laubacher, and Dellarocas 2009), and awareness systems (Hermida 2010).

Hayek's valorization of neoliberal ideals of competition assumed that social actors are motivated by self-interest (generally defined in terms of economic gains), and that competition is what enables the pursuit of self-interest to be appropriately channeled in ways that reward efficient actors (and actions) and weed out inefficient ones, thereby generating adaptive responses to dynamic socioeconomic conditions. Though not strictly a social Darwinist, Hayek accepted without reservation the idea that competition protected social systems, like biological ones, from stagnation and deterioration and was the essential driver of evolutionary development.

Hayek is one of many neoliberal economists to use biological evolution as a metaphor for anointing competition as the natural, self-regulating property of functional socioeconomic systems, but his views of marketplace competition, like those of many of his ideological compatriots, were based on a misunderstanding of the source biological principles. As West, El Mouden, and Gardner (2011, 231) discuss, "Our understanding of social evolution theory has advanced hugely over the last 45 years. . . . Unfortunately, these advances have been communicated poorly to the social sciences. Consequently, in many cases, the evolutionary theory being applied in the social sciences is based on secondary sources that were aimed at non-specialists, some of which contain fundamental errors and do not reflect the current state of the field."

One of the most glaring errors made by these economic appropriations of evolutionary theory is their heavy emphasis on "survival of the fittest" competition for scarce resources and the minimization of cooperative actions and symbiotic relationships that are necessary for organisms to survive in challenging or harsh environments. Evolutionary theorists, including Darwin himself, have long recognized that the cooperative sharing of resources is vitally important to species survival and the processes of natural selection (Hrdy 2009; Kropotkin 1902). Contemporary developments in evolutionary science have cast cooperation in an increasingly central role (Santos and Pacheco 2006). To quote Nowak (2006, 1563), "Evolution is constructive because of cooperation. New levels of organization evolve when the competing units on the lower level begin to cooperate. Cooperation allows specialization and thereby promotes biological diversity. Cooperation is the secret behind the open-endedness of the evolutionary process." A large and growing literature also suggests the importance of cooperation in a wide variety of economic settings over the long span of human history (Bowles and Gintis 2011).

WHERE NEOLIBERALISM FEARS TO TREAD:
CORNUCOPIAS OF COOPERATION

We can now compare the characteristics of plenitude economies to Hayek's neoliberal vision of competitive markets. Many aspects of Hayek's framework, particularly its Gesellschaft assumptions, apply well to the BAU economy, with its global supply chains, vast geographical and informational chasms that separate consumers from BAU means of production, reduction of value to price-quality calculations, and largely impersonal transactions in which contractual modes of governance function as practical surrogates for interpersonal trust and reciprocity. In contrast, the alternative economies profiled in this volume are more consistent with a Gemeinschaft social order.

They are geographically bounded socioeconomic networks, exhibiting a preponderance of social capital and trust-based reciprocity cultivated through face-to-face interactions, and deploying localized modes of production that facilitate richer information flows across the network. It is less a conventional exchange relationship than a social contract; the participants in our case studies are not reduced to using price as an all-encompassing market signal that only gauges efficiency. As a consequence, practitioners of plenitude can assess the extent to which these market-mediated relationships are effective means to accomplish a broader range of social values, ideals, and quality of life goals. For example, members of time-banking barter networks report experiencing these alternative exchange practices as more personalized, rewarding, and affirming of personal worth than those undertaken in BAU markets (Dubois, Schor, and Carfagna's chapter 3 in this volume). Similarly, the communal-provisioning practices discussed by Gowan and Slocum (chapter 1 in this volume) enable participants in the Aude's alternative economy to transcend the commodity fetishism and alienation of labor value characteristic of the BAU capitalist system and pursue new allocations of time that are not constrained by conventional wage labor impositions. Thompson and Press's CSA consumers (chapter 4 in this volume) have traveled a similar trajectory from arms-length food provisioning to a closer personal relationship with farmers.

Prior research shows that cooperative and sharing behaviors most readily occur in social groups that are characterized by tightly knit social networks in which participants are bound together by feelings of moral obligation—reciprocal interdependency (such that gains and losses are shared across participants), a strong sense of common cause, and feelings of participating in a cornucopia (Belk 2007). All of the above are fairly self-evident properties of the plenitude economies analyzed in these chapters, with the exception of cornucopia. Cornucopia is a more complex aspect because it can be experienced in a variety of ways. In the Aude, for example, people have a cornucopia of time, but not of cash. Studies on the collaborative and peer-to-peer economies that have developed online (Benkler 2006; Belk 2007) remind us that social media phenomena such as peer-to-peer file sharing, wiki-type collaboratives, and open-source software creation are cultural contexts in which experiences of cornucopia and cooperative community behaviors also abound. In these settings, participants do not see themselves as competing for control of scarce resources or fighting for a niche in the economic system where they can maximize the remunerative potential of their informational advantages. Rather, they are engaged in a project of personal and collective skill building and creating a richer "commons": processes that lend themselves to a sense of expansive opportunities rather than constraint and scarcity.

In a similar fashion, plenitude economies afford consumers means to cultivate self-provisioning skills and (even in less encompassing manifestations such as CSAs or farmers' markets) to reverse the de-skilling of consumption that has characterized the convenience-oriented BAU economy. By fusing consumption and production (and in the ideal case, reducing individuals' time commitments to working and shopping in the BAU economy), plenitude practices serve as modes of creative self-expression, innovation, emotional enrichment, and a means to forge stronger interpersonal ties. Because plenitude practices forgo the BAU logic of specialization and standardization, they also enable consumers to experience greater variety in their everyday consumption practices and lifestyle routines. In these ways, plenitude economies produce an array of intangible goods that do not have a ceiling on their expansiveness, potential for enjoyment, or even enchantment.

Plenitude's cooperative ethos also circumvents another BAU dilemma that shaped some of Hayek's defining neoliberal propositions: the incompleteness of information. Aside from the fact that digital communication technologies now allow for an ease and extent of information sharing unimaginable at the time of Hayek's most influential writings, the cornucopian qualities of plenitude also engender strong incentives for sharing information that are not replicable in the BAU economy, even though many firms are seeking to incorporate collaborative networks, open-source innovation, and participatory engagement into their business models. What distinguishes the plenitude economy from the so-called Wikinomics model of collaborative business management (see Tapscott and Williams 2006) is the latter's intractable commitment to the BAU norms of profit seeking and maintaining proprietary control of monetizable innovations and resources, all of which place pragmatic limits on the nature and scale of sharing that can actually take place in these participatory adaptations of BAU practices.[4]

While many plenitude economies need to generate revenue to remain viable, conventional competitive pressures are obviated by their localized nature. The craft producers plying their wares in the Aude incur no market risk in sharing information with artisans located in the craft villages of the Scottish Highlands. Time bank members are eager to share skills with others, rather than being worried about losing their market "niche" in the time bank. Even in cases where there is some potential for localized competition (such as in

CSAs or raw milk markets), the economic viability of such small-scale producers, who depend on drawing new members away from much larger (and heavily marketed) BAU enterprises, is enhanced by barter arrangements, information sharing, and other practices of resource pooling. Through these information flows, plenitude practitioners can learn from the experiences and experiments of others and adapt that knowledge to their own local conditions. In turn, these can be shared across the social network in a process of adaptive learning that fills the information void Hayek sought to resolve through his championing of undistorted price signals.

THE PRAXEOMORPHICS OF PLENITUDE:
COLLABORATIVE NETWORKS AND
RESISTANT RHIZOMES

> The way human beings understand the world tends to be at all times praxeomorphic: it is always shaped by the know-how of the day, by what people can do and how they usually go about doing it. The Fordist factory—with its meticulous separation between design and execution, initiative and command . . . was without doubt the highest achievement to date of order-aimed social engineering. No wonder it set the metaphorical frame of reference for everyone trying to comprehend how human reality works on all its levels—the global-societal as well as that of the individual life.
> (Zygmunt Bauman)

If the Fordist factory provided the praxeomorphic reference point for modernity—and one does not have to dig too far back in history to recall a litany of mechanistic models used to explain the operation of nature, society, and all things in between, the World Wide Web—with its vast expanse of interlinkages, hyperlinks, and diffuse and rapid information flows—is a leading contender for the dominant metaphor of the postmodern age. And as we have seen, plenitude is a realm of interconnected activities, values, localized modes of production and communal self-provisioning, and information flows. Embodying the techno-utopian ideals associated with digital communication technologies (Kozinets 2008), practitioners of plenitude have formed collaborative networks that function to create innovations, solve problems, and fashion new assemblages of social relationships, human capital, material goods, ecological systems, and marketplace logics.

However, the network metaphor has itself been thoroughly appropriated by the BAU economy, as the postindustrial, "light-capitalist" tropes of speed, flexibility, decentralization, and just-in-time responsiveness have displaced the "heavy-capitalist" tropes emanating from Fordist-era industrialism (Bauman 2000). The praxeomorphic image of collaborative and dispersed digital networks not only fails to clearly distinguish plenitude from BAU, it also elides two other points of distinction: plenitude economies are grounded in local conditions rather than the deterritorialized commodity flows that characterize the BAU economy, and they present decentralized points of resistance to BAU practices.

Accordingly, we suggest that the defining characteristics of the plenitude economy are better represented by Deleuze and Guattari's (1987) botanically inspired trope of social resistance and transformative potential: the rhizome. Rhizomes are complex subterranean root systems that can spread and thrive in the presence of more dominant arborescent structures.[5] While interconnected, any section of a rhizome has a functional resiliency that allows it to survive and create a new system of offshoots if separated from the larger web. Rhizomes, once established, are notoriously difficult to uproot and have the capacity to radically transform a (socioeconomic) landscape.

Seen in this light, any specific exemplar of the plenitude economy—be it a CSA, a Transition community, a time bank, a community garden, or a barter economy—exists as a localized, heterogeneous node in a more profuse rhizomatic web. Those who fault specific manifestations of the plenitude economy by arguing that an economic empowerment project like Experimental Station does not confront the deeper problems of urban poverty or that CSAs cannot provide food security for the world's population mistake the nature of rhizomatic resistance. Each enterprise or activity in the plenitude-oriented alternative economy poses little if any direct challenge to the BAU economy. The transformative potential of plenitude lies in the totality of its rhizomatic web, which offers ever-increasing numbers of disaggregated sovereign consumers diversified "lines of flight" from the BAU economy and reembeds and reassembles them as collaborative communities.

Unquestionably, the broader structural problems and injustices that pervade the global economy are vitally important to recognize and to combat through organized political action. Plenitude is neither a panacea nor a substitute for broader political engagement. But realpolitik is not a realm of either-or absolutism. For example, the anticonsumerist Burning Man Festival—often ridiculed as being little more than self-indulgent, creative class carnival in the desert—also serves as a platform for recruiting and organizing its participants into ongoing interest groups working on behalf of different social and environmental causes (Sherry and Kozinets 2007). More generally, the web of plenitude-oriented economies can connect with other social networks in the environmental and social justice spheres in ways that dovetail with institution-building approaches to creating a more sustainable and humane socioeconomic world.

In sum, decentralization need not mean atomized individualism, and market-mediated relations need not reproduce neoliberal preferences for price-driven competition (and the corresponding elision of "externalities") when undertaken in market structures oriented around principles of cooperation and mutually supportive rhizomatic connections. Plenitude economies are localized civic engagements that convert "Think globally—act locally" eco-consumerist platitudes into forms of collective and cooperative action that are spreading across the global economy. They harbor the potential to generate a diversified bottom-up impetus for more sweeping transformations of the BAU economy. Rhizomatic resistance is never a full frontal assault but a gradual and incessant process of uprooting and reclaiming.

NOTES

1. While Blue (2010) argues that locavore movements are steeped in a neoliberal logic of sovereign consumer choice, personal responsibility for well-being, and the enactment of life politics through the marketplace, she also suggests that these consumer-centric practices harbor the potential to be pathways into broader forms of political engagement.

2. Hayek was far less doctrinaire in his views on the responsibilities of the state toward its citizens than many contemporary advocates of neoliberal policies. For example, Hayek (1944, 120) believed that the state had a moral duty to provide social insurance against the "common hazards of life against which, because of their uncertainty, few individuals can make adequate provision": an idea that contemporary neoliberal writers condemn as slippage that provokes moral hazard, that is, deleterious opportunistic behaviors. (for example, Block 1996).

3. In the celebrated debate between Hayek and Oskar Lange on capitalism versus socialism, Lange, who won the debate, showed that a central planner could replicate the competitive market solution if information is given to him, thereby establishing that, in theory, socialism could be as efficient as capitalism.

4. For more extensive analyses of the profound contradictions between the communal rhetoric used to recruit participants into Wikinomic customer cocreation processes

and its value-extracting practices, see Humphreys and Grayson 2008; Ritzer and Jurgenson 2010; Zwick, Bonsu, and Darmody 2008.

5. While trees are typically celebrated as symbols of environmental consciousness and revitalization, Deleuze and Guattari used them as metaphoric representations of centralized authority, essentialism, and hierarchal ordering principles (see Best and Kellner 1997).

REFERENCES

Allen, Patricia, and Julie Guthman. 2006. "From 'Old School' to 'Farm-to-School': Neoliberalization from the Ground Up." *Agriculture and Human Values* 23 (December): 401–15.

Amable, Bruno. 2011. "Morals and Politics in the Ideology of Neo-liberalism." *Socioeconomic Review* 9 (1): 3–30.

Barnett, Clive. 2010. "Publics and Markets: What's Wrong with Neoliberalism?" In *The Handbook of Social Geography,* ed. Susan Smith, Sallie Marston, Rachel Pain, and John Paul Jones III, 269–96. London: Sage.

Bauman, Zygmunt. 2000. *Liquid Modernity.* Malden, MA: Polity.

Belk, Russell W. 2007. "Why Not Share Rather than Own?" *Annals of the American Academy of Political and Social Science* 611 (May): 126–40.

Benkler, Yochai. 2006. *The Wealth of Networks: How Social Production Transforms Markets and Freedom.* New Haven, CT: Yale University Press.

Berlinski, Claire. 2008. *There Is No Alternative: Why Margaret Thatcher Matters.* New York: Basic.

Best, Steven, and Douglas Kellner. 1997. *The Postmodern Turn.* New York: Guilford.

Block, Walter. 1996. "Hayek's Road to Serfdom." *Journal of Libertarian Studies* 12 (Fall): 339–65.

Blue, Gwen. 2010. "On the Politics and Possibilities of Locavores: Situating Food Sovereignty in the Turn from Government to Governance." *Politics and Culture,* October 27. http://www.politicsandculture.org/2010/10/27/on-the-politics-and-possibilities-of-locavoressituating-food-sovereignty-in-the-turn-from-government-to-governance / (accessed March 1, 2013).

Bowles, Samuel, and Herbert Gintis. 2011. *A Cooperative Species: Human Reciprocity and Its Evolution.* Princeton, NJ: Princeton University Press.

Brint, Steven. 2001. "*Gemeinschaft* Revisited: A Critique and Reconstruction of the Community Concept." *Sociological Theory* 19 (March): 1–23.

Brown, Wendy. 2006. "American Nightmare: Neoliberalism, Neoconservatism, and Dedemocratization." *Political Theory* 34 (December): 690–714.

Deleuze, Gilles, and Felix Guattari. 1987. *A Thousand Plateaus.* Trans. Brian Massumi. Minneapolis: University of Minnesota Press.

Edgerton, David E. H. 2007. "The Contradictions of Techno-Nationalism and Techno-Globalism: A Historical Perspective." *New Global Studies* 1 (1): 1–32.

Guthman, Julie. 2008a. "Neoliberalism and the Making of Food Politics in California." *Geoforum* 39 (May): 1171–83.

———. 2008b. "Thinking inside the Neoliberal Box: The Micro-politics of Agro-food Philanthropy." *Geoforum* 39 (May): 1241–53.

———. 2011. "If They Only Knew: The Unbearable Whiteness of Alternative Food." In *Cultivating Food Justice: Race, Class, and Sustainability*, ed. Alison Hope Alkon and Julian Agyeman, 263–81. Cambridge, MA: MIT Press.

Hamilton, Clive. 2001. "The Third Way and the End of Politics." *The Drawing Board: An Australian Review of Public Affairs* 2 (November): 89–102.

Harvey, David. 2005. *A Brief History of Neoliberalism.* New York: Oxford University Press.

Hayek, Friedrich A. 1944. *The Road to Serfdom.* Chicago: University of Chicago Press.

———. 1945. "The Use of Knowledge in Society." *American Economic Review* 35 (September): 519–30.

———. 1948. *Individualism and Economic Order.* Chicago: University of Chicago Press.

Hermida, Alfred. 2010. "Twittering the News: The Emergence of Ambient Journalism." *Journalism Practice* 4 (3): 297–308.

Holt, Douglas B. 2002. "Why Do Brands Cause Trouble? A Dialectical Theory of Consumer Culture and Branding." *Journal of Consumer Research* 29 (June): 70–90.

Hrdy, Sarah Blaffer. 2009. *Mothers and Others: The Evolutionary Origins of Mutual Understanding.* Cambridge, MA: Harvard University Press.

Humphreys, Ashlee, and Kent Grayson. 2008. "The Intersecting Roles of Consumer and Producer: A Critical Perspective on Co-production, Co-creation and Prosumption." *Sociology Compass* 2 (May): 963–80.

Jameson, Frederic. 1991. *Postmodernism; or, The Cultural Logic of Late Capitalism.* Durham, NC: Duke University Press.

Johnston, Josée. 2008. "The Citizen-Consumer Hybrid: Ideological Tensions and the Case of Whole Foods Market." *Theory and Society* 37 (3): 229–70.

Kozinets, Robert V. 2008. "Technology/Ideology: How Ideological Fields Influence Consumers' Technology Narratives." *Journal of Consumer Research* 34 (April): 865–81.

Kropotkin, Peter Harry. 1902. *Mutual Aid: A Factor of Evolution.* http://www.gutenberg .org/catalog/world/readfile?fk_files=2138514 (accessed March 1, 2013).

Lamont, Michèle, and Virág Molnár. 2000. "Too Much Economics." In *Do Americans Shop Too Much?* ed. Joshua Cohen and Joel Rogers, 75–80. Boston: Beacon.

Lavin, Chad. 2010. "Pollanated Politics; or, The Neoliberal's Dilemma." *Politics and Culture*, October 27. http://www.politicsandculture.org/2010/10/27/pollanated-politics -or-theneoliberal%E2%80%99s-dilemma/ (accessed March 1, 2013).

Littler, Jo. 2009. *Radical Consumption: Shopping for Change in Contemporary Culture.* Maidenhead, UK: Open University Press.

Malone, Thomas W., and Mark Klein. 2007. "Harnessing Collective Intelligence to Address Global Climate Change." *Innovations* 2 (3): 15–26.

Malone, Thomas W., Robert Laubacher, and Chrysanthos Dellarocas. 2009. "Harnessing Crowds: Mapping the Genome of Collective Intelligence." Working Paper 2009-001, MIT Center for Collective Intelligence, Massachusetts Institute of Technology, Cambridge.

Mitchell, Melanie. 2009. *Complexity: A Guided Tour.* New York: Oxford University Press.

Mudge, Stephanie Lee. 2008. "What Is Neo-Liberalism?" *Socio-economic Review* 6 (4): 703–31.

Nowak, Martin A. 2006. "Five Rules for the Evolution of Cooperation." *Science* 314 (December): 1560–63.

Peck, Jamie, and Adam Tickell. 2002. "Neoliberalizing Space." *Antipode* 4 (July): 380–404.

Ritzer, George, and Nathan Jurgenson. 2010. "Production, Consumption, and Prosumption: The Nature of Capitalism in the Age of the Digital Prosumer." *Journal of Consumer Culture* 10 (March): 13–36.

Ryder, J. Magnus. 2002. *Capitalist Restructuring, Globalisation, and the Third Way: Lessons from the Swedish Model.* New York: Routledge.

Santos, Francisco C., and Jorge M. Pacheco. 2006. "A New Route to the Evolution of Cooperation." *Journal of Evolutionary Biology* 19 (May): 726–33.

Sherry, John F., and Robert V. Kozinets. 2007. "Comedy of the Commons: Nomadic Spirituality and the Burning Man Festival." In *Research in Consumer Behavior,* vol. 11, *Consumer Culture Theory,* ed. Russell W. Belk and John F. Sherry, 119–47. New York: JAI.

Slater, Don, and Fran Tonkiss. 2001. *Market Society: Markets and Social Theory.* Malden, MA: Blackwell.

Surowiecki, James. 2005. *The Wisdom of Crowds: Why the Many Are Smarter Than the Few and How Collective Wisdom Shapes Business, Economies, Societies and Nations.* New York: Doubleday.

Szasz, Andrew. 2007. *Shopping Our Way to Safety: How We Changed from Protecting the Environment to Protecting Ourselves.* Minneapolis: University of Minnesota Press.

Tapscott, Don, and Anthony D. Williams. 2006. *Wikinomics: How Mass Collaboration Changes Everything.* New York: Portfolio.

Thatcher, Margaret. 1987. Interview. *Women's Own,* October 31. http://www.margaret thatcher.org/document/106689 (accessed March 1, 2013).

Tönnies, Ferdinand. 1887. *Community and Society.* Trans. Charles Loomis. Mineola, NY: Dover, 2002.

Wapshott, Nicholas. 2011. *Keynes Hayek: The Clash That Defined Modern Economics.* New York: Norton.

West, Stuart A., Claire El Mouden, and Andy Gardner. 2011. "Sixteen Common Misconceptions about the Evolution of Cooperation in Humans." *Evolution and Human Behavior* 32 (July): 231–62.

Zwick, Detlev, Sammy Bonsu, and Aron Darmody. 2008. "Putting Consumers to Work: Co-creation and New Marketing Governmentality." *Journal of Consumer Culture* 8 (2): 163–96.

Contributors

Lindsey "Luka" B. Carfagna is a doctoral student in the sociology department at Boston College, holds an MA in the social sciences from the University of Chicago, and double-majored in economics and sociology at the University of Vermont. She works as a research assistant for Juliet Schor as part of the MacArthur Foundation's Connected Learning Research Network and is currently studying open learning. Her research interests are in economic sociology and the sociology of education, with specific focuses on cultural capital in digital spaces and how institutional and organizational mechanisms facilitate the reproduction of inequality. Luka grew up outside Pittsburgh, and she recently helped found that city's New Economy Working Group, where she is responsible for training Resilience Circle facilitators.

Emilie A. Dubois is a doctoral student in the sociology department at Boston College and holds an MA in history from Columbia University. She works as a research assistant for the MacArthur Foundation's Connected Learning Research Network, where she analyzes emerging hipster lifestyles in the context of the New Economy movement. Emilie's research interests are in economic sociology, with a special focus on gender within formal organizations and across a range of consumptive practices.

Teresa Gowan teaches ethnography, urban sociology, and the sociology of consumption at the University of Minnesota. Her ethnography *Hobos, Hustlers, and*

Backsliders: Homeless in San Francisco (2010), winner of both the American Socio-logical Association's Robert Park and Mary Douglas awards in 2011, ties its delinea-tion of homeless recycling and other marginal lifeworlds to the seismic shifts in urban form, spatial control, public culture, and U.S. social policy around the turn of the twenty-first century.

Karen Hébert is a cultural anthropologist whose research examines issues of nat-ural resource development and sustainability in the subarctic North. Through long-term ethnographic fieldwork in rural southwest Alaska, she has explored transformations in contemporary commercial fishing economies and markets in environmental goods more broadly. She is currently an assistant professor jointly appointed in the Department of Anthropology and the School of Forestry and Environmental Studies at Yale University.

Douglas B. Holt is founder and president of the Cultural Strategy Group, Boulder, Colorado, and its pro bono subsidiary Planet Strategy. He is also affiliate professor of sociology at Colorado State University and a fellow at the university's Center for Fair and Alternative Trade, and professor of marketing at Southern Denmark Uni-versity. Previously, he was L'Oreal Chair of Marketing at the University of Oxford and a professor at the Harvard Business School. Doug is the author of *Cultural Strategy: Using Innovative Ideologies to Build Breakthrough Brands* (2010) and *How Brands Become Icons: The Principles of Cultural Branding* (2004).

Diana Mincyte is an assistant professor and faculty fellow in the Center for Euro-pean and Mediterranean Studies at New York University. Diana's research focuses on environmental and justice dimensions of agro-food systems, especially in the context of European integration. Focusing on standards of living and quality of life, her new project is a comparative analysis of poverty measurements from a histori-cal perspective. Her work has appeared in the *Slavic Review, Agriculture and Human Values, Sociologia Ruralis,* and *Cultural Studies/Critical Methodologies,* among other journals, as well as in edited volumes.

Melea Press is senior lecturer of marketing at the University of Bath. Her research focuses on market systems and approaches to supply chain relationships that fos-ter innovation and sustainability. She has a special interest in agriculture. Her work has been supported by USDA and USAID grants and has been published in market-ing and sustainability books and journals.

Juliet B. Schor is professor of sociology at Boston College and a member of the MacArthur Foundation Connected Learning Research Network. In addition to *Plenitude* (2010), she has published *The Overworked American* (1992), *The Overspent American* (1998), and *Born to Buy* (2004). She is a former Guggenheim Fellow and a recipient of the Herman Daly and Leontief awards for her work in ecology and economics. She is a cofounder of the South End Press, the Center for Popular Economics, and the Center for a New American Dream. She also founded the Summer Institute in New Economics in 2012. Juliet spent 2011 as a senior scholar at the Center for Humans and Nature working on this volume.

Rachel Slocum is a cultural geographer whose research concerns the way race is formed materially through engagements in food space. Exploring the imaginaries and practices of U.S. alternative food networks in the Northeast and Midwest, she has written about the role of whiteness in these networks, antiracism and emotionalism as part of the local-food movement, and the embodied racial geographies of the Minneapolis Farmers' Market. Most recently she has published on how food studies scholars theorize race. An edited collection, *Geographies of Race and Food: Fields, Bodies, Markets* was published in September 2013 in Ashgate's Critical Food Studies.

Craig J. Thompson is the Churchill Professor of Marketing at the University of Wisconsin–Madison, and he holds an affiliate appointment at the University of Wisconsin's School of Journalism and Mass Communication. His research on the cultural and ideological forces that shape market systems and everyday consumption practices has appeared in leading journals. He is coauthor of the book *The Phenomenology of Everyday Life* (1997).

Robert Wengronowitz is a PhD student in the Department of Sociology at Boston College. He received an MA in the social sciences at the University of Chicago and a BA in sociology at the University of Illinois at Urbana-Champaign. He has two main interests that intersect through transformative praxis. First, he is concerned with social movements, especially climate justice, and the ways we bring about social, political, economic, and cultural change. Second, he is interested in alternative agriculture, particularly how cooperative and community-driven enterprises can lead to a more ecologically sane, and perhaps more meaningful, way of living. Bobby is currently researching sustainable agriculture in New England and the ecological, economic, and social aspects of "beyond organic" in practice.

Index

Page numbers in *italics* refer to illustrations.